SENSIBLE
STOCK
INVESTING

SENSIBLE STOCK INVESTING

How to Pick, Value, and Manage Stocks

DAVID P. VAN KNAPP

iUniverse Star
New York Lincoln Shanghai

Sensible Stock Investing
How to Pick, Value, and Manage Stocks

iUniverse Star
an iUniverse, Inc. imprint

iUniverse books may be ordered through booksellers or by contacting:

iUniverse
2021 Pine Lake Road, Suite 100
Lincoln, NE 68512
www.iuniverse.com
1-800-Authors (1-800-288-4677)

Because of the dynamic nature of the Internet, any Web addresses or links contained in this book may have changed since publication and may no longer be valid.

The information, ideas, and suggestions in this book are not intended to render professional advice. Before following any suggestions contained in this book, you should consult your personal accountant or other financial advisor. Neither the author nor the publisher shall be liable or responsible for any loss or damage allegedly arising as a consequence of your use or application of any information or suggestions in this book.

ISBN: 978-1-60528-010-3 (pbk)
ISBN: 978-0-595-60611-5 (ebk)

Printed in the United States of America

For Sue, With Love

Contents

Introduction..1

PART A. INTRODUCING SENSIBLE STOCK INVESTING

Chapter A-1   Stocks: The Best Way to Build Wealth 7

Chapter A-2   The Sensible Stock Investor 12

Chapter A-3   The Three Steps to Sensible Stock Investing 16

Chapter A-4   Risk and Time Horizons 21

PART B. THE STOCK MARKET

Chapter B-1   What *Is* the Stock Market, Anyway?....................................31

Chapter B-2   Stock Indexes 33

Chapter B-3   What Determines Stock Prices?...41

Chapter B-4   Is the Market Efficient? Is It Rational? 60

Chapter B-5   Bull Markets, Bear Markets, and Bubbles.............................65

PART C. PICKING COMPANIES

Chapter C-1   A Sensible Approach to Picking Companies...........................73

Chapter C-2   Are Established Companies or "Emerging Opportunities" Better Bets? 79

Chapter C-3   Subdividing the Universe of Companies 86

Chapter C-4   Megatrends..92

Chapter C-5   What's the Story? Buy Dominant Companies 101

Chapter C-6   Inherently Unplayable and Risky Companies.......................112

Chapter C-7   The Company as a Financial "Black Box" 118

Chapter C-8   Financial Evaluation Factors 124

Chapter C-9   Dividends as a Company Evaluation Factor 139

Chapter C-10 Bonus Points 145

Chapter C-11 Putting It All Together: A Company Scoring System............. 147

PART D.   VALUING STOCKS

Chapter D-1   What Is Valuation and Why Do You Need It?...................... 153

Chapter D-2   Common Ways to Value Stocks 156

Chapter D-3   Valuation Ratios 161

Chapter D-4   Dividends as a Valuation Tool 168

Chapter D-5   Putting It All Together: Valuing a Stock 171

PART E.   MANAGING YOUR PORTFOLIO

Chapter E-1   Managing a Portfolio Is Different from Picking Stocks 181

Chapter E-2   Managing Risk... 184

Chapter E-3   Types of Stocks 194

Chapter E-4   Momentum 201

Chapter E-5   Timing 208

Chapter E-6   Concentration and Diversification 221

Chapter E-7   Articulating Your Stock Investment Strategy 224

Chapter E-8   When to Buy 230

Chapter E-9   When to Sell... 236

Chapter E-10 Summary of Portfolio Management 250

PART F.   BUILDING A REAL PORTFOLIO

Chapter F-1   Getting Started 255

Chapter F-2   Evolution of Sensible Tools 261

Chapter F-3   Real-Life Buying and Selling..267

Chapter F-4   Focusing the Portfolios on Different Missions..............................273

Chapter F-5   Actual Results..275

Chapter F-6   Lessons Learned..280

APPENDICES

Appendix I   Sample Forms..287

              Sample Form 1 *Easy-Rate™ Stock Rating Sheet*...............................*287*

              Sample Form 2 *Company "Story" Questionnaire*...........................*289*

              Sample Form 3 *Shopping List*..*290*

              Sample Form 4 *Timing Outlook*...*294*

              Sample Form 5 *Portfolio Review*..*295*

Appendix II   Annual Calendar for the Sensible Stock Investor...........................297

About the Author...301

Acknowledgments..303

Disclaimer & Important Information..305

Introduction

Who Are You?

This is a book about individuals investing in the stock market and beating it.

It may come as a surprise, but one does not have to be a financial genius, good at math, a trained economist, or have an MBA to beat the market. More important are qualities like the following. See if they describe you:

- Male or female
- Between the ages of 15 and 90
- Want to build wealth
- Self-directed
- Looking for a road map to cut through the informational clutter
- Logical, objective, and disciplined, at least most of the time
- Looking for a sound stock-investing methodology
- Reasonably self-confident, with an "I can do this" attitude
- Optimistic but not irrationally exuberant
- Believes an individual investor has a chance on Wall Street
- Independent thinker, willing to question conventional wisdom
- Skeptical about "Wall Street," conventional investment advice, and whether traditional brokers' and advisers' interests are truly aligned with your own
- Prudent, but willing to take some measured risks without being a wild-eyed speculator
- Open to the idea that the stock market's challenges and opportunities can be fun
- Willing to approach wealth building in a serious way, yet able to look at it as a game and play it as such
- Willing to devote a few hours a month and to do some research on your own

Does this list describe you? Mostly? If so, this book has been written for you. You are in the book's target audience.

You may have heard that no one can beat the market. Don't believe it. I do it, and I am convinced that thousands of others do it consistently. They do it by being intelligent and methodical, making rational stock selections, holding their stocks for as long as it makes sense, and selling them when the stocks stop working. Such successful investors match their stock selections to their own personalities and knowledge, never straying far from their zones of comfort and comprehension, and making decisions that are sensible to themselves.

This book will show you an approach to doing just those things. It is certainly not the only approach that works. But this book's approach—Sensible Stock Investing—is straightforward and logical. It is easy to understand. It integrates the best features of several different "conventional" approaches (such as "value" and "growth" investing). It is transparent, not obscure. It does not ask you to trust any fact or technique that you cannot verify. It is flexible, and you can tweak it if you see a better way. It is meant as a foundation for rational investment thinking.

As you read the book, it should become obvious why the approach works. It will make sense.

To be a Sensible Stock Investor, the work required of you is comparatively easy. It is not overly time-consuming. We manage or avoid risk in straightforward ways. We use no exotic tools or tactics—just good solid stock picking and a disciplined approach about selling.

I hope that this book helps you in your quest to build your own wealth for whatever purpose you have—educating your kids, ensuring a comfortable retirement, perhaps retiring early. I also hope that you find it easy to read, logical, and perhaps even exciting. If it works for you, and you enjoy reading it, I will have done my job.

* * *

Stock investing is a complex problem. Many people see the markets as impenetrable mathematical "places" where incomprehensible transactions take place, where unintelligible jargon is used, and where only "masters of the universe" make money while most others lose their shirts. Scary places.

But it turns out that the stock markets can be understood on a practical level, stripped of most of their incomprehensibility and high-level mathematics. Markets are places of social interaction that happen to focus on money and investments. They can be understood at a macro level, in the same way that parties, crowds at a football game, or the political process can be understood. Stock prices, in the end, are determined by the behavior of people. So yes, they are complex, but they can be understood and should not be scary.

Many people do not see investing as fun—to them it is a drag, uninteresting, one of the last things they want to think about, dreadful. (Partly that may be because they see the markets as incomprehensible.) But others see the markets as exciting, challenging, a game worth playing, and a road to important goals, such as a comfortable retirement. Selecting individual stocks and managing a stock portfolio requires some work, discipline, and time (so, for that matter, does keeping in shape or becoming a decent tennis player). Fortunately, with the many free and low-cost investment sites on the Internet, the information you need is readily available, and with discount online brokerage accounts, the costs of investing are at rock bottom. As an added benefit of online accounts, you can cut brokers and others with questionable agendas out of the process entirely.

My mission in writing this book is to serve the needs of individual investors who see investing as challenging, rewarding, and fun. I have attempted to explain how the stock market works, how to find companies worthy of your consideration, and how to determine when to buy and sell them. The "system" embodied in Sensible Stock Investing is an amalgam of various approaches. It allows you to come at the game from several directions. It is flexible, not rigid or dogmatic. Sensible Stock Investing beats the indexes. It works. It will take you a few hours a month, but over time, the rewards will be well worth it.

* * *

For more information, please visit our Web site at SensibleStocks.com

PART A.   INTRODUCING SENSIBLE STOCK INVESTING

Chapter A-1.   Stocks: The Best Way to Build Wealth

Chapter A-2.   The Sensible Stock Investor

Chapter A-3.   The Three Steps to Sensible Stock Investing

Chapter A-4.   Risk and Time Horizons

CHAPTER A-1

Stocks: The Best Way to Build Wealth

Money is better than poverty, if only for financial reasons.
—Woody Allen

Your Fundamental Investment Mission Is to Build Your Wealth

The goal of investing in stocks is very simple: You buy stocks to make money. The objective is wealth maximization.

If *building wealth* is not your principal goal, do not invest in stocks. Other reasonable financial objectives—such as the *preservation* of money or the generation of *steady income* streams—may be better accomplished using other investment vehicles, such as cash or bonds.

Investing in stocks embraces capitalism and allows you to practice it in its purest form: You are the capitalist. Investing is therefore significantly different from holding a job. In that role you are not a capitalist—no matter what bonus programs, profit sharing, or stock options you may get. In most jobs, you have to deal with bosses, office politics, managing, being managed, labor laws, office rules, OSHA, and the like. With stock ownership, someone else takes care of all of that for you. In a job, you work for a salary and the owners get the profits. In stock investing, you *are* the owner, and you get the profits.

The reason to use *stock* investing to build wealth is that every historical measure shows that stocks have been the most profitable long-term investment, where "long-term" is measured in years. There is little reason to expect that stocks will not continue to outperform other assets over long time frames. Stocks in general have provided an average 10 to 11 percent annual return since before the Great Depression, and the market has risen in about seven out of every ten years. Prior to the three-year bubble leakage of 2000–2002, it had not taken more than two years for stock market prices to go up since 1939–1941.

Building wealth through stock ownership—capitalism—is about investing money to make more money. The more you make, the more you make, because of the "miracle of compounding"—building wealth in an accelerating fashion on the basis of wealth already built. Albert Einstein said, "There is no greater power known to man than compounding interest." The following table shows how annual percentage gains compound over time:

Compounding—The Multiplication Effect of Gains Over a Number of Years

% Gain	1 yr.	2 yr.	3 yr.	4 yr.	5 yr.	6 yr.	7 yr.	8 yr.	9 yr.	10 yr.
5%	1.05	1.10	1.16	1.22	1.28	1.34	1.41	1.48	1.55	1.63
7½%	1.08	1.16	1.24	1.34	1.44	1.54	1.66	1.78	1.92	2.06
10%	1.10	1.21	1.33	1.46	1.61	1.77	1.95	2.14	2.36	2.59
12½%	1.13	1.27	1.42	1.60	1.80	2.03	2.28	2.57	2.89	3.25
15%	1.15	1.32	1.52	1.75	2.01	2.31	2.66	3.06	3.52	4.05
17½%	1.18	1.38	1.62	1.91	2.24	2.63	3.09	3.63	4.27	5.01
20%	1.20	1.44	1.73	2.07	2.49	2.99	3.58	4.30	5.16	6.19

Note the shaded box in the far right-hand column; it is at the intersection of 10 percent gain per year and 10 years. What the number there—2.59—tells you is that an annual gain of 10 percent compounded over 10 years will multiply your money by 2.59. So in ten years, you would have more than 2 1/2 times the money that you started with, provided that you reinvested your gains along the way. If you began with $10,000, you would have $25,900. *That* is what we mean by building wealth.

While stocks have been the most profitable investment over the long term, they have done it at the expense of significant short-term volatility. Volatility can be scary. That leads us to the questions in the following section.

Are Stocks Right for You? Are You Right for Stocks?

If past history holds, over sufficiently long periods of time you can build wealth by simply *participating in* the market. If you won't need the money over the next few years, stocks are likely to perform pretty well over the long haul. You can participate in the market by simply buying broad index mutual funds, which hold many stocks, mimic the market's overall performance, sport low expenses, and are readily available from a number of sources.

However, in order to accomplish wealth-building even more effectively, you need to ratchet up your goal from *participating* in the market to *beating* the market. The only ways to do this are as follows:

- Buy what are known as "actively managed" mutual funds that consistently beat the market. It turns out that there are very few of these, and there are practically none when measured over terms as long as ten years.
- Buy individual stocks and do it yourself. That is what this book is about.

Stocks are not right for everyone. Before anyone invests in stocks, they should be sure that stock ownership is a good fit for them. Stocks may be right for you if the following conditions are true:

- You have a relatively long investment horizon. A common rule of thumb is to subtract your age from 100 or 110. The resulting number is the percentage of your investable assets that "should" be in the stock market. For example, if you are 55, you are likely to live another 25 to 40 years, and you "should" have 45 percent of your investable assets in the stock market so that you can keep up with inflation.

- You don't need the money within three to five years (such as for a house down payment or college tuition). Both this and the previous guideline are sensibly predicated on stocks' potential to *lose* value over three-to-five year time periods.

- You are comfortable with some degree of risk. Compared to bonds or cash, stocks are volatile, and they can lose value. Stocks are *not* a vehicle for protecting your money. Rather, stocks present the potential for making it grow. That potential is accompanied, however, by risk of loss, especially over short time frames.

- You have enough money. If you have less than about $30,000 to invest, the risk of loss may be too great with individual stocks. It would be better to get started with mutual funds. Mutual funds still bear risk, but they are usually less volatile than individual stocks, because funds purchase many more stocks than you will as an individual investor, and the ups and downs in their many stocks tend to smooth out total performance.

- You do not mind paying attention. Of course, many investors consider this to be fun. You may be one of them.

Why You, an Individual Investor, Can Beat the Market

Many people believe that an individual cannot beat the market. That is, they think that they cannot, over long periods of time, generate better returns on their money than the overall market itself generates, nor outperform professional money managers who, after all, do this for a living. Investing in stocks simply intimidates some people.

Successful investing is not nearly as complicated as many people would have you believe. The idea that you cannot do better than professional money managers, or better than the market itself, is flawed for a number of reasons:

1. As an individual investor, you run your own shop. You have the ability to wait for the right price. Unlike many professional money managers, you don't need to be fully invested, or close to it, at any time. If, during bad market conditions, cash is the best place for your "stock money," you can keep it in cash and no one will fire you. You don't have your boss telling you to get fully invested. You *are* the boss. You decide what to do with your capital.

2. Many mutual funds own unattractive stocks. They get into that bind because they have so much money to invest. So the professional fund managers go through their first tier of good ideas and on to their

second tier, and maybe even into their third. Their fund's charter may require diversification across a broad range of stocks, or it may limit how much stock can be owned in any one company. The bottom line is that mediocre performance is practically assured. A fund holding upwards of 400 stocks is basically a "closet" index fund—a worst-case scenario combining the average returns of an index fund with the high expenses of an actively managed fund. On the other hand, you, as an individual investor, can keep your holdings concentrated in a relatively few number of good opportunities.

3. As an individual investor, you can control your expenses. You can buy and sell using the cheapest brokerage—the execution of stock trades, after all, is a commodity service. You don't have to pay management fees, "wrap" fees, marketing expenses, or any of the other expenses that go into running mutual funds. You do not need to employ armies of analysts or pay for their computers, travel expenses, or assistants. All of the information you need to invest intelligently is available for free.

4. You don't have to "window-dress" your portfolio. In an effort to look good, some mutual fund managers buy certain stocks (and sell others) at the end of a quarter, so it looks like they owned the "right" stocks all along. These transactions cost money and do little for performance. Worse, the effort to look good can drive managers into taking risks that they would not consider if they were not in such a competitive industry.

5. You can keep your own best interests in mind. Sad to say, at many mutual funds, the primary mission is to attract more investors and their money. Incentives are set that way, rather than to encourage taking care of the fund's owners' money.

6. You control taxable events. When stocks "just sit" in a portfolio, no taxable event takes place. Capital gains (or losses) are just on paper. One of the primary advantages in owning individual stocks instead of mutual funds is to gain control over taxes. Mutual fund shareholders own shares in the fund but *not* in the individual stocks that the fund owns. Therefore, they are at the mercy of buy-and-sell decisions made by the fund's managers. Maddeningly, a mutual fund can generate taxable gains for its owners even though the fund itself *loses value*. It happens all the time. The unfortunate fund holder is left not only with a tax bill but also with an investment worth less than when it was purchased. This happens because the fund sells some stocks with gains but does not offset those gains by selling other stocks with losses. So the fund has net profits *on its trades* even if the total value of the fund is lower (because the fund held on to its losers). The net trading profits (by law) are passed through to the fund's owners. Those unfortunate owners will owe taxes on those profits even though they did not sell any shares in the fund itself. By contrast, with individual stocks, no taxable event takes place unless shares of stock are actually sold. If you own individual stocks, you are in sole control of that decision.

7. You don't have to worry about "style drift." For example, the rules for a small-company mutual fund may force the fund's manager to sell a stock if its market size exceeds a certain limit. That's what its prospectus promises its investors. But that growth is just what you are looking for as a capitalist. You *want* your small companies to succeed and become large companies. That's how you make money! All other things being equal, you don't want to sell such stocks. You don't have to be invested in any particular kind of stock. You can pick stocks based solely on merit.

The fact is, depending on market conditions, well over 50 percent and often over 80 percent of all mutual funds underperform the market consistently. The individual investor can do much better.

How This Book Can Help

As you will learn in this book, you can improve your odds of beating the market by investing more intelligently than average. If you succeed at that, you will outperform the vast majority of mutual funds, in addition to beating the returns from bonds and simple cash instruments.

There are three distinct steps to beating the market:

- picking the best companies to invest in;
- valuing the stocks of those companies so they can be purchased at the most favorable times (prices); and
- managing your portfolio well—that is, knowing when to buy and sell.

We call this Sensible Stock Investing. The skills and processes will be explained in this book.

In addition, this book also features the following:

- Two real-life, real-money portfolios, which were started in 2001 and 2002, and which are still running today. These portfolios have helped teach and illustrate the application of the Sensible Stock Investing principles in real life. You can see for yourself what the results have been.
- Forms and worksheets that can be used to organize your research, "score" companies, create a Shopping List of good opportunities, review your portfolio, and the like.
- A monthly calendar of activities you can follow to keep your financial house in order.

Stock investing can be both fun and rewarding. Let's get started!

CHAPTER A-2

The Sensible Stock Investor

Eighty percent of success is showing up.
—Woody Allen

Sensible Stock Investing in a Nutshell

In the field of law, there is a time-honored concept called the "reasonable person." Over hundreds of years, the courts have honed the description of this hypothetical being, endowing him or her with great—but not superhuman—powers.

The reasonable person acts sensibly, does things without serious delay, and takes proper but not excessive precautions. He or she makes reasonable decisions given all the information available and bears a responsibility to actively acquire critical information. The reasonable person is mindful of his or her responsibilities and seldom allows emotions to overbear reason. He or she reacts to new information in a sensible way and always exercises a reasonable amount of *care,* which means giving serious attention to possible dangers, mistakes, and pitfalls, and ensuring that these risks do not materialize, especially when dealing with very important affairs. (All of the foregoing definitions are adapted from *Black's Law Dictionary,* 1999.)

One of the mysteries (to me, anyway) of modern life is, why do so many people treat their investments passively, turning away from them (with fear or disinterest) and exercising almost deliberate ignorance? It's almost as if, once having worked so hard to make the money in the first place (at their primary jobs), they want to throw it over a wall to someone, pay as little attention to it as possible, and somehow it will magically grow into a wonderful nest egg.

Building wealth for your future—a secure retirement, college for your kids, money to help others and for a better life—would seem to be one of the most important human activities. Shouldn't individuals approach investing with interest and care, the same care that the law suggests that a prudent person applies to very important affairs?

Yet we hear stories of people who give practically no thought to the investing dimension of their lives, turn it over to the "experts," act foolishly on hot tips, and play the blame game when they get near retirement and don't have enough money. During the bubble deflation of 2000-2002, stories were rampant of people who became so depressed, so passive, that they stopped opening their quarterly 401(k) statements, because they did not want to face the bad news and apparently thought that there was nothing they could do about it anyway. This is not the way successful people approach other important activities of their lives. Why do people approach investing that way?

I'll leave it to psychologists to answer that question. Meanwhile, a more active attitude—one that puts you in control—is clearly needed. Stock investing needs the financial equivalent of the law's reasonable person.

To fill that void, we hereby invent the **Sensible Stock Investor**. When it comes to building wealth for the future, the Sensible Stock Investor practices what we call Sensible Stock Investing—an intelligent method based on common sense, best practices, sensible risk management, and a reasonable degree of attention and care. In other words, the Sensible Stock Investor acts like the law's reasonable person when it comes to tending his or her wealth.

The individual ideas of Sensible Stock Investing make sense and are fairly simple, but taken together they create a powerful latticework of sound interlocking concepts. The end result, stated simply, is that as a Sensible Stock Investor you will:

- Stay rational.

- Choose a few stocks that are likely to outperform the market, concentrating the bulk of your investments in your best ideas (those with the highest probability of above-average performance).

- Have the fortitude to hold on to them during short-term market volatility (as long as things do not deteriorate too much).

- Keep track of what you own, making sure that your companies are still excellent operations with continuing good prospects.

- Maintain a fiduciary duty to yourself by guarding against losing money.

- Control excessive optimism and pessimism, knowing that both extremes can cause you to make bad judgments.

- Always keep learning about how you can improve your approach and do things better.

Rejecting Rigid or Extreme Approaches

As we shall see, Sensible Stock Investing usually rejects extreme styles and rigid approaches. In the stock market, there are many schools of thought about how to go about making investment decisions. Some of these schools are not only diametrically opposed to one another in their fundamental principles and beliefs, but they are also rigid and unyielding. Some investors—including professionals—cling stubbornly to clearly losing strategies for years. We will help you sort out the various approaches and decide what to embrace and what to reject.

One thing we've found is that hybrid or centrist approaches generally outperform extreme approaches over the long run. Therefore, Sensible Stock Investing is flexible and seeks balance. We try to figure out what makes the most sense and make our decisions accordingly.

In Sensible Stock Investing, we will not just focus on a single factor in making decisions whether to buy, hold, or sell a stock. Instead, we'll be eclectic and agnostic. For example, we will not always veto a stock solely because its price seems too high, and we certainly won't buy one only because its price is low (the price might be low because the company is lousy). Once we own a stock, we won't sell it simply because it has grown too large or increased in value too much. On the contrary, growth is our objective—we should all be so fortunate as to need to decide what to do with a stock that has "grown too large."

The Sensible Stock Investor believes that success is achieved by identifying really good companies, buying their stocks at decent prices, managing portfolios intelligently, and protecting against significant losses along the way. Period.

Because we avoid extreme approaches, the Sensible Stock Investor generally experiences steady, rather than spectacular, results. This is a good thing: A steady portfolio almost always makes more money over time than a wildly volatile portfolio. Consider these examples:

- Stock A: Loses 50 percent in Year 1 and then gains 100 percent in Year 2. That spectacular second year may be worthy of cocktail-party bragging, but after two years, the net gain is 0 percent. You are right back where you started. Not only that, you probably lost some sleep during Year 1, if in fact you held on all year. Because of inflation, you lost purchasing power.
- Stock B: Gains 100 percent in Year 1 and then loses 50 percent in Year 2. Net gain: 0 percent again.
- Stock C: Gains 20 percent in Year 1 and 8 percent in Year 2. Point of arrival: 30 percent gain. (Notice that the total two-year gain is not the simple sum of 20 percent plus 8 percent. The "extra" gain comes from the compounding of gain upon gain.)

Sensible Stock Investing pursues above-average, market-beating total returns. This is not to say that the ride will not be bumpy. Everything in the stock market is bumpy. However, we encourage you to tolerate some bumpiness, because it is so likely that in the long term, the strong underlying economics of the good companies you select, combined with the advantage that you gain by obtaining them at sensible prices, will overcome short-term price fluctuations. And thanks to the effects of compounding, over long periods of time even a little extra return each year will add significantly to your long-term results.

Learning to Spot Common Sense and Reject Nonsense

As you become familiar with Sensible Stock Investing, you will find yourself becoming skeptical or critical of a lot of conventional wisdom about stock investing. Things you read or hear on TV will start to sound different. Some "experts" won't seem as smart as they used to. That may happen when they start to sound rigid, while you are becoming comfortable with flexibility. Or perhaps when it does not sound anymore like they are drawing reasonable inferences from the information available. Or maybe when it becomes apparent that they seem to be able to view things in only one way.

As you go through this transition, you will find yourself discounting or rejecting much opinion and dogma, which seems to be mindlessly repeated. You will also learn to be wary of theories and conclusions based on the historical performance of large categories of stocks, rather than on stocks individually. For example, the daily report about whether the Dow Jones Industrial Average or the NASDAQ Composite Index is up or down tells you little about the individual stocks that you own. Both indexes might fall, while the value of your portfolio goes up. For the Sensible Stock Investor, that happens fairly frequently. And it's a great feeling.

Here are just three examples of common investment "wisdom" that you will find yourself coming to question as you become a Sensible Stock Investor:

- *The efficient market theory.* This is an academic principle that, at any given time, the market has already factored into its prices all known information about every company. Therefore, the market is always "fairly priced," any price that appears too high or too low must be an illusion, and there is therefore no use investing in individual stocks, because your results will track market results. People who believe this tell you to just buy index mutual funds. We reject this theory for a variety of reasons. We firmly believe that the market makes pricing mistakes regularly, that it can be beaten soundly, and that there are thousands of Americans who do it regularly. We do it, and you can too.

- *"Diversify, diversify, diversify."* This principle is so embedded that it has become a mantra. But when the dogma is set aside for a moment and actual facts are examined, it turns out that statistically your best chance for beating the market is to hold a limited number of stocks, say 20 or fewer. This is because the more stocks you hold—the more you diversify—the more your portfolio becomes *like* the market. If your portfolio simply mimics the market, then obviously you cannot *beat* it. You may as well simply buy an index fund.

- *Buy and hold.* This is a passive approach to stock investing which recommends that you simply hold on to stocks once you buy them. There are strong and weak forms of this principle, and they have become embedded in much investment literature. The trouble is, Buy-and-Hold is not always the best approach. It depends on what kind of stocks you own and what prevailing market conditions are. Our philosophy is called Buy-*to*-Hold. That is, when you purchase a stock, your *intent* is to hold it for one to two years or more, but if things are not working favorably, you sell the stock without hesitation. The bottom line is that you will hold some stocks for short periods of time, others for longer, and a few successful stocks for much longer, perhaps for your entire investment lifetime.

CHAPTER A-3

The Three Steps to
Sensible Stock Investing

Sensible Stock Investing has three basic elements:

- Pick the *right companies.*
- Pick the *right price* to pay for stock in those companies.
- *Manage your portfolio* intelligently.

These elements are interdependent. They overlap and operate simultaneously.

Let's take a brief tour of these three elements now. Then in the remainder of the book, we'll explore them in detail and demonstrate how they will guide your Sensible Stock Investing decisions.

Pick the Right Companies

The first element in Sensible Stock Investing is to pick the right companies. A share of stock, after all, is a share in the ownership of a company. So when you purchase a share of stock, you are buying into the future performance and fortunes of the company. Naturally, you want to own superior companies with superior futures.

Remember your objective: to build wealth at a pace faster than the market's pace. As a generalization that is good enough for now, stock prices for the most part track the fortunes of the companies they represent. So the idea is to find companies which will not only build their financial value, but which will do it *faster* than the average company.

Of course, nothing in investing is guaranteed. The stock market's day-to-day vagaries can cause stock prices to become quite detached from the value inherent in their underlying companies. Thus, no matter how well you select companies, there is always an unavoidable element of market risk—the risk inherent in the stock market itself. So it is imperative that you do what you can to tilt the playing field in your favor. The first step in gaining this advantage is to identify truly superior companies. How to do this is the subject of Part C of this book.

Pick the Right Price

The second move for the Sensible Stock Investor will stack the odds even more in your favor. This is to determine an acceptable—or better still, an obviously advantageous—price to pay for every stock that you buy.

The assessment of stock prices is referred to as "valuation." The underlying idea is that there is such a thing as a "fair" price for a stock, or that a company's stock has a certain "inherent value," which market participants will generally agree upon over time. If *today's* price of the stock has become detached from its "fair" price, then history suggests that, over time, the stock will gravitate toward that fair price. So another way to look at this step is that you are trying to determine the *direction* that the stock's price is likely to go in the future.

Naturally, the direction we are interested in is *up*. Since stock prices vary daily, are traded on an open market, and involve the buy-and-sell decisions of hundreds of thousands of people using who-knows-what approaches, common sense suggests that valuing stocks involves an inexact appraisal process of one kind or another. Stock valuation, in fact, has many similarities to home appraisals. If you've ever had a home appraised, you know that the exercise involves comparisons to "similar" properties and the use of imprecise factors (such as the comparative quality of materials used in the homes). Whether an appraisal is of a home, a piece of heirloom jewelry, a used car, or a stock, the process is part art, part science, and part luck. There are different ways to go about appraising anything.

Thus, reasonable minds often differ when appraising what a stock is worth. That's why stocks are traded—each party thinks he or she is getting the better end of the deal. We offer a sensible approach that comes at the problem from a variety of angles, avoids duplication, is relatively easy to compute, and weighs information intelligently—all to put you on the right side of the deal more often than not.

Putting these first two elements of Sensible Stock Investing together—picking the best companies and picking good prices to pay for them—yields the following fundamental tenet of our approach: If you purchase stocks of superior companies at prices that are, for whatever reason, "low," the market's long-range tendency to move stock prices in the direction of company performance will reward you with better returns than the market averages.

You will beat the market.

Surprisingly, the importance of stock valuation is sometimes hotly debated.

- Some pundits actually maintain that the price of a stock is not relevant to your success as an investor. Their reasoning is that if you have succeeded in locating a superior company, it doesn't matter what its stock costs, because it *will go up* over time, as a result of the superiority of the company. Such investors are usually called "growth" investors. Sometimes the extreme form of this philosophy is referred to as the Growth at Any Price approach, meaning that price is irrelevant when you are dealing with "growth" stocks. One heard this philosophy much more during the bubble period of the late 1990s than today.

- A second group of investment experts also maintains that valuation is irrelevant, but for a different reason. These are the efficient market theorists, who believe that today's market price of a stock *is* what the price "ought" to be, because the market is a completely efficient machine in processing all available information. As a result, they maintain that no improvement in investment success is possible based on valuation, because you can never make a better estimate of what a stock is truly worth than the market already has. The Sensible Stock Investor does not buy this, for reasons stated earlier and explored more thoroughly in Chapter B-4.

- A third group of investment theorists is at the opposite end of the philosophical spectrum, believing that valuation is *everything.* Extreme "value" investors believe that the *sole* source of stacking the investing odds in your favor comes from purchasing only stocks that are way undervalued, or "cheap," and that you'll make your money by waiting for the stock's price to rise (as it inevitably must, they say) to the stock's "correct" price. Quite often, for example, you'll hear the manager of a value-oriented mutual fund state that his fund will only consider a stock whose price is no more than 60 percent (or 70 percent, or whatever) of what he or she believes is the stock's intrinsic value (however that may be computed). Proponents of value investing believe that the Growth at Any Price approach is total nonsense, deriding it as the "Greater Fool Theory," meaning that your only chance to make money if you pay no attention to price is if you are fortunate enough to find someone even dumber than you, who will buy your stock from you for more than you paid. So-called value investors had a laugh on the growth investors during the bubble deflation of 2000–2003. However, they were outperformed badly by other approaches in the late 1990s.

What do we think?

Sensible Stock Investing takes a somewhat middle ground. Logic (not to mention math) tells you that price *has to be* important. After all, the lower the price you pay for a stock, the more shares you will receive for your dollars. The benefits of owning those extra shares will magnify the value (the wealth) you receive from that stock for as long as you own it, assuming that at some time in the future the stock's price does rise, either to what it "ought" to be or to some other value even higher.

Therefore, Sensible Stock Investing posits (along with many successful investors) that each stock has a *likely future direction* in its price, which will be played out over a short or long term. Over time, the stock's price will gravitate toward a reasonable value as appraised by participants in the market.

We further posit, from common observation, that from day to day the actual current price of any stock wanders around its long-term price trend, sometimes departing significantly from it, both up and down. Sometimes the price will be higher than it is going to become, and other times it will be less. The latter, of course, represents a favorable buying opportunity for the stock, because if you can buy it when it is selling for less than what the market will later judge the stock to be worth, that obviously tilts the odds of success in your favor.

Valuing stocks is discussed in detail in Part D.

Manage Your Portfolio Intelligently

The third and final element of Sensible Stock Investing involves knowing why and when to buy and sell—in other words, how to manage your portfolio.

Neophyte investors tend to focus solely on stock picking, but before long they realize that actually owning stocks imposes the need for additional decisions about when and whether to buy more of, sell, or just hold on to stocks they have already purchased.

There is a spectrum of approaches to portfolio management. So-called day traders buy and sell stocks furiously, attempting to make money by utilizing minuscule holding periods, fueled by constant monitoring of information about companies, their stocks, and second-by-second price changes. In its purest form, day trading requires selling out every position by the end of each trading day, to guard against the danger of price moves caused by unexpected news overnight. It sounds and is exhausting (although there must be some adrenaline highs along the way), and we don't recommend it. Not many people are successful at it, and the tax consequences of all that trading can be indescribable. Day trading is not the preferred method of Sensible Stock Investing.

At the other end of the scale are the Buy-and-Holders, whom we've already met. Like a dog with a bone, the Buy-and-Holder hangs on to every stock as long as possible, ideally forever. They become very committed to their original decision. That's a good approach *if* one has judged every stock's future price direction correctly as up, and if the investor has unlimited time until he or she needs the money. The Buy-and-Hold approach (i.e., not trading) also works well over shorter time frames when the market is moving generally upward and carrying most stocks along with it.

The Sensible Stock Investing approach, as usual, lies between the two extremes, although in this case we find ourselves closer to one end than the other.

Holding on to stocks (once purchased) has a number of advantages *if* prices are generally moving up, or even if they are going sideways. Three of the most important advantages of holding on are

- the postponement of taxes, which allows tax-free compounding of returns;
- the reduction of the applicable tax rate on gains if the stock is held for over a year; and
- the avoidance of excessive commissions.

Because of these advantages, the Sensible Stock Investing approach to portfolio management is closer to Buy-and-Hold than to day trading. But, as we will show, sometimes clinging to a stock is, well, stupid, and there are many times when the intelligent thing to do is to sell.

We call our approach Buy-*to*-Hold. This conveys that our *intent* is to hold on to our stocks for a long time while they grow and compound in value. But our approach is flexible. We will sell stocks for a variety of reasons when that appears to be the best thing to do.

We'll explore the details of portfolio management in Part E.

And that concludes the mini-tour of Sensible Stock Investing's approach:

- Buy stocks of superior companies.
- Buy them at advantageous prices.
- Hold on to them as long as it makes sense.

CHAPTER A-4

Risk and Time Horizons

Risk comes from not knowing what you're doing.
—Warren Buffett

What Are the Risks in Stock Investing?

While most people have a gut-level understanding of risk, it is actually quite a complicated subject. A library's worth of books has been written about risk. For the purposes of the individual investor, we need to simplify the concept.

Common dictionary definitions of risk are that it means exposure to the possibility of harm or loss, to embark on a hazardous or perilous course of action, or to take a chance. In life, there are numerous risks, and law's reasonable person is expected to make intelligent decisions about which ones are worth taking and which should be avoided. Normally, as knowledge increases, risk level decreases.

In investing, of course, the "loss" under consideration is loss of money, and the reasonable person is you, the Sensible Stock Investor. There are three ways you can suffer an investing loss, which means that there are three fundamental types of risk:

1. The *actual* loss of money, meaning that you end up with less than you started with. It is a fact: You cannot participate in the stock market unless you put your money at risk. That is because stock prices decline as well as rise. This risk is called "principal risk."

2. The *effective* loss of money, which means that the *buying power* of your money erodes over time because of inflation. The math is simple: If the buying power of a dollar declines 3 percent per year (which is typical of the past several years), then after 10 years you might still have the same number of dollars you started with, but those dollars will buy only three-quarters as much as they do today. It is as if you lost a quarter of your money. Your investment is worth less in real value at the end of your holding period than at the beginning. This risk is called "purchasing power risk," meaning the risk of not keeping up with inflation.

3. The *relative* loss of money, meaning that your investment has failed to achieve some target that you expected (say the market's long-term 10 to 11 percent return) or that it has failed to beat the return of another investment where you might have put your money: different stocks, or maybe bonds (which sometimes return more than stocks for a period of time).

Coming at the question of risk from another angle, we find that the risk in stocks is also sometimes parsed into two other categories: market risk and stock-specific risk. Market risk is the chance that the entire market will go down and drag your stocks with it. (The overall market might go down because the economy tanks, terrorists attack, the market hits a bad patch, or the like.) Stock-specific risk is the possibility that your particular stock declines (or underperforms the market) even though overall the market is performing well. (This could happen because something unfavorable happens to the company itself: labor problems arise, bad weather affects retailers, growth or profit margins unexpectedly decline, or management makes a dumb acquisition.)

How Risky Is the Stock Market?

It is almost impossible to put a quantitative value on riskiness, because risk can be measured in so many ways. Ultimately, of course, risk exists because stock prices change, and they change because the stocks are traded in markets. For that reason, most financial theorists and many investors equate risk with price volatility: the week-to-week or month-to-month ups and downs in the share prices of stocks. The more volatile a stock's price, the riskier the stock is considered to be.

Sensible Stock Investing looks with a jaundiced eye at equating risk with price volatility. While it is true that a stock with low volatility will lose less money when the market is going down, it is also true that the same stock will *gain* less than the market when the market is going up. Besides that, a drop in a stock's price can provide an attractive opportunity to *buy* the stock—it's on sale! So overall, relative volatility leaves a lot to be desired as the measure of a stock's risk.

Further complicating the measurement of riskiness is the fact that certain risks can be hedged, or ameliorated, if the investor takes certain defensive measures. To cite an obvious example, the fact that a stock's price drops 30 percent in a year is irrelevant to you if you sold it after the first 5 percent of the drop. Selling, as it turns out, is the most fundamental hedging technique, and there are many others. And of course, risk is reduced in the first place if one sticks to investing in excellent companies and buying them at favorable prices, which you will recall are the first two cornerstones of Sensible Stock Investing.

Another complicating factor in the quantification of risk is the length of your holding period. That is why risk and time horizons have been combined in this chapter. The length of your holding period depends on how you manage your portfolio, which is the third cornerstone of Sensible Stock Investing.

For example, if you have a long-term holding horizon, history tells us that stocks *have made* money for the people who invest in them. Let's ignore our goal of beating the market for a moment and just look at the market itself. On average, since 1926, the stock market has returned around 10 to 11 percent *annually.* That is an excellent rate of return in its own right: At 10 percent compounded annually, money doubles in about 7 years. If we can improve the market's return significantly (which is the goal of Sensible Stock Investing), we can do better. The "better" is brought to you courtesy of the arithmetic of compounding. Refer back to the table in Chapter A-1 and note the difference after 5 years between a 10 percent annual return and a 15 percent annual return. The difference after 5 years on a $10,000 initial investment is $4000, which is 40 percent of the original stake. That is a significant improvement.

One of my favorite notions in Sensible Stock Investing is this: A "paper" loss becomes an actual loss only if you sell the stock. Both gains and losses become real (or "realized") *only* when you sell. Everything before that is just on paper. Thus your holding period can play a significant role in the actual riskiness of your stock investing. Because risk does not ripen into reality until you actually sell a losing stock, volatility and risk are *not* the same thing, except over very short periods of time. For example, if you are selling your stocks day-to-day (which is what day traders do), then risk and volatility are about the same thing: Whatever your stock did *that day* also determines your risk.

If you own the whole market (i.e., an index fund), the risk of actually losing money in stocks *goes down* with time. Averaged across the whole market, the risk of losing money with a broad market index has historically tended to go to near zero over very long holding periods (say 30+ years). That is because the shorter-term volatility in stock prices takes place against the backdrop of a trendline, which has been moving upward at about 10 to 11 percent per year since before the Great Depression.

We might call this the Rip Van Winkle principle: The real risk of investing in the stock market (as a whole, not an individual stock) decreases as the time frame increases. Someone (Rip) could ignore his portfolio for 15 years and then wake up, check his latest brokerage statement, and find that his stocks have gone up 10 percent per year. He would not know that they jumped all over the place in between, *and he wouldn't care.*

As good as that sounds, Rip's approach does not describe how most investors behave, nor does it work as well as you shorten the time frame or apply it to small portfolios. Most important, it does not allow an investor to *improve* on the market's overall performance by making occasional smart moves to avoid losses, lock in gains, or sidestep the worst bear markets. Beating the market, again, is the fundamental goal of Sensible Stock Investing, so ultimately Rip's approach cannot be ours, at least not without some modifications.

The risk of actually losing money (the risk numbered "1" in the first section of this chapter) varies by *asset class:*

- Cash is the least risky (unless you literally do lose it).

- Bonds are in the middle. Bond prices fluctuate, but usually your principal is safe (with bonds backed by the U.S. government's taxing power being the safest of all). And the bonds' price fluctuations are dampened by the flow of interest income that the bonds throw off.

- Stocks are the most risky (except over decades-long time periods as described above).

The risk of money losing its purchasing power to inflation (risk number 2) also varies by asset class. The results are just the opposite of the above:

- Cash is the *most* risky, because cash (and "cash equivalents" such as savings accounts) return either zero or nearly zero over time. They usually do not keep up with inflation.

- Bonds again are in the middle, because their average return is in the middle. They sometimes do, and sometimes do not, keep up with inflation.

- Stocks as a class are the *least* risky over long time periods, because they hold out the promise for the highest rate of return. In the long run, stocks have proven to be the best protectors of purchasing power of any major asset class.

The bottom line is that however you measure riskiness in stock investing, it can be reduced by following sound techniques for picking stocks, valuing them, and managing your portfolio.

The Tortoise and the Hare

Take this little quiz: See if you can guess which portfolio in the table below (A, B, C, or D) ends up with the largest total gain after 5 years. Notice the different returns from year to year of each of the portfolios, especially the mouthwatering 30 to 60 percent returns available in Portfolios B, C, and D. Also notice that if you just arithmetically add the portfolios' returns across all 5 years, they all total 50 percent (shaded column). Does that mean that their cumulative return is really the same?

The Tortoise and the Hare—Part I

Portfolio	Year 1	Year 2	Year 3	Year 4	Year 5	Arithmetic Total Gain
A	+10%	+10%	+10%	+10%	+10%	+50%
B	−30%	+10%	+30%	+30%	+10%	+50%
C	+50%	−40%	+60%	−20%	0%	+50%
D	+10%	+20%	+30%	+40%	−50%	+50%

Which portfolio won? You might be surprised. Steadiness of gains beats out big swings almost every time. Scenario A—monotonous 10 percent gains each year—wins easily. The other portfolios are more exciting, sporting gains as large as 60 percent in some years. But they lose to Portfolio A.

The Tortoise and the Hare—Part II

Portfolio	Year 1	Year 2	Year 3	Year 4	Year 5	Arithmetic Total Gain	Actual Total Gain
A	+10%	+10%	+10%	+10%	+10%	+50%	+61%
B	−30%	+10%	+30%	+30%	+10%	+50%	+43%
C	+50%	−40%	+60%	−20%	0%	+50%	+15%
D	+10%	+20%	+30%	+40%	−50%	+50%	+20%

The reason that Portfolio A wins is the result of compounding: In a stock portfolio, the *cumulative* result after each year is a function of what has gone on during preceding years as well as during the year in question. Each year's final value is *not independent* of what happened in prior years. So the scattered negative years in Portfolios B, C, and D ruin their cumulative results. In fact, the 61 percent total gain of Portfolio A is 42 percent more than the next-best Portfolio B, and a whopping 400 percent more than the intriguing, but ultimately worst, Portfolio C.

You might say that the negative years result in a "decompounding" effect that is just as powerful—but in the wrong direction—as the relentless positive compounding that takes place in Portfolio A. Simple mathematics works against you when you are talking about losses. Consider this: When a stock falls from $100 to $50, it registers a 50 percent decline. But getting it back to $100 requires a 100 percent increase (i.e., the $50 has to double). To illustrate with Portfolio D: If you started out with $10,000, you got to $24,024 after Year 4. But the 50 percent loss in Year 5 brought the portfolio back to $12,012, or just 20 percent more than where you started. Portfolio A, meanwhile, has steadily climbed to $16,105, or 61 percent more than the original $10,000.

The lesson here, of course, is to cut losses short when they rear their ugly head. We will discuss loss avoidance thoroughly in Part E of this book.

Time Horizons in Investing

Time comes into play in a variety of ways in investing. Are you a long-term investor? How long do you hold the average stock in your portfolio? How long *should* you hold it? How long before you'll actually need the money you have invested?

In the lingo of investing, *time* is often coupled with *horizon*, as in "What is your investing horizon?" It's a good idea to take a step back here and consider two specific time horizons that we need to understand.

What Is Your Investment Horizon?

First, your "investment horizon." This refers to how long you'll be investing. The answer is obvious: You will be investing (in something) for the rest of your life, so your investment horizon could be 30, 40, or 50 years or even longer. In that sense, you are a "long-term investor," even if you are a day trader. The key is not how long you hold on to your typical stock; it's how long you're in the game at all. If someone asks you if you are a long-term investor, the answer is always *yes*, even though that is probably not what he or she meant.

What he or she almost invariably meant was: Do you tend to hold on to your investments for a long time? But your investment horizon is *not* the same as your holding period. While you may be invested in stocks for 30 or 40 years, it is awfully hard to peer into the future *that far* and foresee with any clarity *which stocks* you'll be invested in 40 years from now. People at the turn of the 20th century could not foretell the boom in radio and television coming in a couple of decades, although they could clearly see the money pouring into railroads. People in the 1940s or 1950s would have had great difficulty predicting the rise in computers, especially personal computers. By the time personal computers were becoming an important industry in the 1980s, it was very difficult or impossible to see the rise of the Internet.

So your investing horizon is long-term, basically lasting the rest of your life. Within that lifelong time frame, if you are sensible, it is almost inevitable that

- you will not hold on to every stock that you ever buy for as long as you live; and
- you will move money into different asset classes (predominantly bonds and cash) as you age and approach important life events (such as financing your child's education, scraping together the down payment for a house, or retiring).

This book is about stock investing, not overall financial planning. But typically, financial advisers recommend *not* having any money in the stock market that you know you will actually need in the next three years, or more conservatively in the next five years. The reason, of course, is the risk of loss in the stock market. As you get close to the time of needing the money itself, you want it to be in a more predictable place than the stock market. The market is your vehicle for long-term wealth building. It is not a safe parking place for your money.

What Is Your Prediction Horizon?

There is a second time horizon that has been invented just for the purposes of Sensible Stock Investing: the "prediction horizon." Under our approach, the prediction horizon is the length of time that it seems *reasonable to predict the likely performance of a company*. This will vary from company to company according to many factors: how long the company has been in existence, its recent track record, what kind of business the company is in, what its competitors are up to, whether a Hall of Fame—caliber leader is nearing retirement, and so on.

Even though you are hoping to purchase stocks that can be held for a very long time, it is impossible to *know* the future, and the farther out you try to predict it, the more likely you are to be wrong. So in Sensible Stock Investing, we concentrate on looking one to two years out in predicting how companies are going to do.

This time period—one to two years—has been chosen carefully.

- One to two years just seems to make sense in terms of being a length of time that you might be able to predict—with some degree of confidence—the prospects and likely performance of a company.
- One year is the minimum holding time to get long-term capital gain tax treatment.

Choosing a prediction horizon as *short* as one to two years allows us to consider investing in younger, less-proven companies, which just wouldn't be feasible under a longer guideline. While *every* company on the face of the earth is vulnerable to the vicissitudes of the economy or to having its business undercut by a smarter, sharper competitor, younger companies in particular are vulnerable to economic slowdowns and to the sudden appearance of disruptive technologies that make their products obsolete. It is very hard to predict market success for most young companies beyond one or two years. Yet we *want* them in our portfolios, because they often offer the opportunities for rewards that are both startlingly quick and breath-takingly large.

Now with these simple concepts out of the way, let's dig a bit into the stock market, find out what it is, and figure out how we can use that knowledge to our advantage.

PART B.   THE STOCK MARKET

Chapter B-1.   What *Is* the Stock Market, Anyway?

Chapter B-2.   Stock Indexes

Chapter B-3.   What Determines Stock Prices?

Chapter B-4.   Is the Market Efficient? Is It Rational?

Chapter B-5.   Bull Markets, Bear Markets, and Bubbles

CHAPTER B-1

What *Is* the Stock Market, Anyway?

What Happens in the Stock Market

The phrases "stock market" or "the market" refer to a variety of physical and virtual markets where stocks are traded. The New York Stock Exchange (NYSE) is a physical bricks-and-mortar market, located on Wall Street in New York City. Traders literally call out bid and ask prices to each other and make trades face-to-face. The NASDAQ, by contrast, is a virtual market existing in computer networks, where software matches up orders. The NYSE and the NASDAQ are the major two markets in the United States, accounting for the vast majority of stocks traded every business day. In addition to the NYSE and the NASDAQ, there are numerous other stock markets both domestically and in many other countries around the world.

In this book, we use "the market" to refer collectively to all stock markets.

What goes on in the stock market? Think of it as a meeting place for buying and selling, with thousands of individual stocks being traded (bought and sold) whenever the market is open. Every stock has its own set of buyers and sellers. The prices of individual stocks change all the time.

The market is *not* a monolithic entity where all the stocks move in lockstep and everything goes up or down together. As the saying goes, the stock market is a "market of stocks." That is the perspective you want, to think of the individual stocks *within* the market. As a Sensible Stock Investor, your success will be based on the performance of individual stocks, not the market as a whole. Unfortunately, much of what one hears tends to push the mind toward the monolithic view. The daily reports on how the market performed imply that stock prices move up or down together, whereas the truth is that the prices of individual stocks move independently, some up and some down, every day.

That said, there is some truth that a rising tide raises all boats and vice versa. Thus the broad market averages or indexes measure the climate for stock investing and provide a benchmark for comparison. When the market as a whole has a strong up day, for example, probably 60 percent or more of all the stocks in the market went up individually. Strong up (or down) days often reflect the collective actions of institutions—mutual funds, banks, pension plans, hedge funds—which are responsible for the majority of trading volume each day.

Why Does the Market Exist?

The stock market has an important function in our capitalist system. It is a giant capital-allocation machine. Because of the stock market, businesses can get money to start up or to expand. Shares in companies are viable investments precisely because the market provides liquidity—a place to buy and sell them.

The market sets a price for each business through the process of trading. Shareowners who have different beliefs about the worth of shares can sell them back and forth, each trying to gain the greater return. Over time, capital usually finds the areas of highest expected return, and thus it gets distributed rationally. Good companies attract capital, and bad ones (eventually) are denied it.

CHAPTER B-2

Stock Indexes

What Are Indexes, Anyway?

In the world of stocks, an index refers to any average of stock prices. Indexes are meant to provide benchmarks or a general sense for how the market as a whole, or particular segments of it, are "doing."

The granddaddy of all market indexes is the Dow Jones Industrial Average (usually just called the Dow). It was created in 1896 by Charles Dow as a way to track the average behavior of the NYSE. Its early invention and historical significance give it an important position in the minds of most investors. To many in the public, the Dow *is* the market. Actually, however, the Dow is a small collection of only 30 stocks meant to *represent* the overall market, which actually has thousands of stocks and millions of shares traded daily.

Since the creation of the Dow, many other indexes have been invented. They cover different universes of stocks and compute their values differently. Each index tells you a little something different, and each has its pros and cons in terms of its informational value to the individual investor.

What follows is a quick guide to the indexes that you hear about most often. This guide will help you interpret what you hear when it is said that a particular index went up or down during a market session. Pay particular attention in the following to

- what stocks (or types of stocks) each index covers;
- how broad the index is—how many stocks are in it;
- how it is calculated—the proprietors of indexes define "average" differently;
- the pros and cons of each index.

The Most Popular Indexes

The Dow

- *Full name*: Dow Jones Industrial Average (DJIA)
- *Number of stocks in the index*: 30

- *Nickname*: "The Blue Chips." This commonly used nickname is misleading, as if the 30 stocks in the index somehow represent the entire population of blue-chip stocks. (Blue chips are large, strong, usually old companies that are perceived to be bulwarks of the economy and safe long-term investments.) In fact, of course, what the Dow represents is no more or less than its 30 specific stocks. It *is* true that all of the companies in it are huge corporations, with the likes of GE, IBM, Microsoft, Procter & Gamble, and Coca-Cola represented. But in the final analysis, the Dow is a limited portfolio, plain and simple, of 30 stocks.

- *Maintained by*: Dow Jones Corporation, publishers of the *Wall Street Journal*

- *Date created*: 1896. The Dow is the oldest continuing market index in the country.

- *How stocks are selected*: The Dow contains stocks of large companies with long records of stable growth. Stocks in the index are not often changed, but it may surprise some that they are changed at all. The most recent changes took place in 2002, when AIG, Verizon, and Pfizer replaced International Paper, AT&T, and Eastman Kodak. Four stocks were changed in 1999 (Home Depot, Intel, Microsoft, and SBC came into the index), and four other switches were made in 1997. That means that since 1997, over a third of the Dow components have changed. Only one original company from 1896 (General Electric) has survived the entire existence of the Dow. Sheer size is clearly a criterion for inclusion. The Dow Jones Corporation maintains separate indexes for transportation and utility stocks, so no companies of that type are represented in the DJIA. Until a few years ago, its stocks were limited to those traded on the NYSE, but with the addition of Microsoft and Intel in 1999, NASDAQ is now represented too.

- *How the index is computed*: The Dow was originally designed for easy calculation. It was just a simple average of the prices of its original stocks. It still is essentially that, although mathematical factors have been introduced over the years to compensate for stock splits and the substitution of new stocks for deleted ones. This *average price* approach, unweighted for how big each company is, makes the Dow somewhat unusual among indexes: A 10 percent change in an $80 stock influences the index four times as much as a 10 percent change in a $20 stock. Thus, the index is "price weighted."

- *Importance*: The Dow is the best-known and most-quoted index. When the average person wants to know, "How'd the market do today?" telling them what the Dow did—"The Dow was up 75"—is usually a satisfactory answer. In fact, if you just say, "Up 75," the listener will know you are referring to the Dow.

- *Good points*: Best-known index. Reported everywhere and widely followed. The roster of large companies results in a high level of stability. Decent diversification across industries.

- *Bad points*: Contains only 30 stocks. No diversification as to size (they are all huge). Price-weighting method of calculation is unusual and does not track the blended performance of the companies as it would be experienced by actual investors (unless the investor owned the same number of shares of each company).

The NASDAQ

- *Full name*: NASDAQ Composite Average

- *Number of stocks in the index*: Represents all of the thousands of stocks traded on the NASDAQ stock market (that is, the National Association of Securities Dealers' "virtual" stock exchange). The NASDAQ exchange is essentially a computer network that enables brokers to trade among themselves. The NASDAQ market today trades almost as many shares as the venerable NYSE on most trading days. Since the NASDAQ Composite Average is limited to stocks traded on the NASDAQ market, the index does not represent the whole stock market but rather a portfolio (albeit a very large portfolio) of stocks.

- *Nickname*: The NASDAQ Composite Average is often referred to as "the tech-heavy NASDAQ," because many of the stocks on the NASDAQ exchange are technology related. Just as the Dow represents but does not measure the entire universe of blue-chip stocks, the NASDAQ represents but does not contain all technology stocks. (Hewlett-Packard and IBM, for example, trade on the New York Stock Exchange.)

- *Maintained by*: This index is a mathematical by-product of the daily trading on the NASDAQ stock exchange. The NASDAQ Stock Market, Inc., computes it.

- *Date created*: 1971

- *How stocks are selected*: All stocks that trade on the NASDAQ are represented. NASDAQ companies tend to be smaller and younger than NYSE companies, but that is not always the case. Companies used to "graduate" to the NYSE as they matured, but today that is less prevalent. Giants like Microsoft and Intel have spurned the NYSE and continue to trade where they started, on the NASDAQ.

- *How the index is computed*: The NASDAQ is a "capitalization-weighted" index, which means that the larger stocks in the index count more toward the average than the smaller stocks. ("Capitalization" refers to the total market value of each company.) Distinguish this from the simple arithmetic price average method of the Dow. The NASDAQ modifies strict capitalization weighting via a proprietary method to prevent the biggest companies from overwhelming the smallest, but the largest companies still dominate the average.

- *Importance*: In recent years, the NASDAQ Composite has become as well known and as often quoted as the Dow. It seems to have become standard practice, especially on TV, to sum up the performance of the whole market by stating what the Dow and NASDAQ did that day. In most people's minds, the Dow tells you how the blue chips or the "old economy" did that day, while the NASDAQ sums up technology or the "new economy." This is a gross oversimplification, of course.

- *Good points*: While capitalization weighting is sometimes criticized as distorting or skewing an index—because of the larger weighting accorded to the largest stocks—it is generally thought to be a superior method of calculation, because it reflects the reality that the largest holdings in any portfolio do in fact have the greatest impact on its overall returns. More to the point, your own stock portfolio is size-weighted, meaning that it is most affected by the stocks in which you have the most money invested.

The NASDAQ has pretty good diversification across industries, but it does tend to have a higher representation of technology-related stocks than the whole market.

- *Bad points*: Restricted to stocks traded on the NASDAQ exchange. Tends to be more volatile than the Dow. Tends to be dominated by the largest stocks on the NASDAQ, so it can be misleading as to how the "average" stock is doing.

S&P 500

- *Full name*: Standard & Poor's 500 Index
- *Number of stocks in the index*: 500
- *Nickname*: Usually called just "the S&P" or "the S&P 500"
- *Maintained by*: The Standard & Poor's Index Committee, which is a unit of Standard & Poor's, which in turn is a unit of The McGraw-Hill Companies, Inc.
- *Date created*: Precursors of the S&P 500 date back to 1923, when Standard and Poor's introduced an index covering 233 companies. Today's 500-stock index was introduced in 1957.
- *How stocks are selected*: Contrary to a popular misconception, the S&P 500 is not comprised of the 500 largest companies, although none of the companies is small. While often called "unmanaged," there is a fairly continual turnover in the S&P 500. Each year, the Committee changes between about 2 percent and 10 percent of the companies in the index, as they react to mergers or acquisitions, and also as they attempt to keep the index populated with industry-leading companies. For example, a company sinking toward bankruptcy will usually be discarded and replaced, as will a company no longer thought to fairly represent the market or its industry. It is considered somewhat prestigious to be included in the S&P 500, and when a new stock is added, its price usually takes a one-time jump, because all the managers of the many mutual funds that track the S&P must add it to their holdings. This causes a buying binge for a few days around the addition of a stock, which drives the price up. The opposite happens when a stock is dropped from the index. The Index Committee does not usually reveal the particular reasons when it adds or drops a company. Its broad guidelines are available on Standard & Poor's Web site. Companies in the index tend to be large industry leaders, widely held, representative of a variety of industries, "liquid" (commonly traded), and fundamentally sound. Companies are removed from the index when they merge themselves out of existence, go bankrupt, become fundamentally unsound, or no longer fairly represent their industry. In 2002, the Committee purged foreign-based companies, so the index now represents only U.S.-based companies.
- *How the index is computed*: Like most major indexes (but unlike the Dow), the S&P 500 is a capitalization-weighted index, so the largest stocks in the index have the greatest impact on the value of the index, and a relative few dominate the movement of the index.
- *Importance*: The third-most-quoted index. Measures the performance of the large-capitalization segment of the U.S. stock market. The major financial TV channels (CNBC and Bloomberg) keep the Dow, the NASDAQ, and the S&P 500 continuously on the screen or rotating constantly. The S&P 500 is widely regarded and utilized as the best single gauge of the U.S. stock market. Although it focuses on large-cap

stocks, their value covers around 80 percent of the total value of all U.S. publicly traded stocks. The S&P 500 is perceived as a "broader" index than either the Dow or the NASDAQ. We use the S&P 500 as our benchmark in this book.

- *Good points*: Broad-based, representing approximately 80 percent of the value of the U.S. stock market and spanning every important sector of the U.S. economy. Capitalization weighting is considered the best method of calculating an index. Most-used benchmark for the market as a whole.

- *Bad points*: Reflects only large, U.S.-based companies. Capitalization weighting causes the index to be dominated by the price movement of a fairly small number of stocks (approximately 40 stocks account for about half the value of the index). Fair amount of subjective judgment involved in stocks selected for the index. Turnover in roster of stocks may make this more akin to an actively managed (albeit large) portfolio than a more passive reflection of how the total market is performing.

Russell 1000, 2000, and 3000

- *Full names*: Russell 1000 Index; Russell 2000 Index; Russell 3000 Index

- *Number of stocks in the indexes*: 1000, 2000, and 3000, respectively

- *Maintained by*: Frank Russell Company, which is an investment services firm owned by Northwestern Mutual

- *Date created*: 1984

- *How stocks are selected*: Russell ranks all domestic stocks by market value at the end of each May. The top 3000 become the Russell 3000, which is therefore a very broad index to practically the entire market (it represents approximately 98 percent of the value of the investable U.S. equity market). The other two indexes are subsets of the 3000. The top 1000 are the largest third, so the Russell 1000 is therefore a broad index of large-cap stocks (broader than the S&P 500, because it contains twice as many stocks). The bottom two-thirds becomes the Russell 2000, which is a widely used benchmark for mid-cap and small-cap stocks.

- *How the index is computed*: All three indexes are capitalization weighted.

- *Importance*: For whatever reason, the Russell 3000 is not as popular a measure of the "whole market" as the S&P 500, although clearly it is a broader measure, because it contains six times as many stocks, spanning companies of all sizes and stripes. It covers about 98 percent of the value of the whole market versus the S&P's 80 percent. The Russell 1000 is not widely used, even though, again, it is a broader measure of large-cap stocks than the S&P 500. The Russell 2000, on the other hand, is the standard index for measuring how small-cap and mid-cap stocks are doing. Stocks in the Russell 2000 represent about 10 to 11 percent of the total market capitalization of the U.S. equities market.

- *Good points*: No subjectivity in selecting stocks for each index. Indexes are updated on an annual schedule, with no surprise announcements. Russell 3000 is an excellent measure of the "whole market." Russell 2000 is the most-used measure of the small-cap and mid-cap sector of the market.

- *Bad points*: Because of absence of subjective judgments, all three indexes include companies that are nearing bankruptcy, companies that are not leaders in their industries, and so on.

Wilshire 5000

- *Full name*: The Dow Jones Wilshire 5000 Composite Index
- *Number of stocks in the index*: This index was originated to represent literally every stock regularly traded in the United States. The exact number of such stocks varies, but 5000 stocks no longer represent all publicly traded companies. The actual number of stocks in the index currently exceeds 6500, and the roster is adjusted monthly.
- *Nickname*: Wilshire 5000. Also known as the Total Stock Market Index, because it attempts to reflect the performance of essentially the entire U.S. equities market.
- *Maintained by*: Wilshire Associates, an independent investment advisory company
- *Date created*: 1974
- *How stocks are selected*: This index covers all U.S.-headquartered publicly traded companies with readily available price data. Stocks traded via the so-called Bulletin Board system (which are mostly "penny" stocks and stocks of extremely small companies) are excluded.
- *How the index is computed*: Capitalization weighted, similar to the S&P 500
- *Importance*: Because of its comprehensiveness, the Wilshire 5000 is considered by some to be the best benchmark of the whole market, although in fact the S&P 500 is used more often for that purpose.
- *Good points*: The most comprehensive and diverse measure of the U.S. equities market. The world's largest index as measured by the total market value of the stocks in it. Probably the best measure of the overall market.
- *Bad points*: Composition of index and number of companies changes frequently. Tends to be dominated by the largest companies because of cap weighting (the 500 largest companies constitute more than 70 percent of the index's value). Contains no foreign companies, even if they are traded on U.S. stock exchanges.

Other Indexes

The foregoing are the most commonly cited indexes, but they are by no means the only ones. Some other well-known or commonly available indexes include the following:

- The NYSE Composite Index. This is to the New York Stock Exchange what the NASDAQ Composite is to the NASDAQ Market. The NYSE Composite Index averages the prices of all the stocks traded on the New York Stock Exchange. For some reason, this index has never enjoyed the popularity or visibility of the Dow, NASDAQ, or S&P 500 indexes, even though it is the functional equivalent of the NASDAQ Composite.
- Dow-Jones Transportation and Utility indexes.
- A variety of S&P Indexes designed to measure different sectors of the market, such as the S&P 100 Index (very large capitalization companies), S&P 400 MidCap Index (companies with capitalizations

between $1 billion and $5 billion), and S&P SmallCap 600 Index (very small companies representing just 3 percent of the total market capitalization of the U.S. equities market).

- Various Wilshire indexes designed to capture different "cuts" of the market. For example, the Wilshire 4500 measures everything *but* the 500 largest companies.

- Various indexes maintained by Morgan Stanley Capital International (MSCI). Examples include MSCI indexes which measure global, regional, country, sector, and industry slices of the overall stock market.

Caution about Interpreting Indexes

While indexes are a convenient way to get a quick take on how the market is doing and has done in the past, it is important as a Sensible Stock Investor to understand their limitations. The fact is, the academic studies and conclusions one hears often suffer from significant and misleading defects.

For one thing, every index—with the exception of the Wilshire 5000—is based on a *selection* of stocks whose prices have been averaged in one way or another. While broad indexes are often spoken of as if they reflect what the whole stock market is doing, in fact all they reflect is what their particular selection of stocks is doing. Because of this, no index really represents the "whole market," again with the exception of the Wilshire 5000. Since they represent different pieces of the market, indexes sometimes move in opposite directions. It is not unusual to have the Dow go up on the same day that the NASDAQ goes down. It happens all the time. (As I write this, it happened yesterday.)

Second, because of the way they are calculated, it is not unusual for an index's value to go *up* on a day when more of its stocks *decline* than advance. Such a day is called one with "bad breadth." Question: On a day like that, when more issues declined than advanced but the index's numerical value went up, did the market do well or poorly? Your answer is as good as mine.

Third, the conclusions presented by academic studies covering long time periods are sometimes of little practical value. For example, when an academic is looking at data covering 100 or 200 years, he or she can pass off performance variations over 5 or 10 years as slight blips. In a real person's life, 5 or 10 years is a significant time period. So sometimes the conclusions drawn from long time series of data, while mathematically correct, are of little use as a guide to how to invest *now*. Academicians often treat extremely long periods of time as if they do not matter to humans. For example, a chart of the Dow obviously shows that the Dow's return from 1926 (before the Great Crash and Depression) to the present has greatly exceeded the return from, say, bonds. That is true. However, a closer look reveals that for about the first 25 years of that period, the returns from stocks far *underperformed* bonds. Stocks only pulled ahead in the early 1950s. Well, that was an important 25 years in many people's lives. Some people went from being 25 years old to being 50 years old. Presumably, most of them would not have wanted to spend those 25 years "underwater," and *at the time*, there was certainly no guarantee that stocks would eventually catch up and surpass bonds. That is only clear now in retrospect. To the theoretician, the 25 years are just part of the whole 79-year span. To the individual investor, they cannot be treated so cavalierly.

Finally, indexes are *averages*. Each one's actual annual performance varies widely from its long-term average. Again looking at the S&P's long-term 10 to 11 percent average annual performance, guess how many years out of the last 20 that the index actually returned within three percentage points of that, either way. Just three times. The actual annual returns from 1975–2004 varied between −22 and +37 percent. Not only that, the composition of the index itself has been *actively* changed during the time period. It has been changed for the better—there is an unemphasized survivorship bias working in the background: Bad companies are replaced by better ones, bankrupt companies by survivors, weaker companies by the companies that bought them out. The survivorship bias tends to skew the data in a positive direction.

So, for most individual investors, the "average returns" of the whole market over very long time periods of 25, 50, or 75 years are only theoretically interesting. They *do* support a general conclusion that, over time, stocks are a "better" investment than bonds and give you the best chance of beating inflation. But they do not reveal how any particular investor or particular stock did. Few real individuals have enough money or so little emotion to ride out decades of bull markets, bear markets, sideways markets, bubbles, boom times, corrections, and recessions. They are real people with real lives. The major phases of their lives play out over shorter time periods than 50 or 75 years. Be skeptical of what such studies really can teach you.

And this applies to daily market reports too. "Stocks were mixed today" will probably be said if the Dow goes down on a day when the NASDAQ goes up, while if they both go up, it will be said that "the market went up today." The fact is that stocks are *always* mixed, because every day some go up and some go down. When the NASDAQ goes up, that does not mean that every stock in the average—nor that every technology stock—went up. "The markets are up today" may not apply to you, because *your* portfolio may be down.

What's most relevant, of course, is how *your* stocks are doing. Obviously, some of the stocks in every index do better than others. If you find a way to own more of the leading performers than the laggards, you will beat the index. Beating the market is the stated goal of the Sensible Stock Investor. On a given day, the market averages may go down significantly, while your own portfolio of stocks goes up. It happens, and when it does, it gives you a good feeling, like your favorite team pulling off an upset. It means that you're beating the market. In the end, the index that matters most to *you* is your own "index," the performance of your own portfolio.

CHAPTER B-3

What Determines Stock Prices?

Forecasting is difficult, especially when it involves the future.
—Yogi Berra

Because the stock market has thousands of participants, scores of factors influence a stock's price at any given time. It is useful for every investor to have a general understanding of what influences stock prices. So let's ground ourselves with the general principles of stock price behavior.

Short-Term vs. Long-Term

The first step in getting a handle on what determines stock prices requires defining the period of time you are talking about. If you are thinking very short-term (a day, a week, or a month), the answer will be different than if you are thinking about a much longer time frame (say a few years).

It is hard to get two investors to agree on what "short-term" and "long-term" mean. During the call-in segments on financial television channels, some callers ask the experts to give their opinion on a certain stock "for the long term, say 3 to 6 months." They don't mean to be funny, but really it is a joke. The Sensible Stock Investor does not think that 3 to 6 months comes close to being "long-term."

So first off, we need some semantic conventions. Here are the ones that we will use:

- Short-term: Anything under a year
- Intermediate-term: Between 1 and 3 years
- Long-term: More than 3 years

Those will be our definitions. Keep in mind, though, that to some investors, 3 years would only qualify as short-term, while 10 to 15 years would be required for long-term. It all depends on your perspective.

The difference between stock price changes in the short term and long term is like the difference between weather and climate. Every day on the weather report, your local forecaster does his or her best to tell you what tomorrow's weather is going to be, based on a wealth of historical and current information, the finest prediction models, and the most advanced computers available. Nevertheless, on a regular basis, weather forecasts are wrong. A day predicted to be in the 20s with snow turns out to be sunny and in the 50s.

Why? Because the best information and computer models have not yet succeeded in replicating exactly what causes the next day's weather. There are too many factors, and unexpected things happen. That's similar to the stock market: There are thousands of factors, unexpected things happen, and as a result, daily price movements are essentially unpredictable.

On the other hand, every city has its own *climate*. Climate is long-term; weather is short-term. I can't tell you what the temperature will be next July 20 in Buffalo, but I can state confidently that it will be 20 to 60 degrees warmer than it was on January 20. That's because of the nature of Buffalo's climate, as demonstrated by years and years of data. Similarly, I can say confidently that Dallas will have a much higher average daily temperature than Buffalo. Again, this is because long-term data tell us so. This does not mean that on a given day Buffalo won't be hotter than Dallas, but over the long term, the laws of weather probability prevail.

Meteorologists have come to give their forecasts in probabilities: The probability of rain tomorrow is 40 percent, they say. That is not a bad way to think about the stock market—as a collection of probabilities. Your goal as an investor is to predict which stocks will do well and which will do poorly. On a long-term basis, that predicting becomes easier, because the short-term unexpected events tend to cancel each other out, while the fundamental truths about each company—the "financial climate," if you will—come to dominate the answer.

The Stock Market Is an Auction House

Remember that the stock market is a free marketplace. Sellers have a price in mind that they want to get, and buyers make bids that they think are reasonable. If a meeting of minds occurs, the trade takes place. If not, there is no transaction. If eBay's stock price is around $50, and I put in a buy order for 100 shares at $25, the order will not get filled, because no owner of eBay stock will sell the shares for that little.

Remember too that the number of buyers of a stock always equals the number of sellers, despite the occasional misspeaking TV person who tells us, "There were more sellers than buyers today on Wall Street." What the anchor is really trying to say is that sellers were on average *more anxious* than buyers, more willing to give in on their price expectations, more willing to sell. This effectively creates an imbalance between supply and demand, in this case an oversupply. When there is a supply-demand imbalance, one or both of the parties have to give in, which is to say, the price has to change for a transaction to take place. Selling pressure (that is, sellers more anxious) causes prices to fall, while buying pressure (buyers more anxious) causes prices to rise.

Parenthetically, note that in each instance, the buyers and sellers are reacting to different perceptions of risk. Anxious sellers are reacting to the risk of losing money. Anxious buyers are reacting to the risk of missing out on making money.

That's the dynamic of the marketplace. What are the buyers and sellers thinking about as they consider whether to go ahead? Well, any stock sells for what it is *perceived to be worth* by its buyers and sellers. The logical question becomes, what forms this perception of worth?

Over the Long Term, Stock Prices Follow Corporate Earnings

The financial goal of every company is to make profits, or earnings. That's the money that is left over after all the bills and taxes have been paid. Over the very long term, there is near-total correlation between the earnings of a company and the price of its stock. If the earnings go up, so does the stock price. If earnings recede (or go negative), the stock price falls.

Why do stock prices follow earnings? Because that is the way capitalists *behave*. Over long periods of time, investors act the same way over and over again. They want to make money. Thus they are attracted to companies which they believe are going to make money. Therefore, the creation of economic value by a company is rewarded by the market—the reward coming in the form of a higher stock price.

Investors prize earnings for the following reasons:

- Some earnings end up directly in the investors' pockets when the company pays them out as dividends.
- The company can retain some (or all) of its earnings to reinvest back into the company, helping it to develop new products, improve its operations, and grow its earnings even more.
- The company can use some of its profits to buy back some of its own shares. This makes each share still on the market (known as the "float") equal to a larger piece of the company pie and therefore more valuable.
- The company can use some of the earnings to make acquisitions of other companies, thereby increasing the pace of earnings growth.

Companies want to do more than just make a profit. They generally strive to *grow* profits, from quarter to quarter and year to year. Many companies believe in the mantra, "Grow or die." If you don't grow, a competitor will pass you by (or buy you).

Investors, being capitalists, want companies to grow their earnings, because they want their own wealth to grow. Combine that desire with the principle that stock prices correlate highly with corporate earnings, and we arrive at a fundamental tenet of Sensible Stock Investing: We want to own stock in companies that, over time, generate sustained earnings growth.

Let's repeat that, because it is so important:

> The Sensible Stock Investor wants to own stock in companies that, over time, generate
> **sustained earnings growth.**

Are there exceptions? Sure. For a period during the Internet and technology bubble of the late 1990s, there was actually an inverse correlation between profits and some stock prices. Many of the best-performing Internet stocks had no profits at all: They were losing money. Yet investors continued to pump money into those stocks, driving up their prices. The more the companies lost, it seemed, the more their stock prices went up. There's a term for this: "concept stock." This means that investors are buying the concept of the company—specifically, the untold riches that the company is expected to deliver based on its revolutionary ideas—rather than the business success it is actually achieving.

At the time that concept stocks were ruling the roost (and it lasted for well over a year), it sure didn't look like investors were paying any attention to earnings. But over the long term, the capitalists' yearning for earnings prevails. Investors reverted to their characteristic behavior, which means that they began to look for earnings. As a result of this return to common sense, the stocks of many Internet companies crashed beginning in 2000, losing 70 to 95 percent of their value by the end of 2002. Along with the stocks went the companies themselves. Hundreds went out of business. Without profits, they could not finance operations or expansion, and after a while, other sources of money (such as venture capital, bank loans, or the issuance of more stock) dried up. Therefore, they couldn't continue.

By the way, the result of this correlation between earnings and stock prices over many decades is that the stock market has gone up, because the American economy has grown as its companies have grown. The overall long-term trend in the U.S. economy is to grow, punctuated by occasional periods of stagnation or recession (shrinkage).

Daily-Weekly-Monthly Stock Prices

On a given day, the price at which a stock changes hands is the composite estimate of what all of those people trading in the stock think is a fair deal. The price is a blend of appraisals made by people with wildly different approaches, including:

- day traders (someone who trades in and out of stocks extremely frequently, perhaps several times a day);
- market timers (investors who anticipate rallies and swoons in the stock market through the use of signals about the economy, interest rates, market trends, month of the year, phases of the moon, or other factors which they consider to have an effect on the market);
- institutional investors (managers of large sums of money such as pension funds, mutual funds, hedge funds, and the like);

- "value" investors (who look for stocks that are priced attractively relative to some measure of their "true" worth, the theory being that at some point the market will "discover" the true value of the stock and bring the price up);

- "growth" investors (who look for companies that are growing faster than the average company);

- fundamentalists who focus on the fundamental, published numbers of a company (such as earnings, book value, cash flow, and the like), as well as less quantitative but still fundamental aspects of the company (such as its market position, business model, and its industry);

- market technicians (who examine stock price charts to discern patterns that they believe foretell future price movements); and

- news-watchers, news-ignorers, computerized trading programs, short-term speculators, long-term thinkers, sane people, irrational people, impulsive people, greedy people, frightened people, uncertain people, cautious people, aggressive people, and people who just need to cash out so they can buy something.

What influences all of these people? Information. Information such as reports of earnings, *estimates* of earnings, press releases, geopolitical news, professional analyst reports, rumors, company or industry news, and God knows what else.

Since investors are people, all of this information is processed both rationally and emotionally. Needless to say, these forces are seldom all pulling in the same direction, nor do they all work on every stock in the same way. Every day, every minute, the influences swirl around, creating a fundamentally unpredictable effect on each stock. As a result, it is a fact that over very short terms (a day, a week, a month), the stock market is as much (or more) influenced by emotional, short-term, incomplete, and illogical thinking as it is by rational, long-term analysis of the likelihood of sustained corporate earnings growth based on valid evidence. The result is that day-to-day price movements are for all practical purposes random and unpredictable.

If you don't believe this, try a simple experiment: Predict the *direction* of the S&P 500 each day for two weeks. Don't worry about the magnitude of the move, just whether it will go up or down the next day. You'll find that you are right about 50 percent of the time, the same result you would get by flipping a coin.

Looking into the Crystal Ball

When they are acting rationally, investors try to look to the future, not to what is happening right now. That's because they want their investments to *grow,* and growth is a future-oriented phenomenon.

It's an old saw on Wall Street that the best time to invest is when the economy is at its worst and there is no good news—the theory being that when things are at their worst, the economy is at the inflection point between things continuing to get worse and starting to get better. As the economy starts to get better, earnings start to get better, and stock prices (following earnings) start to go back up.

And studies have shown that the old saw is true. For example, in the 13 recessions (periods of general economic shrinkage) going back to 1926, stock returns in the 12 to 24 months *following* the recessions were well above historical norms. The best returns came on investments made right in the middle of the recessions—when the economy was at its worst.

One problem with actually investing this way, of course, is that it is emotionally difficult, because when the economy is at its worst, it is hard to be optimistic. A second problem is that the "middle" of a recession is impossible to recognize *at the time.* A couple of years later, of course, looking at graphs of the economy, the moment will be obvious. Nevertheless, stock prices do tend to "look ahead" by a few months, as investors achieve some collective success in trying to divine future prices. This suggests that composite investor behavior—as reflected in the stock market—is, in a way, remarkable, in that the combined perceptions of future economic changes are often correct. Because the market tries to anticipate the future, stock prices often decline *in advance of* earnings declines and rise *in advance* of earnings growth. Typically, the time lag is anywhere from 6 to 12 months.

As stated earlier, historical total returns from the stock market have been around 10 to 11 percent per year. But in getting there, the market has tended to alternate between periods of optimism (when the market goes up) and pessimism (when it goes down). Obviously, separating each pair of cycles is a turning point. Just as with graphs of the economy, if you look at historical charts of market performance, the turning points are pretty clear. The trick is in *predicting* them.

Because it is mass behavior that causes every upward or downward market trend, at each turning point the majority of investors—by definition—are wrongly positioned in relation to future performance. They are selling when they should be buying, or vice versa. Recognizing this, many investors like to call themselves "contrarians." What they mean is that by "going against the crowd," they are on the "correct" side of whatever trend is coming next. How can this work? It works because the contrarians themselves are the ones who in fact cause the trend to turn—they create the buying (or selling) pressure that makes stock prices hit the tipping point and begin to go in the other direction.

Investor Sentiment

We've just been talking about attempts to make rational business forecasts, left-brain thinking. Now let's add in the right side of the brain, where emotions rule. The stock market (or any market) is fundamentally a social/business system, not a machine. "Investor sentiment" refers to what investors are expecting will happen, based on their combined rational and emotional interpretations of the information they have.

So part of investor sentiment is emotional. Commentators often remark that the two emotions that control investor sentiment are fear and greed. While those two define perhaps the most striking points on the emotional spectrum, I would also add some other emotions that invariably come into play—hope, confidence, exuberance, and optimism on the positive side, and uncertainty, pessimism, doubt, and depression on the negative side.

Investor sentiment is powerful. It can create hot and cold sectors of the market. It can create bull and bear markets (discussed in Chapter B-5). It can be so powerfully negative that some people decide that the stock market is a fearsome place, never to be entered again. (This happened to a great number of people during the Great Depression.) Or it can create the "irrationally exuberant" feeling that the only thing stocks do is go up, so just put all your money into the market and become rich automatically. That creates bubbles.

For a concrete example of the latter, let's look again at the Internet/technology stock bubble and focus on the many dot-com companies that sprang up in 1998-1999. In a nutshell, for a year or two, emotions such as hope, confidence, and greed drove investor behavior. Concept companies had no trouble getting people to invest in them. Some would say that investor behavior with respect to these stocks was characterized by irrational exuberance, mania, or idiocy. But as actual business performance made it clear that these companies were not generating profits and were unlikely ever to do so, their shares became less desirable investments, owners turned into sellers, buyers turned their backs, and—by the grinding processes of supply and demand—the share prices came down. Way down.

News

Investors react to news. What sort of news? The most prominent types of news which impact stocks and markets include the following:

- Buy/hold/sell recommendations and stock upgrades/downgrades, which are issued daily by stock analysts at the big investment houses and reported on TV, in newspapers, on the Internet, and in phone calls from brokerage houses to their clients.

- Profit estimates, and changes in them, made by the same analysts and disseminated in the same way.

- Whatever is being said in the business media (print, television, and the Internet).

- Expected or unexpected news about mergers, acquisitions, corporate surprises (either happy or calamitous), strategic shifts, executive changes, new products, and innumerable other events that happen every day in the business world.

- Profit warnings issued by companies. These can come at any time but often come a few weeks before their actual earnings are announced. They are "warnings" because the company is giving a heads-up that its quarterly profits are not going to be what most investors expect.

- The inverse of profit warnings, namely announcements that the company "is comfortable with" current estimates of their profits or even believes that they are too low.

- Positive or negative "guidance" issued by companies about where their business is going.

- Actual earnings figures and other financial data announced by companies and submitted quarterly to the SEC. This can often lead to investor reactions, depending on whether the real earnings come as a "surprise" (in being more or less than expected) or in other ways delight or disappoint investors.

- The release of economic data on subjects like unemployment rates, the creation of new jobs, inflation, consumer confidence, and innumerable other economic topics.

- News about geopolitical factors (such as anything having to do with war) that are believed to impact American companies in one way or another. (Another old saw: The market hates uncertainty. Remove an uncertainty, such as the outcome of a war or a presidential election, and the market will "like" that, i.e., the market will go up.)

Short-term-oriented traders react, sometimes with startling swiftness, to new information, whereas long-term holders react more slowly (or not at all). Therefore, news may produce price changes that are proportional to the new information available or wildly out of proportion to it. And then again, sometimes news that on its face appears to be significant has no impact at all, and it is difficult to say why.

Interest Rates

One kind of news that many investors are very sensitive to is news about interest rates.

In our country, the Federal Reserve System is charged by law with maintaining stable prices and growth rates in the economy and then (secondarily) with keeping unemployment low. Note that the Federal Reserve is *not* charged with protecting, boosting, or having anything to do directly with the stock market. Their charter concerns the economy. That said, the Fed does seem to watch the stock market over its shoulder. The market, after all, is part of the economy.

All things considered, over the years the Federal Reserve has become pretty good—but not perfect—at attaining its goals. The Fed's primary tool is a blunt instrument: the power to adjust federal short-term interest rates. The Federal Reserve tends to reduce those rates when the economy is growing sluggishly (or contracting) and needs a boost, and to raise rates when the economy is "overheating" or growing too fast. For several years, the Fed's overall target goal for growth in the economy has appeared to be around 4 to 4.5 percent per year, this being seen as a "neutral" growth rate that will meet all the goals of low inflation, stable growth, and sufficient employment.

The Fed's interest rates work their way into the whole economy and affect basically everything, including individual and corporate spending, capital investments, and (most importantly) corporate earnings. Since, as we have seen, long-term stock prices are strongly correlated with corporate earnings, interest rate changes often impact stock prices as investors react to the news. In general, the relationship between interest rate changes and stock prices is predictable, although sometimes it takes months to fully manifest itself.

- Interest rate *cuts* tend to *boost* the stock market.
- Interest rate *increases* tend to *lower* the stock market.

Why do rate cuts almost always boost the stock market?

- They lower corporate borrowing costs, which helps boost corporate profits. Lower interest costs means that more revenue can fall to the bottom line (rather than being used to pay interest).

- Lower interest rates encourage additional corporate borrowing, which can be used to improve facilities, expand operations, bring efficiency up a notch, and accomplish other good things.

- Lower borrowing costs and lower returns on interest-bearing investments encourage both companies and individuals to *spend* more, which tends to boost profits.

- Lower mortgage rates give homeowners an incentive to refinance their homes, which often gives them more cash to spend. Non-homeowners get an incentive to purchase their first home. Current homeowners seek opportunities to move up. Everyone buys furniture.

- Rate cuts lower the return on bonds and certificates of deposit. Thus more money is tempted to flow into stocks, raising their prices by the law of supply and demand.

- Falling interest rates motivate investors to anticipate better times ahead (they know that the Fed lowers rates to boost the economy), so they buy stocks. The buying pressure tends to raise stock prices.

To illustrate the effect of interest rate changes: Since 1913, the Fed has lowered rates four times in a row ten times. Nine of those times, the Dow was up 35 percent (on average) 18 months later. And rate cuts usually do come in bunches. All six rate cuts since 1980 (excluding 2001–2002) were multiple in nature, and on average the S&P 500 was up 17 percent twelve months following the action. During 2001–2002, the Fed set a record by lowering rates eleven times, and most economists agree that these unprecedented cuts cushioned and shortened the recession of 2001. The S&P 500 gained 26 percent in 2003.

All of the above having been said, sometimes the stock market does not react as just described. The interest rate *increases* that the Fed initiated in 2004 provide a perfect example. The Fed raised rates five times in 2004 (a quarter point at a time, starting from historic lows), and it did not seem to affect the stock market at all. The reason would appear to be that market participants were looking for reassurance that the economy was in fact getting better after the recession of 2001 and what felt like stagnation in 2002–2003. So the Fed's series of rate increases helped to remove the uncertainty surrounding the economy. In this case, it could be said that the removal of an uncertainty "trumped" the usual effect of rising interest rates.

The Economy

"The economy" refers to the overall economic activity of the United States. Investors are interested in whether it is growing, stagnant, or receding. The rule of thumb is that changes in the stock market tend to lead—even to predict—changes in the economy. The lead time is typically thought to be 6 to 18 months.

Over history, the economy has tended to move in cycles, with boom or good times followed by bust or bad times. That's why the Fed is charged with trying to smooth out the cycles and keep the economy growing at a steady pace, while avoiding excessive inflation and unemployment.

While legendary investor Warren Buffett has famously said that he does not care and it would not make any difference to him if he knew for sure what the economy was going to be doing in the future, or what interest rates were going to be, the fact is that stock prices, interest rates, and the economy are linked as just described. Therefore, it seems that the Sensible Stock Investor should have at least a general idea of what is going on in the economy, in order to raise the quality of his or her investment decisions. There are periods of time—sometimes very long periods—when it is quite unprofitable to own stocks, because of the impact of business cycles.

"The Dance"—Earnings Guidance, Estimates, Warnings, and Surprises

Prior to the well-publicized corporate accounting scandals of 2001–2002, it had become virtually standard practice for major corporations to "guide" analysts to earnings expectations that were intended to be right on the nose or a penny or two below what the company truly expected to earn. While some companies never played this game (Warren Buffett's Berkshire Hathaway being the best-known example), and the practice has diminished in the wake of post-Enron reforms, in fact it still takes place as many companies try to "spin" their data. The motivation is that a company which consistently produces "positive earnings surprises" (i.e., beating expectations by a penny or two) will be rewarded in the stock market. And you know what? It often works, at least over the short term.

Earnings "guidance"—which companies typically provide via press releases, conference calls, and executive TV appearances—kicks off a predictable minuet, which goes something like this:

- A company provides earnings guidance. Earnings "preannouncements" (referred to as "confessions" if they are bad) typically begin around the end of each quarter (in early January for the quarter ending in December, early April for the quarter ending in March, etc.). Note that *anticipated* financial results are given out via press release (so they may be different from the corporation's ultimate quarterly results), and the earnings preannouncements may contain manipulations (things left in or out) that will cause them to be different from the actual quarterly results. Typically the manipulated earnings are called "pro forma" earnings.

- Analysts covering that company consider this material and may recompute their earnings estimates for the next quarter.

- Financial information companies poll the analysts, average out their estimates, and publish the "consensus estimate" for that company. These are referred to as the "expected earnings" for the company for the quarter.

- The financial media reports all of this. That is, it becomes news that influences investors.

- A few weeks later, the company comes out with its reported earnings, computed according to Generally Accepted Accounting Principles (GAAP). These are released about 30 to 60 days after the end of the quarter. They are accompanied by more press releases and conference calls to explain them.

- If the actual reported earnings differ from the analysts' consensus estimate, that's a "surprise." If the earnings exceed the estimate, the company "beat expectations" and is credited with a "positive surprise."

If the earnings fall short of the estimate, that's a "negative surprise." If the earnings equal the consensus, the company "met estimates."

- The financial media reports all of this. More news.

- Investors and analysts react to the situation. Those with a short-term orientation may react by buying or selling the stock, depending on what kind of surprise (or no surprise) was recorded. As a result, typically a negative surprise pushes the stock price down and a positive surprise pushes it up. Investors with a longer-term orientation react more slowly, perhaps by using the new information to refine their estimate of what a stock's fair value is, which may eventually lead to a buy or sell decision down the road. In the case of a price dip accompanying a negative surprise, they may *buy* the stock to take advantage of the low price. Many investors do nothing at all.

Prior to Enron-inspired reforms, it was amazing how much difference there could be between the original preannounced earnings and the actual earnings reported a few weeks later. Example: For the first three quarters of 2001, Cisco, Dell, and Intel reported combined pro forma earnings of +$4.4 billion. The real quarterly results later reported to the SEC were a *negative* $1.4 billion (source: *Fortune*, Feb. 18, 2002).

There is no standard definition of "pro forma." Since pro forma reports are not official, companies can basically report whatever they want, adding or excluding various items so they can tell whatever story they want. Companies manage expectations via the guidance dance. For many companies, there is a managerial obsession with meeting consensus earnings estimates and with showing smooth progress in earnings, quarter-to-quarter or year-to-year.

Pro forma reporting is not inherently evil. It can help resolve an ambiguous situation. For example, when two companies merge, a pro forma report can show what performance would have looked like if the companies had been merged a year ago, making it easier to compare last year's earnings to this year's. But pro forma reporting can also be abused, because it is really hypothetical thinking. In its extreme worst case, it can become a complete fantasy, "earnings without all the bad stuff."

The 2001–2002 spate of accounting scandals prompted Congress to pass the Sarbanes-Oxley Act of 2002, which created an Accounting Oversight Board and includes many provisions designed to curtail corporate chicanery. One provision prohibits "material misstatements or omissions" that would make pro forma numbers misleading and requires any company giving pro forma earnings to explicitly reconcile them with the quarterly results reported to the SEC.

Stock prices—which are volatile anyway—often become even more volatile around earnings season. For example, if one company announces that its earnings aren't going to be as strong as the latest consensus estimates, not only may its stock price get hammered, but also its entire sector—sometimes the entire market—may be affected. Investors get jittery around earnings season.

The Multiple

We have seen that investors value earnings. A fair question is, by *how much* should an investor value earnings? Is a dollar in corporate earnings worth just that (a dollar), more than a dollar, or less to someone who owns shares in that corporation?

The answer is found in the stock's "multiple." The most famous mathematical ratio in stocks is the price-to-earnings ratio (abbreviated P/E), colloquially known as the multiple. Mathematically, it is simple: The company's stock price per share (P) divided by its earnings per share (E) equals its multiple. The multiple tells you how much investors value a company's earnings. A higher multiple tells you that investors are placing a higher value on each dollar of a company's earnings. Stocks with high P/E ratios are considered "expensive," while stocks with low P/E ratios are considered "cheap," like a TV on sale.

Counting all the years since before the Great Depression, the average multiple for the market as a whole has been around 17. That is, if a company's earnings over the previous 12 months (E) equal $1 per share, the stock's price (P) has been, on average, $17 per share. The multiple is 17. Later on in this book, we will see that there are other ratios that investors use to value stocks, but for now let's just concentrate on this most classic of ratios. (Notice that the P/E ratio is unitless; it's not 17% or $17—it's just 17.)

Companies announce their official earnings (E) quarterly, while the stock price (P) changes by the minute whenever the market is open. Since P is changing constantly, so is the P/E ratio. Say that a company with $1 in E is selling for $15 per share when you leave for lunch but for $19 when you return. Its P/E ratio has just rocketed from 15 to 19.

Obviously, not every stock, at every point in time, has a multiple of 17, even though that is the long-term market "norm." What are some of the reasons that investors might more highly value a company's earnings?

* Predictability. Investors tend to place a higher value on earnings that are predictable than on those which are not. We have already encountered the old Wall Street saying that uncertainty is an investor's enemy. The opposite of uncertainty is predictability, making it the investor's friend. Historically, a stock that consistently delivers 10 percent annual earnings growth is considered a more attractive investment than a stock whose earnings growth rate might average 10 percent but which hops around a lot.

* Sustainability. Investors tend to more highly value a stock that—because of its competitive advantages, healthy industry, fine management, etc.—looks like it will sustain its earnings growth over long periods of time.

* High growth rate. Investors prize stocks that look like they are going to display above-average earnings growth rates over an extended period.

So investors tend to "award" higher multiples to stocks that appear to have predictable, sustainable, and/or significant growth in their earnings. By doing so, investors place a *higher value* on the stocks of such companies. That is why $1 in earnings by Company A may be "worth" more to the investment community than $1 in earnings by Company B.

The P/E ratio has a multiplying effect on a stock's price. The greatest price run-ups occur when a company has *simultaneously* a steady growth in E combined with a growing P/E multiple. Conversely, the fastest crashes in a stock price come when you get the unfortunate combination of earnings slowdown combined with negative investor sentiment resulting in a drop in the multiple.

It is not at all uncommon for a stock to bear such a high P/E ratio that it is said to be "priced for perfection." This means that its high P/E ratio reflects investor sentiment that *everything* is going to turn out perfectly for the company. Indeed, this is how bubbles form. Occasionally, a very high P/E ratio can be justified only with the most extreme or even manic logic. Certain industries (especially technology) tend to carry a certain "excitement factor," which leads investors time and again to award high multiples that may not be sustainable.

The principles listed above, of course, also work in reverse. Companies with earnings that are unpredictable, unsustainable, and not growing will tend to be "punished" with negative investor sentiment and lower multiples. When the pace of a company's earnings growth slows or decelerates over a long period, the pace of its stock's price growth will also decline or actually go into reverse. This often happens when a company reaches a certain stage of maturity and simply cannot grow as fast as it used to. Similarly, when a company's earnings decline or are expected to decline over the long term, its stock price will also decline over the long term, the result of the combined effect of lower earnings multiplied by a lower multiple.

Historically, P/E ratios vary by sector. For example, technology, telecommunications, and health-care stocks tend to carry higher-than-average multiples, while basic materials and utilities tend to carry below-average multiples. This is the result of human behavior, plain and simple. There is no strictly economic justification for it. Basic materials and utilities are just not very exciting, I guess.

Most P/E ratios range from below 5 to around 40 or 50. It is not unknown, however, for a stock to have a P/E in the 80s or the hundreds, if the company has demonstrated (or investors believe that it has) an ability to generate very rapid earnings growth. In recent years, the P/E ratio for the S&P 500 (the sum of all prices divided by the sum of all earnings) has tended to stay near 20, compared to its historical value of 17. It is difficult to say whether this higher-than-historical P/E level is a residue of the 2000–2002 bubble or whether it represents a "new normal."

Caution: Be Sure Your Multiples Are Calculated the Same Way

This is a good time to note that the E number used in the P/E calculation can cover varying time frames, and investors must be careful that they are comparing apples to apples when they are comparing two companies' P/E ratios. The financial media are not always clear on what E they are using. There are at least two common approaches:

- If the E is the company's officially reported earnings over the past 12 months ("trailing 12 months"), the P/E ratio is the "trailing" P/E ratio. The trailing P/E has the advantage of being booked and involving no estimates. Its disadvantage is that it is old news.

- Some calculations invoke estimates of the ongoing and future quarters' earnings. The calculation may use both already-booked numbers and estimated numbers for the rest of the year, or it may use all estimates to "look" a full year ahead. Either way, such analyses are called "forward earnings," and the resultant multiple is the "forward P/E." This has the advantage of being future oriented but the huge risk of being completely based on estimates.

It is of paramount importance, when you are comparing P/E ratios among different stocks, that you verify that they have all been calculated the same way. After all, if a company is expected to be growing its earnings, its forward P/E will *always* be lower than its trailing P/E. Since many investors look to the P/E ratio as a measure of whether a stock is selling at a bargain price, the forward P/E of a growing company will *always* make it look like a better deal. So be sure that you are using identical timeframes when dealing with P/E ratios.

Seasonality

The stock market has in the past displayed seasonal patterns. They were well documented in the December 2002/January 2003 issue of *Bloomberg Personal Finance,* based on stock returns from 1971 to 2000. Graphs on page 23 of that issue show that:

- The best time for stocks in general is November through April.
- The best time for technology stocks is from mid-October to mid-March.
- The best time for "growth" stocks is October through December.
- The best time for "value" stocks is January through March.
- The only months that the S&P 500 has averaged +1.5 percent or more are December and January.
- The only months that the NASDAQ has averaged +1.5 percent or more are December, January, and February.

Notice that all of the "good" months for stocks cluster around the end of the year and the beginning of the following year. Historically, market returns to investors have been minuscule or negative in July, August, and September. Of course, these are averages, and no particular year necessarily follows the pattern.

One other seasonal factor runs over a longer cycle: The third year of the presidential election cycle has historically been the best-performing year for the stock market, presumably because that's when presidents really pay attention to the economy so that they or their party will be reelected.

Sector Rotation

Sometimes, different sectors of the market—large industry segments or slices—seem to go in and out of favor with investors. An article in *In the Vanguard* (Spring 2000) illustrated how performance "rotated" among major sectors of the stock market during the bull market of 1982–1999. The following table is adapted from that article.

Performance Rank among Market Sectors Based on Three-Year Returns

Economic Sector	1982–1984	1985–1987	1988–1990	1991–1993	1994–1996	1997–1999	Average Rank All Years
Consumer cyclicals	1	6	8	2	11	3	5
Consumer staples	2	1	2	8	6	6	4
Utilities	3	5	5	9	10	10	8
Financials	4	9	9	1	3	7	5
Communication services	5	4	3	7	8	2	5
Technology	6	10	11	4	1	1	5
Capital goods	7	7	6	5	4	5	6
Health care	8	3	1	10	2	4	4
Transportation	9	11	7	3	9	9	9
Basic materials	10	2	10	6	7	11	8
Energy	11	8	4	11	5	8	8

The main conclusions to be drawn from the table are that over three-year periods, different sectors rise and fall in terms of performance, and that success over one period is no guarantee of success over the next period.

Another conclusion to be drawn from the table is that over very long periods (like the 18 years covered by this data), every dog has his day. For example, in the table,

- every sector ranked at least as high as fourth during at least one three-year period,
- five of the eleven sectors ranked #1 at least once,
- every sector except one (capital goods) ranked as low as eighth during at least one period,
- six of the eleven sectors ranked dead last at least once.

Note the rightmost column. It shows average rank across all 18 years. No industry sector really stands out over such a long time; the best were consumer staples and health care.

Migration

Closely related to the idea of sector rotation is the concept of migration, as in money migrating from one part of the market to another. "Migration to quality" is a phrase often heard, and it suggests that investors are moving their money to less speculative stocks—that is, from smaller, more volatile companies to larger, older companies that are more likely to still be with us, say, 5 years from now.

Another phrase sometimes heard is "Migration to defensive stocks," which are those thought to be least sensitive to economic cycles, such as food, because people must eat; pharmaceuticals, because people will not stop taking drugs; and so on.

The underlying concept would be sound if it worked. But if you listen to TV or read the money sections of newspapers, over time you will see nearly every kind of company listed as "defensive": food, pharmaceuticals, financials, utilities. But common observation tells you that any category of stock can have down periods. In the table in the preceding section, health care had one period when it ranked tenth (out of eleven). Consumer staples (which includes food and beverages) had a period where it ranked eighth.

Here's a commonsense piece of advice: If you really feel the need to *defend* your money, don't have it in the stock market at all. Such money should be in bonds, in cash, or in the bank.

Market Volatility

"Volatility," in investing, means about the same thing it does when talking about a person: the tendency to change, sometimes abruptly. Moodiness, if you will.

Stock prices can be wickedly volatile. Even among so-called defensive companies, it is not unheard of for stock prices to change 10 to 20 percent, or even more, in a single day. Price changes of 1 to 2 percent in a day are very common.

Volatility, of course, refers to changes both up and down. Let's look at downward volatility. A price drop can be *favorable* to you if it is a stock that you want to own, and you have been waiting for a bargain price. In a generally rising market, a Sensible Stock Investor will utilize temporary price dips to acquire desired stocks (so long as the price drop does not reflect something going fundamentally wrong with the company). There is a great deal of price fluctuation in most stocks every year—often 50 percent or more. So if you are patient, you can buy many stocks at a 50 percent discount to where they will trade at some other time during that year.

Downward volatility, however, can be scary if you already own the stock. I don't know about you, but once I own a stock, I'd prefer to see it go up, like, forever. When it melts down, it raises questions like these:

- Was it a mistake to buy it in the first place?

- Will the price continue to go down, turning the stock into a loser that you'll have to sell, at a loss that you'll never make up?

- Do other investors know something about the company that you don't know? Are they correctly dumping the stock while you're hanging on like a chump?

- How far should you let it drop before you unload it?

This list of questions illustrates why, in Sensible Stock Investing, you will try to remain emotionally detached so that you can dispassionately decide whether short-term price movements are a clue to a longer-term trend or are just part of normal volatility.

What Are the Components of Total Stock Returns?

Viewed from a purely economic perspective, there are three elements that make up the financial return you get from stocks:

- Inflation ("nominal" price increase)
- Capital appreciation beyond inflation ("real" price increase)
- Dividends

The long-term average 10 to 11 percent return from stocks has been made up of these elements. So is the return you get from any individual stock. Let's examine the elements one by one.

Inflation

All else being equal, the average company—just by being in business—can raise its prices and increase its earnings by the rate of inflation. This is not considered any great accomplishment, and returns from this source are not considered "real" by academics and economists. Rather, they are referred to as "nominal." The company and its stock are just riding along with the general increase in prices in the economy.

According to a table available on the Federal Reserve Bank of Minneapolis' Web site, the early part of the 20th century was characterized by wildly gyrating annual rates of inflation—from double-digit positive to double-digit negative. In more recent years, with the Fed working to fight inflation, annual rates have smoothed out considerably. Between 1980 and 2004, the annual rate has averaged just over 3 percent. There seems little reason to believe that this is going to change much, so a future expectation of inflation at around 3 percent per year is a reasonable expectation.

Real Capital Appreciation

The second element of stock returns is "real" capital appreciation, which is the increase in the price of the stock above and beyond the inflation rate.

The stage is set for real capital appreciation when a company "creates value" by generating profits. A good company ingests capital and then utilizes the skills of its people, research, development, manufacturing, marketing, and all its other functions to make the company worth more than the capital it took in. The increase in worth happens because the company's operations create earnings.

With the stage thus set, real capital appreciation in the company's stock takes place when the market recognizes the increased value of the company and therefore prices its stock more highly. So the real capital appreciation component of total stock returns requires the market both to recognize the value that has been created *and* to place an appropriate multiple on the increased value of the company. As already seen, investors tend to view increased earnings as evidence of the company's increased value *and* to place a multiple of about 17 on earnings. So the average company with $1 in earnings per share is worth $17 in stock price. If the earnings increase 15 percent, to $1.15 per share, the "proper" stock price would be 17 times that, or $19.55. Thus is the increased value of the company recognized (and rewarded) by the market.

Remember that we are talking about an ideal situation here, one that would be produced by automaton-investors acting with perfect knowledge and consistent behavior. In the real world, the actual multiple varies widely from stock to stock, as does the market's recognition of each company's "true" value. But—accepting that the market operates weirdly sometimes—the foregoing paints a useful picture of where real stock price increases, based on real earnings, come from. These form the second component of any stock's total return to its shareholders.

Dividends

The final component of stock returns is dividends. Dividends are cash payments returned to the shareholder by the company from its profits. The shareholder can keep the cash, reinvest it in the same company, or reinvest it elsewhere. Some companies issue no dividends (retaining all of their earnings to fund growth), some issue very small dividends, and some pay out significant dividends.

The ratio of any dividend payout to the stock's price is called the stock's "current yield." So if a stock is selling for $20 per share and sends out $1 in dividends this year, its current yield is 1/20, or 5 percent.

Dividends are also a "real" return. They are actual cash in your pocket, nothing illusory about it. In the last few years, the dividend yield for the S&P 500 has hovered between 1.5 and 1.9 percent. As of this writing (early 2006), it is 1.8 percent.

Putting the Components Together

The total return from stocks, or any particular stock, is the sum of the three components just described. In Wharton Professor Jeremy Siegel's book *The Future for Investors* (2005), he demonstrates that over very long periods of time the average stock's total *real* return (that is, after inflation and including dividends) has stayed pretty much in the 6.5 to 7 percent range. For the investor, "real" returns represent actual increase in purchasing power. The stock's price increases and dividends propel its return ahead of inflation and make stocks the investment of choice for beating inflation. With inflation at around 3 percent and real returns of, say, 7 percent, we get an estimated total annual return of stocks of 10 percent. Actually, owing to differences in measuring periods and variations in all three components (inflation, real capital appreciation, and dividends), the average annual return from stocks since 1926 (just before the Depression) has been 10 to 11 percent. Remember, however, that this picture is built upon averages and requires long terms to play out. But given those cautions, it is a real picture of the returns that stocks have provided over time.

In Summary

We have seen that stock prices often don't correlate with much of anything over short terms (days, weeks, months). Or perhaps more accurately, stock prices can be subject to the influence of *anything,* with so many diverse factors impacting them that they are essentially random. From either point of view, the bottom line is the same: Stock prices are pretty unpredictable over short time periods.

Over longer time periods, however, stock prices follow patterns and directions that are *relatively* predictable. Over the long term, stock performance *correlates well* with company performance. All of the short-term influencers work their effects every day, but over the months and years, transient and emotional factors tend to cancel out, and the more fundamental economic factors can be seen as really in control. Thus, there is, over time, logic underpinning a stock's price. Companies that are good performers will, over time, have that performance reflected in their price. Those that are not good performers will drop or stagnate in price.

CHAPTER B-4

Is the Market Efficient? Is It Rational?

Markets can remain irrational longer than you can remain solvent.
—John Maynard Keynes

What Does "Efficiency" Mean in the Stock Market?

In academic theories about the stock market, there appears the concept of "efficiency." This does not refer to the smoothness with which trades are executed, the adroitness with which indexes are recalculated, or other forms of effectiveness in the operation of the market. Rather, market efficiency refers to the idea that, at any given time, stock prices perfectly reflect all publicly available information concerning every stock.

Under the Efficient Market Hypothesis (EMH), the market as a whole knows all available information, and the market's participants process that information intelligently, fully, and realistically to maximize their own best economic interests. The inevitable result, under EMH, is that every stock's price is always equal to its true or "correct" value, because that price has been determined rationally in a market operating flawlessly. Going forward, future prices will instantly adjust to new information as it becomes available, because all market participants have equal and instantaneous access to all relevant information, and they act on it perfectly.

The EMH gained widespread academic credence in the 1960s. Strong EMH believers contend that all public information is always processed so efficiently that the market even adjusts prices ("discounts") in advance for events (like upcoming earnings announcements or anticipated changes in interest rates) that haven't even happened yet. That's why you'll hear that some particular anticipated event "is already priced into" a stock.

While unquestioning belief in EMH is not nearly as prevalent today as it was a decade or two ago, it still has plenty of adherents. If one believes EMH, then one must also believe that, absent inside information or other forms of "cheating," the following must be true:

- An investor cannot pick fortuitous times to enter the market, because the market is "correctly" priced at all times. Market timing is impossible.

- One cannot zero in on individual stocks on the basis of their being "mispriced" bargains. The market already knows everything about them, and they are not mispriced.

Belief in EMH has led many investors (and investment advisers) to conclude that there is no way to "beat the market" and therefore that the best one can do is simply to ride along with the market. This means that an investor should simply buy index mutual funds, hold on to them, and hope that the future performance of the market will match its historical average annual 10 to 11 percent rise.

Is the Efficient Market Hypothesis True?

Many well-respected stock market experts believe in the Efficient Market Hypothesis, while others believe it is nonsense.

What do we think?

Well, common sense suggests that the market *cannot* be perfectly efficient. Over a long period of time, it is true that stock prices rise and fall based on available information, but when you focus in on one particular time and a single particular stock, and take into account all of the factors which influence stock prices discussed in the last chapter, it seems impossible that every stock's price always is an exact and "correct" reflection of what the stock ought to be worth.

So Sensible Stock Investing, while recognizing that stock prices certainly do move on the basis of information, rejects EMH. There are many reasons for this conclusion.

First of all, the stock market is just that, *a market,* and in the final analysis, things are "worth" what people are willing to pay for them. We saw earlier all of the factors that influence a stock's price. With so many factors in play, it does not make sense that a stock's price always perfectly reflects all available information. The price of a stock at any given time is based on the aggregate appraisal of the stock's value by active participants who are trading that stock. This composite perception has a strong emotional component to go along with hard information. Not only that, some players are ignorant of a portion of the available information, some of the "information" is mere speculation about the future, and some of the traders do not process their information very intelligently.

Second, it is observable that a stock's price may rise or fall 5 percent or 10 percent in a given day when there is basically no news (that is, no new information) about that stock. The stock couldn't possibly be "perfectly" priced at both the beginning and end of such a day. Why would a stock's price *fall* on the very day that the company announces strong earnings? Or how could every price be exactly correct one day, only to have the whole market plunge or rise 2 percent the next day? These things happen, and no amount of new information explains such phenomena.

What *is* happening is that *perceptions* of the stock's true worth are changing—minute by minute, day by day, month by month, year by year. The best way to look at it is that, over longer periods of time, movements in the stock's price *directionally follow* what might be called the "correct" price, but there are constant adjustments being made, up and down, based not only on the rational processing of valid information but also on emotions, erroneous perceptions, ignorance, irrational processing, and incorrect information.

Examples of gross pricing inefficiencies are not difficult to find. Here's one: In early 2000, 3Com announced its intention to spin off its Palm division (at the time, Palm was far and away the market leader in handheld personal digital assistants). At the time, 3Com owned 95 percent of Palm. Yet after the spin-off, the market valued Palm at billions more than 3Com, its former parent. In terms of market efficiency, this makes no sense. If the market thought that Palm *by itself* was really that valuable, then the value of its parent 3Com should have included that value *before* the spin-off. Obviously, either 3Com had been markedly undervalued, or the market had assigned newly independent Palm an unjustifiably high (i.e., "incorrect") valuation. Given the time frame (early 2000) and the benefit of hindsight (that was the very height of the tech bubble), we know what happened: Palm was given way too high a valuation by the market. Within a year, Palm's shares dropped to a tiny fraction of their post-spin-off price. That price had not been "correct" in any sense of the word. Everybody was simply caught up in the excitement of the times and the enthusiasm about Palm's products. It was a concept stock.

Don't mistake what's being said here for the idea that the market is totally inefficient. To the Sensible Stock Investor, the commonsense alternative lies between the two extremes. The sensible approach is to believe that the market is *approximately efficient,* meaning that it is often (or even usually) efficient, within reasonable limits (plus or minus a few percent). Over long periods of time, stock prices generally correlate with business success and reasonable expectations of future business results. The longer the term you look at, the stronger the correlation becomes, because the moment-to-moment inefficiencies become just blips in the long-term pattern.

By not believing in total efficiency, we leave open the possibility that, from time to time, we will be able to find stocks that are individually underpriced. These will represent investable opportunities that will help us beat the market. It works in the opposite direction too: There will be times when we cannot find such stocks, when they all seem overpriced. Those conditions will be caution flags that it may be prudent to sell in order to take profits off the table or prevent oncoming losses when the market corrects itself. As we will see later, sidestepping losses is perhaps the most important component in beating the market.

The Market Is Rational over the Long Term and Rewards Sensible Investing

While the concepts are closely related, there is a subtle but important difference between efficiency and rationality in the market. Efficiency focuses on rapid, instantaneous adjustments in stock prices as new information becomes available. Rationality focuses on whether those price adjustments make sense. Efficiency relates to the speed with which information impacts prices. Rationality concerns whether the prices are what they "ought" to be.

So it is important to ask whether the market is *rational*. We have already seen the answer. While the market is often irrational in the short term, it is more or less rational in the long term. That is, as stated before, over the long term, stock prices reflect business results and reasonable expectations of future performance as measured by sustained earnings growth. Over time, the market tends to correct its "mistakes."

If you combine the market's approximate efficiency with its tendency to be more or less rational over the long term, you arrive at the fundamental strategies that Sensible Stock Investing uses to beat the market.

1. First, we know that some companies are simply *better companies* than others. They are in expanding industries, are better-run, command more market share, enjoy pricing power, attract more revenue, and more effectively convert that revenue into profits. They add value to the capital they ingest and have superior prospects for sustained earnings growth. Superior companies make more money than others, and they do it more consistently and faster. The first step in Sensible Stock Investing—picking superior companies—exploits the market's long-term rational tendency to reward the stocks of companies that have sustainable growth, stability, and predictability. Over long periods of time, the basic rationality of the market means that investors will believe that those companies are more valuable than the others. Investors will award them higher P/E ratios, which, when combined with their more rapidly growing earnings, means that their stock prices will rise more than the market averages. And if those are the stocks you own, you will beat the market. It's as simple as that. Any conclusion that it is useless to try to beat the market through individual stock picking is false.

2. Second, because the market is *not* perfectly efficient, the stocks of some of these superior companies will, from time to time, be undervalued—priced too low. Therefore the Sensible Stock Investor—rather than accepting the market's price as the "correct" one—makes his or her own independent judgments of the worth of superior companies. He or she knows that there are times when the prices of individual stocks are simply "wrong," meaning they have strayed from their long-term "correct" values. The second element of Sensible Stock Investing—valuing stocks—takes advantage of short-term market inefficiencies, by leading you (and disciplining you) to take these anomalies into account when you are considering buying, holding, or selling a stock. As the market's overall long-term rationality brings these prices more into line with their "correct" values, an initial bargain price will act as a magnifier of the return that these stocks provide. By the same token, a current "overprice" of a stock will act as a warning to collect profits or not to buy a stock, even if the company is a superior one.

3. Third, because the market is neither perfectly efficient nor rational over the short term, there will be occasional opportunities to take advantage of price trends to make money in an individual stock

regardless of whether the company is superior or the entry price is a bargain. The Sensible Stock Investor happily takes advantage of inefficiencies and irrationalities that work in his or her favor. Some would pejoratively refer to this as "speculation" rather than "investing," but it is simply recognizing how markets operate and how stock prices get determined. The risks of riding price trends can be managed, and the potential rewards are great. So this becomes the third leg of the Sensible Stock Investing strategy for beating the market: Manage your portfolio intelligently, which includes taking advantage of occasional special opportunities when they present themselves.

CHAPTER B-5

Bull Markets, Bear Markets, and Bubbles

How do we know when irrational exuberance has unduly escalated asset values, which then become subject to unexpected and prolonged contractions?
—Alan Greenspan, 1996

Bull markets, bear markets, and bubbles represent extremes in investor behavior in the stock market. They are the most vivid outcomes of the market's pricing mechanisms described in the previous chapters. They are what happen when investor sentiment and behavior go consistently in one direction for an extended period of time. Understanding them is the final foundational component for understanding how the stock market works.

Bull and bear markets are important because they tend to impact most stocks, both those that "deserve it" and those that don't. Research consistently shows that 60 to 75 percent of all stocks tend to move directionally with the market averages over extended periods of time. Because bull and bear markets represent extremes in groupthink, they take on a life of their own, sometimes sending individual stock prices into areas unexplainable by economic factors alone.

Bull Markets

The standard definition of a bull market is whenever there is a 20 percent or more rise in the market as measured by a major index such as the Dow, the NASDAQ, or the S&P 500. There is no set time over which this rise must occur, but generally "bull market" suggests a prolonged period of rising stock prices lasting at least several months and often for years. According to the *Stock Trader's Almanac*, a respected investment reference guide, the average length of a bull market is almost two years. The longest bull market ever, by general agreement, lasted from 1982 until early 2000.

Bull markets usually take place against a background of a healthy growing economy and rising corporate earnings. A bull market requires an influx of money from individual and institutional investors. This money creates the buying pressure which causes stock prices to rise practically across the board.

Beyond definitions based on math (20 percent rise), time frames (a few months or more), and money inflows, a bull market is usually accompanied by—and at least partly caused by—a general psychological optimism about the stock market. This spate of optimism creates a positive tailwind that pushes stock prices along. Investors become "bullish," which is to say optimistic or exuberant about a stock, an industry, a sector, or the whole market. Investors are more willing to take risks. Negative news is dismissed or downplayed. Investors become greedier, and their fear is not of losing money but rather of being left out of the moneymaking. The bullishness creates an upward pressure on prices. Investors develop a strong conviction that the stock market is the best place to have their money.

There is a chicken-and-egg dimension to a bull market. What causes what? Do rising prices create optimism, and therefore further upward pressure and the bull market, or does optimism cause buyers to become enthusiastic and push prices up? The answer probably does not matter: Think of it instead as a virtuous circle, with rising prices creating more optimism, optimism creating buying enthusiasm, enthusiasm creating money flows and buying pressure, and buying pressure producing higher prices. During the course of a bull market, bad companies as well as good ones tend to get bid up.

One can see a bull market shaping up by looking at the generally rising trend in the value of an index. The picture is often clearer if, instead of looking at day-to-day price levels, you look at the 50-day and 200-day moving averages of an index. (Moving averages smooth out daily volatility and show longer-term trends more clearly.) At the start of a bull market, as investor sentiment shifts to the optimistic and pushes prices up, you will observe the daily level of the index rising (maybe in fits and starts) and eventually crossing through its 50-day moving average and later through its 200-day moving average. These crossover points "confirm" the bull market if price levels stay above the moving average lines for a while—say a couple weeks or more. If the general rally continues, eventually the 50-day moving average itself will cross through the 200-day moving average line. By that time, it is fair to say that a solid bull market is under way.

A long-lasting bull market—say one lasting two years or more—is called a "secular" bull market. Such an upward run probably will not be uninterrupted. Occasional "corrections" may bring prices down by about 10 percent, but these corrections are short-lived and often seen as healthy, bringing the market back into line if it has "gotten ahead of itself." Market corrections are simply normal volatility that reaches 10 percent in a short time, thus justifying the special label. General market corrections are natural and normal adjustments in free markets, and they are considered to be just part of the game. A correction in the midst of a secular bull market may last anywhere from a few days to a few weeks. The correction does not end the bull market, because the underlying optimism and financial fundamentals still exist. In fact, price corrections during a bull market are often seen as buying opportunities—called "buying on the dips"—and these spates of buying end the correction and propel the bull market to even higher highs.

Shorter bull markets (under, say, two years) may alternate with bear markets of roughly equal length, meaning that the market cycles between short-lived up and down trends. This happened, for example, in the 1970s. At the end of a series of up and down cycles, the market may be roughly where it started. Using a wide-angle lens, you could say that the market went sideways, perhaps for many years. Looking more closely, however, you will be able to see that during that very long period of time several short bull markets and bear markets took place.

In an extended bull market, stock prices may go irrationally high—in an individual stock, an industry, or even the whole market. The market may be "momentum-driven," with stocks going up simply because people are buying stocks—which they are doing because the market is going up. The market runs on its own momentum, like the car engines of old that kept running after you turned them off. If this keeps going on, a "bubble" may be created in which stock prices get totally out of line with fundamental notions of value. See the next section of this chapter for a discussion of bubbles.

We have seen earlier that, mathematically, stock prices are the product of stocks' earnings (E) times "the multiple" (P/E ratio). Upward movements in both of these factors characterize most bull markets: Companies generate more earnings (probably because of an improving economy), the multiples go up (because of optimism about the future), and the combination creates a perfect storm of conditions for stock prices to rise and rise.

The upward momentum of prices in a bull market is often led by high-valuation, risky, young, untested stocks and companies. Such issues become market leaders, moving upward 1½ to 2 times or more than the general market.

As stated earlier, the most recent secular bull market lasted from 1982 through 1999, the longest of all time. During those 18 years, the S&P 500 rose to its highest-ever level of 1527 on March 24, 2000. The NASDAQ Composite, often seen as a proxy for the technology sector, reached its highest-ever level of 5049 on March 10, 2000. And the granddaddy of all indexes, the Dow, rose to its highest all-time level, 11,723, on January 14, 2000.

Bubbles

There is no standard definition of a bubble. If a bull market exists after stock prices have gone up 20 percent, then a bubble takes more—probably much more—than that. Magnitude aside, the more important point about a bubble is that stock prices not only rise fairly steadily to form the bubble, but they also get totally detached from normal notions of value.

If a bull market represents generalized investor optimism, exuberance, a willingness to take risks, and a belief that the stock market is the place to be, a bubble is characterized by extremes of all those beliefs and behaviors. Intense speculation takes hold, and investor enthusiasm becomes totally exaggerated. In a bubble, investors ignore financial fundamentals, "buy on the buzz," pay any price to get in the game, accept hype as truth, and extrapolate high rates of return indefinitely into the future. Actual information that doesn't support the overoptimistic sentiment is dismissed as irrelevant or old-fashioned thinking. Speculation and greed prevail. The market's basic function as a capital-allocation machine breaks down, as capital flows not to where it is most needed or deserved but to companies with the sexiest concepts. Fear of loss drops. Normal investor ground rules for sufficient, stable, and predictable earnings (E) to justify high P/E levels disappear. The E of some of the most highly valued companies may be tiny or nonexistent, mathematically causing P/E ratios to become astronomical or infinite.

By their nature, bubble prices are not sustainable. That's why they are called bubbles. But they may last a long time if good news keeps flowing. In the sustained bull market of the 1990s, increases in the typical P/E ratio accounted for a great deal of the change in stock prices as a whole. The average P/E for the S&P 500 crept into the high 20s, compared to its historical average of around 17. Technology stocks were particularly big contributors to this phenomenon. If you do the math, a P/E of 25 makes a huge difference in the price of a stock compared to a P/E of 17. Through this increase in the multiple alone, a $50 stock becomes one selling for over $73 per share, a 46 percent increase in the stock's price unsupported by any increase in earnings.

It is generally agreed that somewhere in 1997 or 1998, the U.S. stock market—which had already been in a bull mode for 15 years—inflated into a bubble. The bubble itself lasted a couple of more years, before finally beginning to deflate in early 2000.

Eventually with a bubble market, the collective mania wears off, widespread selling pressure develops (pushing prices down), and the bubble deflates. Stocks return to prices and valuations that are more logical based on financial fundamentals. The deflation can come in the form of a crash that happens quickly, or it can take a long time, more like a leakage as prices descend slowly but steadily.

In the deflation or crash of a bubble, prices may overshoot their "proper" level significantly to the downside. Some commentators believe that until this happens, the bubble mentality has not in fact been wiped out. The deflation process can take a long time. At the time of this writing (early 2006), it is not clear that the 1990s bubble has yet deflated, even though there was a yearlong bull market from early 2003 to early 2004, with another uptick at the end of 2004. The question is whether these were just interruptions to the secular deflation of the bubble or truly marked the end of the bubble.

In any event, during the deflation from 2000–2002, investors lost more than $7 trillion in the market value of U.S. stocks, and literally hundreds of companies went out of business. Because things like this happen, bubble markets are often derided, with pundits saying that they always "end badly," turn into "a debacle," and the like. But for the Sensible Stock Investor, there is no need to look at bubbles like this. Instead, just remember that markets cycle, bull markets and bubbles happen, and stock prices often overshoot "correct" valuations. Bubbles can become nice ways to *make* money. The trick is to depart before the huge losses in value occur. The horribilizations of the pundits are based on buying *and holding* stocks while they are collapsing. You don't have to do this. As we will discuss later, the Sensible Stock Investor approaches his or her portfolio attentively, with a particular focus on managing risk and avoiding losses.

Bear Markets

A bear market is a lasting downturn, the exact inverse of a bull market:

- The standard definition of a bear market is whenever there is a 20 percent decline (or more) in the major indexes over an extended period of time.
- Bear markets reflect falling corporate earnings, falling P/E multiples, or usually both.
- Moving average lines cross through each other in the opposite direction from a bull market. That is, they fall. First the actual index's daily value will fall through its 50-day moving average. Then the 50-day moving average (if the bear market lasts long enough) will fall through the 200-day moving average.
- Long-lasting bear markets are called "secular" bear markets. A secular bear market may be interrupted by "bear market rallies," which are similar but opposite to the corrections that interrupt secular bull markets. A secular bear market creates a headwind for stock prices, and most stocks (around the same 60 to 75 percent as with a bull market) are affected sooner or later. Good companies as well as bad companies lose value.
- There is usually negative investor sentiment toward stocks, so the price declines are a reflection not only of deteriorating company financials but also of a loss of faith and confidence in the stock market as the place to be. Someone who loses confidence in the stock market is "bearish." Hope and confidence diminish, replaced by fear, uncertainty, and pessimism. Investors lose their appetite for risk, and the market's P/E contracts. Whereas in a bull market the thing most feared is losing out on a sure way to make money, in a bear market the fear is literally over losing money. After the 1929 stock market crash, many individual investors—some of whom lost their life savings—generally avoided stocks until around the 1950s. They became scared of stocks. After all, it took 25 years—until 1954—for the Dow to finally close at a level it had first attained in 1929. Even though stock ownership began to climb again in the 1950s and 1960s, investors did not really regain an overall favorable sentiment about stock ownership until the 1980s. Although the Dow first hit 1000 in 1966, it did not hold a sustained level above 1000 until 1983. That means it was basically stagnant for 17 years.
- Conviction about stock ownership reverses from favorable to unfavorable. Whereas in a bull market stockholders would probably say that they are confident in their stocks, in a bear market stockholders become skittish, unsure, fearful, and alert to any reason to "get out." Investors formerly committed to long-term stock ownership begin to doubt that commitment, look for reasons to sell, and do sell more readily than before. Their tolerance for poor performance dries up.
- The virtuous circle of positive factors that drives a bull market reverses in a bear market and becomes a vortex of negative factors. "Flushing" is not a bad analogy. Just as rising earnings and rising multiples characterize bull markets, deteriorating earnings and falling multiples characterize bear markets. Just as an extended bull market can lead to valuation bubbles, an extended bear market may not end until

stock valuations actually are significantly "too low." Again, this is investor psychology at work: Investors are pessimistic in a bear market, and as a result they keep selling until eventually the multiples go right down through normal historic levels.

- High-valuation, risky, aggressive "growth" stocks, the kind that often lead the charge in a bull market, may get hammered two to three times as hard as the average stock during a bear market. Since bear markets are bull markets in reverse, they often pull down stocks that don't "deserve" to be punished. In the bear market of 2000–2003, the first stocks hit were those which had led the late-1990s bull market into bubble territory—technology and telecom companies. But further along, practically every kind of company got hit: health care, media, finance, retail, and industrial conglomerates all were affected.

The inverse of bull market corrections may take place from time to time—prices might rise during a short period without really interrupting the overall downward trend of the bear market. These are called bear-market rallies, and they typically last only a few days or weeks. However, the spurts can be dramatic. According to the *ChangeWave Investing* service, the ten biggest *up* days in the Dow's history happened during bear markets. Just as optimistic investors use corrections to buy on the dips during a bull market, pessimistic investors use these bear-market rallies to sell off their stocks, getting themselves out at slightly better prices. That selling pressure, of course, causes a halt to the rally.

We saw that market bubbles are not sustainable, because eventually the mania subsides, investors realize that they have taken prices and valuations too high, and selling pressure replaces buying pressure. The same thing—in reverse—causes bear markets to end. Investors realize that stocks of good companies have become bargains, various uncertainties clear up, and investors move in to buy the underpriced stocks. An improving economy bolsters corporate earnings (E), confidence begins to return, multiples go up, the desire to get back into stocks grows, and the bear market is over.

Bear markets can last anywhere from a couple months to several years. If the bear market is deflating a bubble, it will last longer, because it will take that long to wring out the excesses of the bubble. The bubble won't be fully deflated until valuations return to levels close to what they "should" be. The bear market may not stop at that point: Prices may continue to drop until they undershoot "correct" values, creating bargains in some stocks.

As the market cycles from the end of a bull market to the beginning of a bear market, individual stocks will "turn" at different times. This underscores the basic principle that the stock market is a market of individual stocks.

PART C.   PICKING COMPANIES

Chapter C-1.   A Sensible Approach to Picking Companies

Chapter C-2.   Are Established Companies or "Emerging Opportunities" Better Bets?

Chapter C-3.   Subdividing the Universe of Companies

Chapter C-4.   Megatrends

Chapter C-5.   What's the Story? Buy Dominant Companies

Chapter C-6.   Inherently Unplayable and Risky Companies

Chapter C-7.   The Company as a Financial "Black Box"

Chapter C-8.   Financial Evaluation Factors

Chapter C-9.   Dividends as a Company Evaluation Factor

Chapter C-10.   Bonus Points

Chapter C-11.   Putting It All Together: A Company Scoring System

CHAPTER C-1

A Sensible Approach to Picking Companies

It is better to buy a great business at a fair price than a fair business at a great price.
—Warren Buffett

This Part C details the first stage in Sensible Stock Investing: In this stage, you identify companies to *possibly* invest in. The other two stages—valuation and portfolio management—are treated later in Parts D and E.

Overview: A Rating System for Companies

Let's sneak a look ahead at where we are going with "a sensible approach to picking companies." We are going to develop a simplified point-based scoring system, called Easy-Rate™. Using a standard form, we will award points to companies based on how they stack up against a list of criteria and benchmarks of excellence. The criteria themselves come from three angles of view as we home in on the best companies:

1. The company's **Story**. This is a word-based, broad overview of the company—what makes it a good (or not-so-good) company based on its business model?
2. The company's **Financials**. How has the company's financial performance compared to that of other companies? Are the financials going in the right direction?
3. **Bonus Points**. We award points for third-party assessments of the company.

Those of you who do not wish to read the detailed explanations of how these factors have been derived—who just want to get to the Easy-Rate techniques themselves—can skip right now to the summary of the scoring system in Chapter C-11. However, I suggest that all readers at least skim the intervening chapters before doing that. And of course as you get more deeply involved in scoring companies, you can come back to these chapters to see how the criteria and benchmarks work.

The Goal: Finding Candidates for Investment

The first step in Sensible Stock Investing is picking companies as *candidates* for investment.

Among the goals of the company-picking stage are the following:

- To have a disciplined approach in order to avoid hype and emotional elements.
- To identify companies whose business prospects are most favorable.
- To have it work: to actually identify "better" companies.
- To be fun and involve as little tedium as possible.
- To be not costly in time and money. This is particularly important for the individual investor.

As it turns out, all these goals can be fulfilled.

We want to be on the lookout for factors that tend to be *predictive* of the fortunes of companies. Therefore, to meet the goals just stated, we'll devise a sensible, systematic rating system that utilizes the most reliable predictive factors in companies' business success. The scoring system will elevate the most investment-worthy companies while downgrading those with the least attractive prospects.

We will develop the Sensible Stock Investing scoring system in the following chapters, ending with a handy summary in Chapter C-11. Then, to illustrate it in actual use, Appendix I, Form 1 contains a completed Easy-Rate scoring sheet for a well-known stock. The approach is completely transparent. You will see exactly how the scores were compiled. There are no "proprietary formulas" in Sensible Stock Investing. This allows you to judge for yourself how sensible they are.

Getting Started with the Easy-Rate™ System

Our system awards "points" for the positive characteristics of companies. With just a couple exceptions, there are no negative points in the system; a company cannot have a total score below zero. Rather, the system builds up from zero. You will come to see that companies that score anywhere near zero are of no interest to us. A low total score means that the company has failed too many of our tests.

In developing the points system, no effort has been made to have the points total 50 or 100 or any other round number. Rather, the idea is to assign the right number of points to each rating factor to properly "weight" it against the other factors. So the total number of available points is simply the sum of the maximum points possible for each individual factor. Another way of looking at this is that the system is open-ended. Thus, if you wish, you can add, delete, or reweight factors, without having to worry about unbalancing an artificial 50-point or 100-point system. As you see how the factors and points are developed, the benefits and flexibility of this open-ended approach will become apparent.

In rating companies under the Easy-Rate system, points are awarded in three general categories:

- **The Story.** This is a narrative summary which articulates why the company might make a good investment. The Story, which has both objective and subjective elements, covers the company's business history and future prospects, focusing on whether it is a dominator (or an also-ran) in its industry, whether it has a good business model, whether it has sustainable competitive advantages, and whether it is in a promising line of business. Up to 10 points are available for the company's Story.

- **Financial characteristics and strength.** Here, we focus on the company's numbers. We look for companies that have both a history of creating value and apparently good prospects for continuing to do so. This is obviously an important line of inquiry; therefore up to 48 points are available to companies with great financial profiles.

- **Bonus points.** These are extra points based on analyst recommendations and how much the company is admired. Points available: 5.

Adding the three categories, the total points available to a company is 63. As of this writing (early 2006), the best companies' scores are around 40. So you can see that our system is tough on the companies, as it must be. To be successful investors, we *have to* separate the contenders from the pretenders, and weak tests won't get the job done.

Putting the ranking system into practice requires some research and analysis, but a company can usually be scored in less than an hour. It's really not that hard; that's why we call it Easy-Rate. For now, don't worry about *how* you would find and compile the data. Instead, focus on the principles involved. Later on, when we actually rate companies, we'll list the sources of all the data used and show how to compute the scores.

Schools of Investing and Their Relationship to Sensible Stock Investing

As you read through investment literature, you come to realize that there are various genres of stock picking. Each comes at the problem from a particular perspective. This is as good a place as any for a brief review of the most common approaches, because they form a foundation for understanding the Sensible Stock Investing approach. These are the predominant schools or "styles" of stock picking:

- Approaches that emphasize the *market capitalization* (total company value: shares multiplied by price per share) of the company. Common categories bear terms like micro-cap, small-cap, mid-cap, or large cap.

    In Sensible Stock Investing, we do not pay much attention to capitalization in deciding whether a company has investment potential. We're looking for a company that has the ability to *grow*, and that does not necessarily correlate with the size of the company. There are better ways to pin down growth potential. Indeed, our approach will turn up companies of all sizes, from well-known behemoths to small young companies that you have never heard of.

- Approaches that emphasize the *value* of the stock compared to its actual price, looking for bargains in the stock market.

  In our approach, valuation is very important. In fact, it constitutes the second major phase of Sensible Stock Investing. We don't use valuation in the process of identifying the best *companies*, but we use it in deciding whether the company's stock is *a good buy at its current price*. Bargain opportunities emerge and disappear, because stock prices change every day. Unfortunately, a highly rated company's actual stock price may never come down to where it is a bargain, so the market's "overvaluation" of a stock can effectively prevent it from ever being purchased under our approach. That's unfortunate from one point of view, but it promotes success for us: Not all great companies are great investments.

- Approaches that try to identify *dominant companies.*

  We'll do this big-time. It is a fundamental tenet of Sensible Stock Investing that market dominance is an important factor in picking companies. We will search for companies whose dominance in their industry appears to be sustainable. Such companies normally have the best prospects for our holy grail, sustainable earnings growth.

- Approaches that emphasize *new and emerging* companies.

  As with market capitalization, this is no more than a moderate consideration for us. New and emerging companies often present wonderful growth potential, but they are also fraught with risks and unknowns because of their very newness. We'll aim for a balanced approach.

- Approaches that emphasize proven *earnings growth*, which presumably suggests the company will be able to continue to grow its earnings.

  We'll use this approach. Ideally, we want to find companies that we can predict, with some degree of confidence, will grow their earnings rapidly and consistently, at least over a one- to two-year "prediction horizon." As we have seen earlier, over the long haul, stock prices show a high correlation with earnings growth.

- Approaches that emphasize financial *fundamentals,* which are measurable, quantifiable financial numbers about the company (such as its rates of revenue or earnings growth, how much it uses debt to finance operations, and a host of other numbers).

  We use this approach. It is the "financial characteristics and strength" category mentioned above. Once we're comfortable with the company's Story, it is the numbers that provide the best clues as to whether, how fast, and how consistently a company is likely to grow.

- Approaches that focus on the *dividends* paid by a company.

  Dividends play an important role not only in this first stage of selecting companies but also in the later stage of valuing their stocks. The consistent payment of dividends and regular increases in dividends are signs that a company is financially healthy. After all, a company has to be profitable and have cash available in order to pay a dividend.

- Approaches that emphasize *charts and graphs* of past market or stock performance, on the theory that past patterns repeat themselves and therefore have predictive value. This is commonly called "technical analysis."

    We won't use this in evaluating companies or in valuing their stocks. However, in the portfolio-management stage, we will investigate a stock's chart before we make any purchase decisions. Occasionally, we will make a purchase based almost solely on upward price momentum. Loss of upward momentum can also play a role in deciding when to sell a stock.

- *Indexing,* in which the stock picking is done mechanically, simply by duplicating the stocks in an index, such as the Dow Jones Industrial Average or the Standard & Poor's 500 Stock Index.

    We won't do this. Our goal is to beat the indexes, not buy them. (This is not to denigrate index funds. Indeed, for many people these represent core investments and perhaps should be the only way they buy stocks. It is simply not what we are trying to accomplish here.)

- Approaches that emphasize *market sectors,* focusing on particular industries or slices of the economy that are expected to fare well or poorly over the coming months or years.

    We will pay attention to this. Some sectors just have better prospects than others. Some are going to benefit more from megatrends in science, demographics, and the like. When we can put such information to use, we will do so. However, it is not our starting point, as our approach is more accurately characterized as bottoms-up stock picking, which means that we examine companies one at a time based on their own merits. The industry or sector in which a company plays is one factor that works its way into the company's Story.

These schools are not mutually exclusive. There is nothing illogical or contradictory about using *fundamental analysis* to identify *growing companies*—in fact, that's how it is usually done.

Thus, the philosophies of these basic schools may be and often are combined. One sees this in many mutual funds. For example, a particular fund's charter may describe its objective as being to invest in *mid-cap* stocks at *bargain prices*. A mutual fund using this approach might have a name like XYZ Mid-Cap Value Fund.

That said, in reading through investment literature, you will sometimes run across *very strong* adherents to particular schools or approaches to investing, sometimes to the point of zealotry that their way is the only right way. They will talk about "pounding the table" in favor of a particular company that they feel strongly about.

We won't ever pound the table. We recommend a more relaxed point of view, with healthy doses of flexibility, balance, open-mindedness, and willingness to borrow from different schools of thought. *Don't* restrict your stock picking to a particular investing style. Instead, come at it from a variety of perspectives. Multiple approaches provide checks and balances, preventing any one methodology from dominating and perhaps misleading you by causing you to overlook other important factors. Judge companies one at a time by applying your investing principles to each company's own characteristics.

As you will see shortly, our Easy-Rate system balances points allotted for fast growth with points allotted for slow, steady gains and the company's payment of dividends. In this way, a fast-growing company like Google can amass a lot of points and come out near the top of the company rankings, but a slower-growing but proven, steady, dividend-paying behemoth like Johnson & Johnson can also come out on top. This promotes our underlying mission of staying flexible and open-minded.

CHAPTER C-2

Are Established Companies or "Emerging Opportunities" Better Bets?

Everything that can be invented has been invented.
—Charles H. Duell, Commissioner, U.S. Office of Patents, 1899

The Pros and Cons of Established Companies

There are several significant advantages to investing in established companies.

One is that the company has a track record. Once a business is well established, all the factors we use to evaluate them have a history. The essential facts and numbers can be retrieved and assessed. The qualities necessary for long-term success—sound finances, growth potential, market dominance, sufficient resources, strong execution, a culture of integrity and honesty—are already there (or not). This track record makes it easier to predict the likely future direction of the company. Such companies usually are heavily followed by Wall Street analysts, so predictions about company performance tend to be on target more often than with lesser-followed (or completely un-followed) smaller companies.

While the prospects for extremely rapid growth may seem smaller with an older, more mature company, many terrific investment opportunities are available from companies whose success is already obvious. The basic idea in picking investable companies is to select market-leading companies that demonstrate strong potential for sustained earnings growth. Some established companies do this consistently, so even though past performance does not guarantee future results, there is often less risk in betting on companies with superior established records. And in fact, many of the best-performing stocks over the years have been those of slower-growing companies. They compensate for their slow growth with consistency plus the ability to generate cash above and beyond what they need to fund their own growth. With their excess cash, they pay dividends (thus contributing directly to your returns), and/or they buy back significant amounts of their own stock (thus contributing indirectly to your returns by making each remaining share more valuable).

Note that not all established companies are huge in size. They are simply "established." Companies can become established—where we feel we can get to know them—in 3 to 5 years. (The company does not need to have been publicly traded for that entire time, just in existence.) Many investors consider a ten-year (or even longer) track record to be the minimum, but we won't get that picky. Again, our multifaceted approach will help prevent us from getting misled very often.

Not everything about established companies, however, works in their favor during our search for possible investments. For one thing, some established companies—such as the 30 in the Dow Jones Industrial Average—are huge in size, precisely because they have been successful for a very long time. At some point in a large company's life, the "law of large numbers" sets in, making the continuation of earlier growth rates nearly impossible. It is practically a mathematical certainty that large businesses cannot grow year after year as fast as smaller companies.

Let's consider this for a moment. The following table shows how many additional dollars in earnings a company with current earnings shown in the left column would have to produce next year in order to achieve the percentage growth rate shown along the top.

Law of Large Numbers

Present Earnings	5% Growth	10% Growth	20% Growth	30% Growth
$100 Million	$5 M	$10 M	$20 M	$30 M
$500 Million	$25 M	$50 M	$100 M	$150 M
$1 Billion	$50 M	$100 M	$200 M	$300 M

Look at the highlighted box at the intersection of $500 M in earnings and 20 percent growth. It tells us that in order to achieve a one-year earnings growth rate of 20 percent, a company with $500 M in earnings this year would have to *increase* its earnings by $100 M, to a total of $600 M next year. An additional $100 M, of course, is a huge amount of money. It is far more than most companies make in the first place, and here we're looking for that much growth on top of an already sizable base.

And remember, we're talking about growth in after-tax profits here, not just growth in revenues. Let's say that the company converts 20 percent of its revenues into after-tax profits (which would make it an extremely effective profit-creator). To profit by an additional $100 M, the company would have to increase its revenues by five times that amount, or $500 M, *in one year*. Needless to say, that is difficult. It will be even more difficult next year, when the respective numbers will grow to +$120 M in earnings and +$600 M in revenue. That's why a significant portion of the annual growth in many large companies comes from acquisitions of other companies—they literally have to buy the growth, because they cannot generate it from their existing operations alone.

Fifteen percent per year is often seen as the practical maximum growth rate achievable by very large companies. Growth of around 10 percent or the high single digits is more typical of highly successful—but huge—companies. Since stock prices over the long term generally correlate with earnings growth rates, it follows that on average the annual percentage growth in the stock price of an established company will not approach the growth rates achievable from the stock of smaller companies.

But—and this is a big "but"—the large companies often achieve a greater total return than faster-growing smaller companies by feeding back money to their shareholders in the form of dividends, which most small companies do not issue. Furthermore, the fact is that if you are able to identify dominant companies in important, fast-growing industries, you will find some large ones that do post amazing achievements in terms of sustained growth rates.

For example, in 1999, GE posted earnings of $10.7 B (that's billion). The next year, 2000, it earned $12.7 B, an increase in dollars of $2 B, and a percentage increase of 19 percent. GE, one of the most successful companies in history and the only remaining original member of the Dow Jones Industrial Average, has been achieving that sort of performance for decades. Its profits doubled between 1993 and 1999. Clearly, the law of large numbers has not yet caught up to GE.

The Pros and Cons of Emerging Companies

Emerging companies in emerging industries can become dominant with startling quickness. A good small company will often target a particular market niche, perhaps one that is not yet recognized by— or is too small to be of interest to—larger companies. (Remember, large companies are fighting the law of large numbers, so they may perceive small niches as being beneath their needs.) Small companies can be successful by inventing new products (sometimes creating hitherto unknown markets), improving on existing products and thereby stealing market share, or being more efficient than their larger competitors. Many small companies are the beneficiaries of businesses outsourcing. They spring up to perform "noncore" tasks for the behemoths or for other small companies that can't do everything themselves. A nimble young company with a hot product or service, strong management, and plenty of room to grow can weave a very compelling Story.

Plus, common sense suggests that a young growth company can offer a great possibility of percentage earnings gains. This might be called the "law of small numbers." For example, a company that made $10 M profit last year only needs to earn $15 M—or $5 M more—this year to have a *50 percent* earnings growth rate. Since history tells us that, over time, the rate of stock price growth generally tracks the rate of earnings *growth* (as opposed to the actual magnitude of the earnings), one might conclude that fast-growing small companies are invariably better investments than ponderous large companies.

Several studies have shown that—taken as a group—small-company stocks, over the very long term, have outperformed their large cousins. Figures from Ibbotson Associates show that small-company stocks had total returns of 12.5 percent annually between 1926 and 2001. Large-company stocks returned an average of 10.7 percent. That 1.8 percent difference is significant when compounded over 76 years, or even over just 5 to 10 years. This earnings growth advantage to smaller companies comports with common sense: It is logical that certain emerging, breakthrough companies and industries can—in their infancy—be fabulous investments with prospects for staggering growth rates. Plus, smaller companies do not have to fight the law of large numbers.

The figures above were compiled over 76 years. When the data is broken down into smaller time increments, one discovers that there are "runs" of years when large-cap companies do better in the market, and then there are other runs when the smaller companies take the lead. Large-cap companies were the leaders during the bubble period of the late 1990s, while more recently small-cap companies have been performing better (2003–2005).

Another point about small and new companies pertains to stock valuation rather than the company itself. This factor can cut either way. In favor of small companies, the mere fact that they *are* small and new means that a fair percentage of good young companies are not followed by Wall Street analysts or perhaps are followed by only one or two analysts. This can help create pricing undervaluations, providing more advantageous purchase points for their stocks. On the other hand, new companies often seem so "exciting" that they are in the news a lot and become overvalued by the market. This can diminish their potential for market-beating returns despite their high growth rates.

While the long-term data and common sense suggest that younger emerging companies have a growth advantage, it would be incorrect to conclude that all small companies are fast-growing and all large companies are ponderous. That is simply not the case. Furthermore, small companies' higher potential reward is accompanied by proportionately greater risk. Younger companies are harder to evaluate for several reasons:

1. They have a *short track record*. The numbers and facts needed for a thorough analysis are simply not in existence. This introduces extra risk into trying to predict their future prospects.

2. New companies are often in *new or emerging industries* with more competition than well-established companies in industries that have already sorted themselves out. For example, the information and communications revolution we are living through is undoubtedly as important as the Industrial Revolution of the late 19th century. This revolution is profoundly changing the way we learn, shop, communicate, entertain ourselves, and transact business. But investments in transformational technologies have not always rewarded investors. Electric power companies, railroads, airlines, and television manufacturers all transformed our lives, but many of their early investors lost their shirts. New industries are like experiments, and it is typical to have industry shakeouts as part of a Darwinian competitive process. A common characteristic of any emerging industry is a flock of competitors. Only by picking the eventual winner—or one of the eventual two or three dominators of that industry—can you make the best investment. In such shakeouts, sometimes the most able early companies achieve long-term dominance, while other times later entrants are the ultimate winners. The so-called "first mover advantage" is vastly overrated. Benjamin Graham, in his classic *Security Analysis* (1934), stated that unseasoned companies in new fields of activity provide no sound basis for determination of intrinsic value. He viewed such companies as highly speculative, and he stated that the buyer of such securities is not making so much an investment as a bet.

3. Young companies will at times deliberately *try to grab market share* by spending disproportionately on marketing or sales promotions. Many dot-coms in the late 1990s did this, because the whole Internet field was seen as a one-time land grab situation, and the early grabbers (it was thought) would achieve permanent advantage. Relatively tiny companies, for example, paid huge sums for Super Bowl ads, and a couple paid millions to have stadiums named after them. But as the companies burned through their cash without ever getting on a path to profitability, they basically doomed themselves. They did not have long-term winning strategies. First place in market share without profits does not make for a sustainable company. Many of those dot-coms have since gone out of business, and a couple of stadiums now bear different names. This is another reason why the early leader in a new field is not always the eventual long-term winner. Microsoft certainly was not the first company to come out with an operating system for PCs, but they ended up totally dominating that product line.

4. Less-established companies usually have *limited product lines, smaller or unestablished markets, dependence on just a couple of key employees, dependence on just a couple of key customers, and leaner financial resources.* All of these are potential disadvantages that make them more vulnerable to adverse business or economic developments.

5. The securities of newer and smaller companies may trade less frequently and in lesser volume than more widely held stocks, and as a result their *prices are often more volatile.* Price volatility in, say, a 20 percent range may not bother you, but how about price volatility in a 50 or 70 percent range?

6. Some young companies simply are *doomed to failure.* Again using the Internet bubble companies as whipping boys, it is now clear that many dot-com companies were not created with a clear vision for the future or even, it seems, with the intent to actually create a lasting company. The goal appears sometimes to have been simply to take the company public and make its founders rich. They were aided and abetted in this by greedy venture capitalists and bankers trying to get into the Internet gold rush. So in evaluating an emerging company, the individual investor must keep his wits about him and not get carried away by "the concept." Look instead for companies that have staked strong claims in industries with probable excellent growth trajectories, capitalizing on visible trends. Most important, try to confirm an intent by the company's leaders to build a true company, one that will generate earnings and enhance shareholder value for years to come. As we will see later, one way to do this is simply to insist that a company has actually made a profit before investing in it.

Picking "emerging" stocks is thus a blend of analysis and intuition. When a company is still in its early growing stages, all an investor can do is look at the early record of the company and the industry and guess what the outcome might be. The mission when looking at young companies is a matter of not only finding the innovators and facilitators of the future but also identifying which of them have staying power. Remember that many variables will be important, not just the best or newest product, but the best combination of product, demand for the product, innovation, management, early dominance, sustainable competitive advantage (to fend off the latecomers), pricing power, and brand-building. Luck and randomness play their usual roles too.

This evaluation is so difficult that it is impossible for an investor to attain as successful a batting average with young companies as with established companies. Venture capitalists, who invest in companies at their earliest stages, do well to pick 10 percent winners. The lure to even try, of course, is the possibility of ridiculously large gains when you do pick a winner.

In Sensible Stock Investing, we subject youthful or emerging companies to the same rigorous tests that we apply to all companies. For example, we articulate the Story of why to buy or hold a youthful stock, just as with established companies, even if the explanations are more subjective. We examine the same financial factors and look for the same "bonus points."

What you will find is that some of the information you would like to have simply will not be available, and as a result, the emerging company will score zero points on that ratings factor. This is actually a helpful outcome. It will tend to lower the company score of many youthful companies, which in turn will provide a measure of protection in deciding whether to invest at all. Since these are riskier investments by their very nature, that helps protect us. To garner enough points to reach our threshold requirements for investment consideration, an emerging company will *really* have to be superior.

An Advantage for the Individual Investor

Pity the manager of a "pure" small-cap mutual fund, which, in order to stay true to its charter and prevent "style drift," must sell its most successful companies when their capitalization exceeds the fund's upper limit. A really successful small company doesn't stay small forever—it becomes a mid-cap or large-cap stock. That is its goal. But a small-cap fund manager may be forced by his or her fund's charter into selling a successful company. As an individual investor, you don't have to be bound by such counterproductive rules. You can let your winners run until you have a better reason to let them go than the fact that they have passed a certain size limit. In fact, if you are fortunate, these companies will turn out to be the best investments you ever make.

A Word on Investor Sentiment

As noted earlier, studies show that sometimes small-cap stocks are "hot," and then other times they are supplanted by large-cap stocks. It's hard to tell whether this is because

- every investor is evaluating each stock individually, selecting the best stocks, and the "drift" to large- or small-cap stocks is simply a by-product of such rational analysis; or
- investors really are "flocking" to large caps or small caps at particular times for less rational reasons or as part of a herd mentality.

No matter. We'll accept that the phenomenon happens. The bottom line is that we won't pay much attention to cap size. We take the point of view that essentially the large-cap vs. small-cap distinction is irrelevant.

Our decisions will be based on factors other than the sheer size of the company, its market capitalization, or how long it has been around.

We will apply the same tests to all companies, regardless of their size. In the end, the commonsense approach is to put high-growth, newer firms on a level playing field with lower-growth older firms in our company scoring system. We will give high-growth firms credit for their rates of growth. But we will give slow-growth firms credit for their steadiness, stability, and dividends. In this way, we will create a company rating system that favors neither established nor emerging companies as a class but rather judges them on their respective merits.

CHAPTER C-3

Subdividing the Universe
of Companies

Why Subdivide the Stock Market?

While the stock market as a whole comprises a distinct asset class (the other two principal ones being cash and bonds), it contains upwards of 6500 commonly traded stocks in the U.S. alone. Therefore it is not surprising that much thought has gone into organizing companies into groupings or sectors. It not only makes things easier for investors to analyze smaller groupings, but it can also be significant when you want to have a well-rounded portfolio rather than a portfolio dominated by one "kind" of stock.

Subdividing by Sheer Size

Probably the most common method of categorizing companies is according to size. The most famous listing of companies on the planet, the *Fortune 500,* is a list of all U.S. companies arranged according to their size, as measured by each company's total revenue. Companies in the *500* are listed from highest revenue to 500th-largest revenue. While this list is justifiably famous, and total revenue is certainly important, it is not the most common way that investors subdivide companies. Investors are more interested in a company's ability to generate future value than in its revenue.

Subdividing by Market Capitalization

The most ubiquitous categorization method in stock investing is market capitalization. That is because market capitalization reflects the total value that investors place upon a company. It is another way of measuring size.

"Market capitalization" (or "market cap") is the total value of a company as measured by its stock's total worth. It is calculated by multiplying the price per share by the number of shares outstanding. Clearly, market capitalization reflects, at any given moment, what the market deems a company to be "worth."

There is no universal definition for different market-cap ranges, although most of the systems in use are pretty similar. In Sensible Stock Investing, we will use these definitions:

- Mega-cap: $100 Billion or more
- Large cap: Between $10 Billion and $100 Billion
- Mid cap: Between $1 Billion and $10 Billion
- Small cap: Between $400 Million and $1 Billion
- Micro cap: Under $400 Million

Just for some examples, these are the market capitalizations of a few well-known companies as of mid-April, 2005:

Anheuser Busch	$35.5 Billion	Large
Bank of America	$181.2 Billion	Mega
Cheesecake Factory	$2.6 Billion	Mid
Eastman Kodak	$8.8 Billion	Mid
General Electric	$383.6 Billion	Mega
Mattel	$7.6 Billion	Mid
Microsoft	$268.4 Billion	Mega
The Men's Wearhouse	$1.5 Billion	Mid
Wal-Mart	$202.3 Billion	Mega

The vast majority of stocks are small- or micro-cap in size.

Subdividing by Economic Sector

Another very common sorting method is to organize around industry clusters.

A great deal of research has tried to identify characteristics of different stock market sectors that might be useful to investors. Much of it is not that helpful. The simple reason is that the research often cannot reliably be applied to individual stocks—even stocks in the sector under study. In fact, there is a danger in applying sector-wide presumptions to individual stocks, because this can obscure your ability to select individual stocks based on their unique characteristics.

That said, there is nevertheless some usefulness to classifying stocks into sectors or industries. The main reason is that the stocks in individual sectors often do move similarly in both magnitude and direction. Therefore, a stock portfolio's well-roundedness (or lack thereof) in regard to industry sectors is one of the factors that determine overall performance. For example, when the technology bubble burst in 2000–2002, an investor would have had much better results if his or her portfolio had no technology stocks in it at all. The prior few years when the tech bubble was forming, of course, were a different story: Technology ruled, and that's where the most wealth was created in the market.

In an individual portfolio, the Sensible Stock Investor will usually want to have some degree of well-roundedness, with different economic sectors represented. Therefore, we need a scheme for classifying companies into sectors of the economy.

There are very many systems in use for classifying industries. There is no "official" way to divide the world of companies into chunks and categories.

Let's keep things simple and divide the universe of companies into these eleven categories:

1. **Basic materials** (such as wood, iron, aluminum, other metals, paper, and mined products).

2. **Energy and utilities** (including companies that produce electricity, companies that refine oil or gas, drillers, energy equipment and services, oil field equipment, pipeline operators, traditional regulated utilities, and newer deregulated energy companies).

3. **Consumer products and services** (including entertainment, consumer electronics, retail stores, foods and beverages, restaurants, household and personal goods, clothes, home builders and supplies, motor vehicles and auto parts, leisure goods and services, personal services, recreational items, and all other consumer goods and services not more specifically classifiable into one of the other categories). Note that this sector includes both so-called "cyclical" (tied to the economy) and "noncyclical" consumer products.

4. **Financials** (including banks, savings and loans, insurance companies, finance companies, brokerages, money management firms, and diversified financial firms).

5. **Health care** (including drugs, biotechnology, genomics, health devices and supplies, hospitals, HMOs, home health, assisted living, health providers and services, and pure research).

6. **Industrial** (including defense, aerospace, chemicals, heavy equipment and machinery, building products, construction and engineering, road and rail transportation infrastructure, and industrial parts).

7. **Technology** (including computers and peripherals, software, electronic equipment, semiconductors, components, office electronics and instruments, and electronic contract manufacturing, but *excluding* companies better classified as communications and media and also excluding companies which, though they heavily *use* technology, are not really straight technology businesses—see the text following this list).

8. **Communications and media** (including communications equipment, telephone companies, communication services, networking, wireless systems, Internet software and services, broadcast networks, diversified telecommunication services, newspapers, printing, publishing, and content creators and providers).

9. **Outsourcers and business services** (firms whose end customers are primarily other businesses, although they may serve consumers too; includes advertising, airlines, consulting, hotels, waste management, engineering, construction, payroll processing, computer processing, security services, distributors, shippers, and transportation companies).

10. **Real estate** (mainly REITs—real estate investment trusts).

11. **Conglomerates and miscellaneous.**

A word about sensible classification in the area of technology: You will find that many classification systems tend to overemphasize technology by calling a company that heavily *uses* technology a "technology company," totally overlooking the fundamental business the company is in. A classic example is Amazon.com. Most brokerages and analysts characterized Amazon from the start as an "Internet" company (and many still do), causing them to miss the point that Amazon was and is a *retailer* and that it should be analyzed as such. Its competitors are other retailers, not other Internet companies (such as Internet service providers). The fact that its business model would be impossible without the Internet is certainly important, but it is not determinative of what business Amazon is really in or whom they compete against.

Subdividing by "New Economy" vs. "Old Economy" Companies

This is probably as good a place as any to deal with the "new economy" and its impact on your investment thinking.

"New economy" is a phrase that sprang up in the late 1990s to describe information- and technology-based companies, as opposed to "old economy" companies that have been around a long time, are "mature," don't grow fast, and are, well, boring. In a vast oversimplification, the common use of the phrase signified information technology companies vs. industrial companies.

This oversimplification, while rampant for a few years, was always dangerous from an investor's point of view. The fact is that there *is* a "new economy," but it is composed of companies that best utilize and benefit from technological advances, not only companies directly *in* the information, technology, and communications business. Therefore, any company is in the "new economy" if it does the following:

- *Uses information well.* An old-line manufacturing outfit that uses enterprise software to manage its supply chain and lower its costs is participating in the new economy, no matter whether it makes steel or computers. Wal-Mart is a perfect example of an old-economy-sounding business (retailing) that uses information technology to succeed. Its use of interlocked computer systems to trade information with suppliers, schedule deliveries, and the like, is legendary. Wal-Mart is a new-economy company even though it is in one of the oldest businesses in the world.

- *Makes money from ideas as well as (or instead of) from traditional hard assets.* The "New Growth Theory" originated by Paul Romer (an economics professor at Stanford) holds that long-term economic progress comes from advances in technology and the human ideas that produce those advances. Wealth isn't created chiefly by having more of old things; it comes from having entirely new things. Change is a foundation for wealth creation. Thus, companies that are keeping up with change are participating in the new economy. As Paul Saffo of the Institute of the Future has said, "In a two-year period, less happens than we would have thought, and in a ten-year period, more happens than we could have imagined."

- *Invests in and effectively uses technology.* If they keep up with technology better than their competitors, the largest and oldest companies can make themselves even more impregnable by using their huge financial resources to continually reinvent themselves, introduce new products, expand their sales channels, and improve their internal processes. Companies like this use technology to gain or widen their competitive edge.

- *Keeps costs low by continually improving productivity.* American productivity grew twice as fast from 1995 to 1999 as it did from 1970 to 1995. That allowed corporations to maintain healthy growth rates and keep people employed without raising prices significantly. Improved productivity, judging from statements from the Fed, makes possible overall economic growth perhaps 33 percent greater (i.e., 4 percent rather than 3 percent) than was formerly thought possible without stoking inflation. That is huge, and it is a by-product of the "new economy."

The Revenge of the "Old Economy"

During the late 1990s, investor sentiment definitely went with the then-conventional view of the new economy. Stocks so perceived—that is, technology, telecom, and information technology stocks—were usually accorded much higher P/E multiples than highly profitable but "stodgier" stocks, with the differences often hard to explain by looking at fundamental numbers. In fact, between late 1998 and early 2000, the tech-heavy NASDAQ index just took off from the more balanced indexes. During that time, the NASDAQ rose 256 percent, the Dow just 28 percent. It was no longer tethered to reality.

The "tech wreck" of 2000–2002, of course, brought the divergence back to realism.

We now know, of course, that the late 1990s was a technology bubble. The key cause was corporate capital spending of unprecedented magnitude, as businesses embraced new computer and communications technologies. From 1994 to 2000, capital expenditures on information technology grew at rates of 20 to 25 percent annually. The climax was fueled by all the spending on Y2K projects (remember them?).

Of course, 20 to 25 percent growth was unsustainable, but at the time it led some to conclude that the technology industry had transcended business cycles, that it was immune to recession. Historically, however, corporate capital expenditures have been one of the most cyclical components of the economy. When technology and telecom became half of all corporate capital spending in the late 1990s, the technology and telecom vendors became frighteningly vulnerable to a reduction in capital spending if corporate profit growth slowed. And that's what happened. Beginning in late 2000 and extending into 2002, capital spending on technology fell off a cliff.

While the magnitude of that spending boom may have been an aberration, the long-term trend of substituting capital equipment (including technology and software) for labor has been going on forever and will continue as long as businesses try to become more efficient.

The most sensible approach to thinking about a "new economy" and "old economy" is that which appears to hold at the Federal Reserve. As frequently articulated by Alan Greenspan, former Federal Reserve Chairman, there is, in fact, a new economic reality at work, because previously unimaginable rises in productivity—most of them spurred by technological advances—are making it possible for the economy to expand at historically high rates without spurring ruinous inflation. The productivity increases allow prices to grow more slowly than before (because companies can produce more without proportionate increases in costs). Looking at it this way, one can see that there is, in fact, a new economy. But it is not limited to "technology" companies. Rather, technology is allowing the whole economy to improve its productivity. Traditional companies are using technology to reengineer their cost structures. Procurement costs, supply chain management, sales costs, order tracking, customer relationships, and shop floor production are all being revamped by new technological capabilities.

Subdividing by Company/Stock "Type"

A final way we will subdivide companies and their stocks is by "type." A company's or a stock's type is determined by how it typically behaves. There are a lot of parallels to human behavior. Just as there are Type A humans, there are Type A companies, and so on.

The details of dividing companies this way appear in Chapter E-3.

CHAPTER C-4

Megatrends

Follow the money!

—Deep Throat (in the movie version of *All the President's Men*)

Following the Money

In the film *All the President's Men,* Deep Throat tells Bob Woodward and Carl Bernstein to follow the money in order to solve the Watergate mystery. That turned out to be key guidance. It is equally excellent advice for the Sensible Stock Investor looking to increase his or her wealth.

Following the money means identifying companies that, for one reason or another,

- are receiving more than their "fair share" of the economy's nominal average 4 percent (or so) long-term growth;
- are effectively converting that rising revenue stream into profits to create wealth at an above-average rate for their shareholders; and
- appear capable of sustaining that superiority in value creation over an extended period of time.

How do we find such companies? In most cases, you want to pick stocks of companies that are in "leading" industries into which money is flowing faster than the economy as a whole. A good beginning place for analysis is to identify companies that are riding strong economically significant trends, such as demographic shifts, scientific advances, and the like. Whatever the underlying reason, such companies have a leg up on attracting money (from customers and investors) that can lead to further growth and better stock performance. That is "following the money."

What Is a Megatrend?

As used here, a "megatrend" is a medium- to long-term secular change, meaning that it is an ongoing, durable shift in economic direction. A megatrend goes beyond the normal expansions and contractions associated with the business cycle. Rather, we are interested in trends or shifts that are transformational. Under their force, entire industries, business practices, and our own individual lifestyles change.

If possible, you want the benefits of secular megatrends operating with you (or at least not against you) when you invest. A megatrend tilts the economic playing field. Because we have set our prediction horizon at one to two years, we are looking for trends that we expect to continue for at least that long. Most true megatrends last much longer than that. Very short-term trends or fads are not of interest when looking through the megatrend lens (although they may present interesting investment opportunities from other points of view).

Importance and Limitations of Megatrends

Long-lasting secular changes create the environment that innovative companies exploit to create value at a faster rate than the general economy. The greater or faster the degree of change, the greater the profit opportunity for the companies that take advantage of it.

That said, however, note that simply because a company is benefiting from a favorable megatrend does not mean that its stock is a fine investment. You can make plenty of bad stock picks by relying only on "theme investing." It is simply one of many screens that the Sensible Stock Investor puts candidates through under our multifaceted approach.

We do not rely *solely* on megatrends for these reasons:

• Success breeds competition. The very identification of a new, exciting opportunity may attract so many participants that none of them has a chance to make money. This commonly occurs in two ways. First, the participation of many companies can lead to hopeless fragmentation of a market among them. Unless one company (or just a few) attain dominance, it is hard for any of the companies to make money and grow. Second, the participation of many companies can lead to so many products that the whole area becomes swamped, perhaps even commoditized. It is generally agreed that this has happened, for example, in the personal computer industry. PCs, once the most innovative product under the sun, are now commodities. They are generally purchased based on price. Industry leadership has gone to the low-cost supplier (Dell). Going back a little further, some of you can remember when electronic calculators were incredible things of wonder. Now they are sold in blister packs at Wal-Mart for practically nothing. They are commodities.

• A company poised and positioned to ride a megatrend may nevertheless have problems of strategy and execution. The investor must be diligent and analyze companies individually. Superiority does not come automatically from jumping on a megatrend.

• Megatrends might unexpectedly change direction or evaporate. This is a particular risk in technology and pharmaceuticals, but it can apply to any societal, technological, or demographic shift. Every megatrend is at risk of displacement by another one.

• Money flow is a function not only of megatrends but also of perennial human needs and wants. Warren Buffett, perhaps the most famous investor of our time, has made a fortune investing in businesses that are the antithesis of the new and the trendy. In fact, he owns huge stakes in, or just outright owns, companies that make Coca-Cola, furniture, paint, and bricks.

Summary List of Megatrends

With that as a background, these are the secular megatrends that seem likely to be with us over the next several years and which may help point toward superior investing opportunities:

1. **Aging of the population.** The baby boomers are in their 40s and 50s, and other age groups are moving through life. This overwhelming demographic megatrend, in turn, spawns several subordinate themes, all having to do with the tastes, needs, and activities of an older population. The most important of these corollary needs—health care—is so significant that it qualifies as the next megatrend in and of itself.

2. **Rising importance of health care.** This is partly the result of the aging of the population, but it is also a function of the tremendous strides being made in health sciences.

3. **Continued innovation and growth in information technology.** This covers both the "basic capabilities" of technology and the practical uses of it. Basic capabilities refers to advances in fundamental chip capabilities and speed, innovations in electronic storage, digitization capabilities, and the build-out of the Internet. Practical uses of these capabilities include communications, productivity, commerce, and entertainment. Often the biggest beneficiaries of technology are not those who create or produce it but those who use it.

4. **Search for business efficiencies and growth.** Companies are always looking for ways to grow and to do things more efficiently and effectively. This causes them not only to constantly try to improve their own internal processes but also to outsource "noncore" functions to other companies. It spawns mergers and acquisitions that are based on perceived efficiencies and the elimination of duplication.

5. **Security and defense.** The events of September 11, 2001, made this an instant megatrend. It covers not only obvious areas like national security and intelligence but also computer security and identity protection.

6. **Globalization.** This trend is typified by the global nature of major corporations (such as McDonald's or Coca-Cola); by the strong presence of foreign companies in some industries (like Nokia in cell phones or Sony in consumer electronics); and perhaps most intriguingly by the huge population of China lurching its way toward a market economy.

7. **Need for More Energy.** This megatrend has been around for decades, but it shows no sign of losing steam.

That's the summary list. Now let's look more closely at each of these megatrends and discuss how they may point us in the direction of profitable investments.

Megatrend 1.   Aging of the Population

According to the American Association of Retired People (AARP), there are currently 76 million baby boomers, defined as those born between 1946 and 1957. The first boomers began hitting age 50 in 1996. The Census Bureau predicts that the number of Americans 65 or older will double to about 70 million by 2030. Due to higher life expectancies, the number of people 85 or older is expected to increase to 8.9 million by the year 2030.

Needless to say, this is a huge megatrend. Within it are several sub-trends.

- Probably the most significant is the increase in the need for health care. As mentioned earlier, health care is itself so important that we reserve it for treatment as Megatrend 2, below.

- Research shows that historical graphs of the S&P 500 and birthrates mirror each other—with a 45-year lag. That makes sense—it lines up stock investing with the peak earnings years of people. If the historical relationship continues, that suggests that there will be net inflows of money into the stock market until about 2012, when the last of the baby boomers hits 55.

- Leisure-based companies are likely to benefit. Members of the 55+ age group who are healthy (and more of them will be, thanks to improved health care) will spend more of their wealth on recreational activities. Specific industries likely to benefit from this trend include travel (including cruise lines); motor homes; travel and tour services; resort hotels, condos, and fractional home ownerships; gambling; in-home entertainment; casual dining; health clubs; and golf.

- Any industry that benefits from the growth rates of particular age groups and what they buy is fueled by the "Aging of the Population" megatrend. For example, as people age, their taste in clothes changes. Companies such as Chicos FAS—which focuses on fashionable clothing for the over-35 set—are already taking advantage of this.

Megatrend 2.   The Rising Importance of Health Care

Health care includes drugs, drugstores, biotechnology, genomics, wellness products, fitness, health devices (such as pacemakers), cosmetic surgery, digital diagnostic machines, new therapies and treatments, hospitals, innovative forms of health-care delivery, distribution of medical goods, health insurance, and pure health research.

Dependence on prescription drugs increases with age, and four out of five drugs are prescribed to people over 50. Nearly half the elderly take three or more prescriptions, up from 35 percent a decade ago. People in their 50s, 60s, and 70s get sick more often than younger people. Longer life gives people more time to consume health-care goods and services, and it afflicts more and more of them with conditions associated with aging, such as heart disease, type 2 diabetes, and joint problems. Within the next few years, inevitably, baby boomers will start spending more time in hospitals.

According to U.S. Health Care Financing Administration projections, total health-care spending will increase by 6.5 percent annually from 2001 through 2008, at which time it will account for approximately 16 percent of the total economy. Drug expenditures are rising even faster, around 18 percent per year, according to the Centers for Medicare and Medicaid Services.

A dramatic sub-trend within health care is the rising importance of generic drugs. Generics become legal to manufacture when branded drugs come off patent protection. It is estimated that branded drugs generating over $100 billion in annual revenue (in their branded form) will come off patent by 2010. Generic drugs are highly favored by health insurers and individuals due to their enormous cost advantages. The Food and Drug Administration is helping generics along by showing increasing willingness to grant fast approval to applications for generic drugs. Generic drug makers employ armies of lawyers to fight patent protection on branded drugs. Not only that, generic drug makers are continually increasing their products' quality and attractiveness by adding time-release features, reducing side effects, and so on. (Branded-drug manufacturers fight back by protecting their patents fiercely, making improvements to drugs nearing patent expiration, attempting to have improved drugs repatented as new drugs, and employing direct-to-consumer advertising.)

Once generic equivalents become available, it is usually only a short time before sales of the branded drug drop 50 to 70 percent or more. There is tremendous room for growth in the generic industry, because at this time generics account for only about 10 percent of the revenue produced by branded drugs.

We should also mention biotechnology here. The drug industry generally divides into two large categories: traditional chemical-based drugs, and biotech-based drugs created through study of the human genome. Some pundits feel that biotechnology may become the most powerful value-creating industry over the next few decades. Biotechnology research has been greatly accelerated by advances in computer analysis, which have allowed scientists to decode one of the most complex puzzles of all, the makeup of the human body.

Megatrend 3.   Continued Innovation and Growth in Information Technology

The third megatrend—technology—is mostly a function of scientific advances, product development, and marketing. New discoveries or engineering feats, the development of applications that utilize them, and the adoption of these applications by customers determine growth cycles in technology.

While the word "technology" can be applied to any scientific- or engineering-driven change, the trend we are focusing on here is *information* technology, or "IT." IT—accelerated by the Internet—has revolutionized business processes, communications, consumer commerce, news, and entertainment.

Technology growth rates have their own rhythms. The adoption rate for any new IT capability is a function of willingness to change over to new machines and processes. The rate is fueled by enthusiasm, promises of efficiency, and quite often a "coolness" factor, while it can be constrained by skepticism, resistance to change, high switching costs, and budget restraints. Generally, new technological products are first purchased by a sliver of enthusiasts and hobbyists, then by a larger group known as "early adopters," then by the large mass in the middle, and finally by recalcitrants who only change when they are forced to. When a new product reaches the stage where it is adopted en masse (and not all technology products reach this stage), a relatively rapid transition can take place from one technology "generation" to another. The bottom line is a transformation that starts out slowly, accelerates to high speed, and finally levels off when the market becomes saturated. (When graphed against time, this adoption pattern looks something like an *S*, so technology adoption is sometimes said to follow the "S curve.")

From a Sensible Stock Investing standpoint, the most important point on the curve is the time when mass adoption begins (or just before that). Investments made too far ahead of that point are usually quite speculative. The mass-adoption, high-growth phase is the best time to own a company. Following the high-growth stage comes an inevitable slowdown. The high growth rates of the mass adoption stage become unsustainable, either because of market saturation, commoditization, or the replacement of the formerly new technology by an even newer one.

The best way to think about the technology megatrend may not be as pointing to investment in companies which *produce* it but rather as helping companies that *use* it. The benefits of many technological changes flow not to the producers of the change but to consumers and to corporations that incorporate the technology to improve their own productivity. As the technology spreads to more corporations, the earlier adopters may see their profitability at first rise but then revert to the mean as more of their competitors also adopt it (or even better versions of it). So technology is a two-edged sword that contributes to both productivity and competitiveness.

Because "information technology" is itself a sprawling category, we need to subdivide it. Let's utilize these categories, one for the basic machinery of technology and the others for the most interesting areas in which that machinery is being utilized:

- Basic materials and hardware
- IT for productivity
- IT for communications, information transfer, commerce, and transactions
- IT for entertainment

Megatrend 4.   *Search for Business Efficiencies and Growth*

The search for business efficiencies and growth is a kind of "perpetual trend." Businesses have tried to grow and to become more efficient since there have been businesses.

IT solutions have been adopted by all kinds of businesses, and capital spending on IT systems, equipment, and advice has grown over the past decade. Beyond IT, businesses in recent years have turned in these directions for increasing their efficiency:

- Outsourcing: Companies potentially can outsource any process (although most do not risk disrupting their most important core tasks). So we see companies outsourcing manufacturing; the running of their computer systems; payroll; human resources; employee education and training; and management of 401(k) programs. Clearly this benefits companies that provide those services to other companies (such as ADP and Paychex in payroll processing or IBM in running computer systems).

- The use of temporary employees to sidestep the extra expenses (such as health care and pensions) associated with permanent employees. Beneficiary companies are those in the temp services industry.

- Hiring consultants to advise on practically everything—process re-engineering, computer systems, or strategy development. Beneficiaries are consulting companies.

As you can see, business-to-business services are motley and varied. Spending on business services has grown significantly, increasing from 3.5 percent of GDP in 1990 to 5.8 percent in 2000.

Beyond business-to-business services, another avenue for both growth and efficiency is consolidation. Consolidation occurs when one company acquires another in the same business and integrates their operations, which often results in savings by eliminating duplication—combining call centers, for example, or human resources departments. Acquisitions of this sort are Darwinian, the strong (usually the larger) business swallowing the weak (usually the smaller). Acquisitions of one business by another have been occurring since the dawn of capitalism.

Megatrend 5.   Security and Defense

In the past several years, the security and defense industries have had an awakening which figures to carry on for quite some time. For most people, of course, the dawn of this era came with the attacks of September 11, 2001. The trend has implications for such industries as biometrics, airport security, weapons manufacturers, global positioning systems, videoconferencing, and antiterrorism technology, among others.

Another facet of security is computer, network, and data security. We have seen how important "soft assets" have become in the corporate world. Everyone who is connected to a network—whether at home or at work—is vulnerable to computer viruses, worms, hacking, and the like. Since so much of modern business depends on IT, companies that have never had disaster recovery plans are developing them, and those that did are updating them.

Disaster recovery is in turn supported by outsourcing to specialist companies that provide services such as off-site storage and backup for physical documents and computer data, software that simplifies the backup process, and systems which facilitate network recovery services to keep things operating in crisis situations.

Megatrend 6.   *Globalization*

Globalization—the spread of companies and markets into new countries and the growing interdependence of business activities across countries and continents—is an inevitable outcome of companies' efforts to grow and to become more efficient. For some companies, acceptable levels of growth are available only if they expand beyond their domestic markets. Many well-known American companies are globalized. Coca-Cola, IBM, and General Electric, to name just a few, derive a significant portion of their revenues from overseas.

Globalization in turn creates expansion opportunities for companies involved in business services: Because many of their customers are becoming global in their operations and markets, business service providers are forced to become global too, or else they will lose business to competitors who can help their clients on a global basis.

China, the world's most populous nation, is also now the world's fastest-growing economic power, growing nearly 8 percent annually over the past decade. It appears to be moving inexorably toward a market economy (from a centrally controlled economy), and if this continues, China represents the largest geographic market for potential growth. Other countries developing market economies include Russia, India, and Brazil.

Besides providing new markets, globalization is having a dramatic impact on labor markets. Workers across the world, aided by IT, can now perform routine and some complex services to corporations anywhere.

Megatrend 7.   *Need for Energy*

The need for energy is another "permanent megatrend." The need for energy is global and growing. Simply put, growing economies require more energy.

Each year, Exxon-Mobil, the world's largest energy company, issues an energy outlook, as does the U.S. Department of Energy. Here are highlights from their December 2004 reports. These points pretty well define the energy megatrend:

- Expansion of the global economy will increase energy demand by 50 percent over the next quarter century.

- Emerging Asian countries will account for 50 percent of the global energy demand growth. China and India will have the most impact on increasing demand.

- Part of the demand will be met by non-fossil fuel sources. However, hydrocarbons will remain the principal source of energy for many decades to come.

- The world has plenty of global oil reserves. Most estimates put the world's proven oil reserves—those economically recoverable today—at one trillion barrels, or about the same as people have consumed to date. Beyond "proven" reserves, it is estimated that the globe has more than six trillion barrels of conventional oil in the ground, plus several trillion barrels of unconventional supply such as oil sands and oil shale.

- Higher prices for oil and natural gas are expected to have limited impact on energy consumption in the United States over the next two decades. That is, demand is generally "price inelastic": Within limits, demand grows with the economy no matter what the price.

- The United States will continue to import the bulk of its energy. To meet our country's and the world's oil demand, OPEC (the Organization of the Petroleum Exporting Countries) will need to produce more oil (although that will be hampered by inattention to their infrastructure over the last few years). Similarly, the United States' dependence on natural gas imports will witness an enormous increase.

The companies that will benefit from the energy megatrend include oil and gas companies, companies that supply them with equipment and services, exploration companies, pipeline companies, oil and gas transportation firms, Canadian oil sands and shale companies, companies that liquefy and gasify coal into usable oil, companies that increase energy efficiency, and companies that develop successful energy alternatives.

CHAPTER C-5

What's the Story?
Buy Dominant Companies

The race is not always to the swift, nor the battle to the strong—but that's the way to bet.
—Damon Runyan

Invest in Dominant Companies

An essential theme of Sensible Stock Investing is to buy dominant companies. There are any number of instructive quotes from famous investors that capture this idea. Here are two:

- Your goal as an investor should simply be to purchase, at a rational price, a part interest in an easily understandable business whose earnings are virtually certain to be materially higher 5, 10, and 20 years from now (Warren Buffett, 1996 Letter to Berkshire Hathaway Shareholders).

- The best growth comes from companies that dominate an industry that is expanding faster than the overall economy. When a company clearly becomes the leader in its field, not just in dollar volume but in profitability, it seldom gets displaced from this position as long as its management is competent. Focus on the leaders with lasting business models (Philip A. Fisher, *Common Stocks and Uncommon Profits*, 1957).

A company that dominates its industry has already proven itself against its competition and established its brand(s) among its customers. If it is in an important, growing industry, good management will parlay this dominance into further dominance, as the company brings its superior resources to bear against its competitors. Dominant companies attract the best talent, form the best alliances, and have the best growth rates relative to other companies in their industry. During hard times, dominant companies not only survive but also apply relentless pressure on their competitors (through price wars, for example), which actually strengthens their dominance *during* the hard times. They emerge even more dominant and perhaps with less competition. For example, during the tech recession of 2000–2002, Dell used its superior low-cost business model to create continual pricing pressure on No. 2 Compaq. Eventually, Compaq was forced into accepting an acquisition offer from Hewlett-Packard. One less competitor for Dell.

Seeking out dominant companies is often called "franchise" investing, i.e., you are looking for companies with dominant franchises. I prefer to call it "dominance" investing, or even "legal monopoly" investing. Select companies with dominant businesses, with strong earnings growth potential, in important growing industries, and with superior management. A legal monopoly is ideal—that is, a company that has earned overwhelming market share due to the superiority of its products or services, all while "fighting fair."

Figuring Out the Stock's Story

At a very early stage in researching a company, you should determine its "Story." While not devoid of numbers, the Story is a word-based rather than a numbers-based exercise. You use facts, of course, but the Story also has a strong element of intuition and feel—you are looking for a Story that makes common sense.

From Peter Lynch's *One Up on Wall Street* (1989):

> Before buying a stock, I like to be able to give a two-minute monologue that covers the reasons I'm interested in it, what has to happen for the company to succeed, and the pitfalls that stand in its path....Once you're able to tell the story of a stock...so that even a child could understand it, then you have a proper grasp of the situation.

For example, years ago when Microsoft had a near monopoly in PC operating systems (at a time when PCs were selling like hotcakes), not to mention being the leading software developer on the planet, it was *intuitively obvious* that Microsoft was a dominant company. It was, in fact, the reigning poster child for dominance investing at the time. (Its top-of-the-heap status was later weakened by the rise of the Internet, the maturing of the PC industry, and a plethora of antitrust suits against the company.)

Any company's Story is distilled from a mosaic of factors. In creating the Story, think about how the company employs its assets to create sustainable competitive advantage and value for its customers and shareholders. The assets may be intangible (such as institutional knowledge, patents, trademarks, brands, business processes) or more traditional physical assets (like plants or a fleet of trucks).

General Business Dominance

The most ideal investment situation arises when a company achieves monopoly or near-monopoly status—clear industry leadership, a dominant brand, and an impregnable position.

It is important here to note that monopolies by and of themselves are *not* illegal. *Anticompetitive practices* to build or maintain monopolies are illegal. But just being way out in front of your competition is not against the law if you play fair.

Not all dominant companies are monopolies, of course. Sometimes an industry has room for two or three strong leaders, any one of which (or all three) might make for good investing. So while you are looking for a monopoly to invest in, look for other characteristics that suggest that a company is outstanding in relation to its competition. All of these are durable competitive advantages, often called "moats"—they protect the company from attack and allow it to earn superior profits on a sustainable basis. The more of these characteristics you can find, the better:

- Dominant market share. This does not necessarily require 80 or 90 percent market share; a number higher than about 40 percent usually signifies market dominance.

- A geographic advantage. Classic examples include local newspapers.

- A regulatory or government-based advantage. Examples would be companies with long-term defense contracts, traditional regulated utilities, or the two satellite radio companies (XM and Sirius).

- A coherent package of complementary products, as distinguished from "one-trick pony" companies that depend on a single product and are vulnerable because of that.

- Unique new products or superior services which have high demand.

- A high-quality executive team, as shown by an articulated and understandable vision, absolute integrity, sensible strategies, adaptability to changing market conditions (without chasing fads or repeatedly changing direction), and a regard for shareholder returns (as distinguished from lining their own pockets).

- Control of a key economic "tollbooth" through which other companies or consumers must pass. Microsoft's Windows operating system is such a tollbooth, because it is the industry standard.

- Economies of scale, where the increased size of the company is leveraged by skilled management to reduce the per-unit cost of production or distribution. In a well-scaled company, fixed costs can be spread over a much larger customer base than competitors have.

- A track record of increasing profits at a greater annual percentage rate than revenues, indicating that wealth is being *created*, not just collected. So if a company is growing its sales 10 percent per year and its earnings at 12 or 14 percent per year, it is probably dominating its industry; otherwise it would be unable to do that.

- Highly effective sales and distribution systems. A dominant company is likely to have resources for marketing and sales that can overwhelm its competitors and allow it to maintain or increase its leading market share.

- Inept competition.

- Intellectual property protections, such as patents, trademarks, copyrights, and licenses. Patent or copyright protection of an industry standard creates, in effect, a monopoly situation. A drug patent would be an example.

- Other high barriers to entry for potential competitors, such as unique and nonreplicable institutional knowledge or huge capital start-up costs.

- A healthy balance sheet—plenty of cash, little or no debt, and the like.

- High switching costs for customers to go over to a competitor. This is sometimes seen, for example, with software companies that have embedded themselves in their customers' processes. Any company that has revamped its entire production and back-office processes to install SAP's "enterprise software" systems—and trained all its people in SAP's unique requirements—is unlikely to switch to some other enterprise system very soon, even if the other software offers discernable advantages. It's easier to lobby SAP to improve its software than it is to rip out SAP and substitute the other company's software. Autodesk also benefits from high switching costs—designers are trained on AutoCAD early in their careers. It's become the industry standard. Look for the tendency for corporate customers to sign long-term contracts.

- Products with unique (as opposed to commodity) characteristics, with meaningful product differentiation—provided that the features *are important to customers*.

- Companies that benefit from the "network effect," that is, a product or service that becomes more attractive to new customers because others are already using it. Growth of the network all but ensures success for the providing company. Great examples of this are eBay (sellers go where all the buyers are, and buyers come to where all the sellers are); and Adobe Systems (whose Acrobat software has become the standard for electronic publishing and the transmission of documents—everybody uses it, so everybody uses it).

- In commodity industries, lowest-cost provider status (examples: Dell in PCs, Southwest in airline travel). Being the low-cost provider allows you to squeeze your competitors, especially if you can continue to bring your costs lower than they can. Dell has confounded its competitors for years with its build-to-order, direct distribution system—its competitors cannot replicate it (because they have middleman distributors to protect), and they cannot beat it.

- Extremely strong brand name(s), along with a commitment and the ability to promote, protect, and expand the good brand position. A strong brand creates trust among customers. They know what to expect based on many years' experience or the brand's reputation for quality or fine service. A strong brand creates effective product differentiation in the minds of customers—they're willing to go at least somewhat out of their way, maybe pay a little more—to get *that brand*. This translates into pricing power and better margins for the company.

As you can see, the idea is to look not only for how strong a franchise a company has but also for how long it can be perpetuated. No individual factor guarantees dominance by itself, and you'll probably never find all of the foregoing attributes in one company. But for your investment dollars, you want companies that are truly superior to their competition or have little true competition.

Test your concepts; look for concerns. Ask "why" and "how" questions. How did the company attain dominant market share, and why aren't competitors taking customers away? Why can't a competitor start and win a price war? How does the executive team function? Why do the company's customers accept price increases?

Expanding Industry

Beyond the company's own excellence, another thing to look for is the expanding nature and future prospects of its industry. Over the long haul, you'd rather be in a growing industry than in a declining industry.

One avenue to identifying investable industries is to look for those that are benefiting from impressive growth curves. Expanding possibilities can result if a company is riding a megatrend or driving a transformational change. Notice that transformational change can come about in any industry, not just the technology industry. Wal-Mart has transformed retailing just as much as Microsoft changed computing. A caution on hot new industries: By their nature, such industries are often hypercompetitive. Ideally, you want a single industry dominator. Lacking that, you want an important, growing industry with room for several leading firms who can all be profitable.

Another avenue to identifying investable industries is to identify slow-growth industries with just one or two dominators. These winning companies can be great investments because the industry has already sorted itself out. The surviving company (or couple of companies) has undoubtedly demonstrated superb productivity, discipline, careful employment of capital, and a propensity to invest only in projects that enhance their business prospects. They are true Darwinian survivors.

Prospects for Growth in Sales and Earnings

Another factor characteristic of a strong Story is the likelihood that the company can build its revenues *and* earnings significantly over the next few years. We're looking for companies that are growing faster than the average company in the market (because our goal is to beat the market). Not all great companies are 20 or 25 percent growers, but it is rare that we would be interested in a company that cannot consistently grow its earnings at least 10 percent per year. While any company can have a bad year, we want to find solid, stable growers, preferably with a good track record of growth spanning several years.

Strong *sales* growth is just as important as strong *earnings* growth. Consistent sales growth demonstrates that there is a sustained demand for the company's products or services and that the company has the sales and distribution systems capable of satisfying that demand. In contrast, rising earnings unaccompanied by rising sales may just be the result of one-time cost cutting. Over the long haul, demand from customers is a must. After maybe one or two rounds of belt-tightening or internal process improvements, a company *cannot* simply cost-cut its way to the kind of sustained earnings growth we need. All earnings begin with revenue, so sustainable earnings growth begins with consistent revenue growth. Strong sales growth can be found in either established or emerging companies.

Companies that score high on this dimension usually exhibit the following characteristics:

- *Unique or exceptional product(s) or service(s)* that are perceived to be superior. Often, but not always, the product(s) or service(s) are relatively new.

- *Pricing power.* This is the ability to charge more than competitors because of the quality, functionality, exclusivity, "coolness," or other unique characteristics of your company's products and services. Occasionally it comes because a company has become embedded in its customers' work processes, resulting in high switching costs for customers. Having pricing power is the opposite of being in a commodity business, where the only competitive variable is price (all the products being essentially the same).

- *Consistent development of new products* that will further increase total sales and replace revenues when current product lines play out. A strong product pipeline is often the result of management's consistently devoting significant dollars to research and development every year, even during hard times.

- *A track record of creating value.* Some management teams actually destroy value by mis-deploying the resources at their disposal. Often this happens in companies that are acquisition-happy for egotistical reasons, making overpriced acquisitions that they then fail to integrate effectively (because their minds have already turned to the next acquisition target). Or they have a history of investing in low-return, capital-eating projects.

- *A growth orientation,* with the wisdom to focus on growth areas that have a logical business relationship to current products, activities, or markets—as opposed to ego-driven acquisitions or projects that take a company away from its core competencies.

- *Repeat-purchase business models.* Look for companies in which most of the revenue growth doesn't have to come from new customers, which are invariably more expensive to attain than current customers are to retain. Great example: Hewlett-Packard's printer business, where most of the profits come from repeat sales of ink cartridges. Another classic example: Gillette ("Give 'em the razor, sell 'em the blades").

Outstanding Labor and Personnel Relations

Steer clear of companies or industries that have periodic (or seemingly perpetual) labor difficulties. The legacy airlines and domestic automotive companies come to mind.

Unquestionable Integrity of Management

Avoid companies that display any signs of lack of integrity. Examples:

- Companies being sued on antitrust grounds.

- Companies that produce unsafe products and attempt to evade responsibility.

- Companies whose reported financials are questioned. (Has the company had a formal SEC investigation in the past year or two? Does the company have a reputation for practicing "aggressive accounting"? Has it repeatedly taken "one-time" charges year in and year out?)

Occasionally, a company's CFO will resign unexpectedly or under questionable circumstances. This is usually a surefire danger signal.

Depending on your point of view, a variety of factors can lead you to question a company's integrity. For example, Microsoft has been adjudged in court decisions to have used illegal tactics to preserve its monopoly in operating system software. You may consider this proof of a lack of integrity and refuse to invest in Microsoft for this reason. For another example, consider Daimler-Chrysler: At the time of the "merger" of Chrysler and Daimler-Benz, Jurgen Shrempp (CEO) said that there would be equality of the companies after the merger. Shrempp later retracted these statements, publicly acknowledged that he had misled, and appointed a German to head Chrysler. Many of Chrysler's executives left the company as the truth of the situation emerged. So did a lot of investors: From early 1999 to early 2001, the stock dropped 50 percent.

Consistent Operating History or Positive Life Cycle Change

Look for companies with a history of outstanding performance under a variety of economic conditions. Stable management often makes such a history possible.

While this criterion tends to favor long-established companies, the desired qualities can sometimes be found in companies that are three to five years old. What you want is a consistent operating history, as opposed to an inconsistent or nonexistent operating history.

Somewhat conversely, you can sometimes find a positive Story element in a company experiencing a major change which is expected to achieve advantageous results. Examples of such changes may be new management, new products, new technologies, restructuring or reorganization, or merger and acquisition. Of course, any of these can work in the opposite direction too and be negative indicators. Just because a company brings in a new CEO does not mean that its fortunes are going to change for the better. Sometimes they get worse. Companies undergoing significant change (or in perpetually changing industries, such as technology) are inherently less predictable and therefore more risky.

Distilling the Story

The Sensible Stock Investing Easy-Rate™ scoring system rates companies on a 10-point scale for their Story. In our book, a company worth 10 points would be:

- A monopoly or effective monopoly, but not being attacked or likely to be attacked by the government on antitrust grounds for its monopoly characteristics. In other words, it has won its monopoly position by fighting fair.

- Free of significant competition and devoid of *likely* significant competition, either from someone else in the same business or from a new or disruptive technology that might obsolete the business or industry.

- Not subject to significant government regulation or the likelihood of regulation; or, in some instances, *protected* by government regulation.

- One whose competitive advantages are protected by patents, copyrights, and the like.
- In a fast-growing, important industry, one with probable staying power over the prediction horizon (one to two years).
- Not subject to rapid shifts in tastes or fashion; accordingly, one not appealing principally to kids or teenagers.
- In an understandable business (from a high macro level).
- Possessing a good strategy and a history of good execution.
- Fast growing for its size, and with an obvious growth orientation on management's part.
- One with very strong prospects for sustained and relatively steady earnings growth for the next few years.
- One with a strong and sustainable brand or brands.
- Usually, one not in a commodity business.
- One free of significant questions about the excellence and integrity of its management.
- A company unburdened by significant litigation and potential legal liabilities.
- One with good labor relations.
- One with strong fundamental financials: having little or no debt, being cash-strong, plowing significant dollars back into the business, displaying good earnings growth, and the like. Note that we will evaluate financial factors separately, but a general sense of them can show up in the Story. Example: The fact that Johnson & Johnson has increased earnings an average of 10.5 percent per year for *100 years* is certainly part of its Story.
- One that keeps the interests of shareholders in mind, for example, via stock-buyback programs or a steady history of increasing dividends.

At the time of this writing (early 2006), I have current evaluations of 95 companies for their Story. Only five have Story scores of 8; none has a 9 or 10. The five are Chicago Mercantile, General Electric, Johnson & Johnson, Starbucks, and Wal-Mart.

Turning the above list inside out gives you the profile of a company that no one in his right mind should invest in. Remember, no single item is necessarily a knockout factor, and it is next to impossible to find a company with all positive characteristics. But viewed in combination, see if you wouldn't rather own a company from the left column and run away from a company in the right column (no matter how "cheap" its stock):

Comparing Great and Lousy Companies

GREAT COMPANIES TO INVEST IN	LOUSY COMPANIES TO INVEST IN
Monopoly or dominant position in its markets	Also-ran in its industry; industry fragmented
Little, no, or ineffective competition	Up against strong competitors; a clear also-ran
Not in any kind of trouble	In trouble with the government (e.g., antitrust), auditors (e.g., questionable financial statements), regulators (e.g., environmental concerns), shareholders (e.g., lawsuits), or customers (e.g., product liability problems)
Unregulated; little prospect of regulation	Regulated, unless the regulation serves to protect the company's dominant status
In a fast-growing or reliably slower-growing industry	In a stagnant or shrinking industry or in an industry threatened by disruptive technology
Company growing; management has growth orientation and strategies	Company shrinking (*unless* the shrinking is part of a deliberate strategic process of refocusing the business on its core strengths); management has "preservation" or "conservation" orientation
Not subject to unpredictable shifting tastes or fashion	In markets dominated by shifting tastes or fashion
Understandable business, at least from a general level	Incomprehensible business; hard or impossible to figure out how the company can make money from what it does
Plausible long-term vision and sound strategies	Improbable (or no) long-term vision, questionable strategies, or strategies that are difficult to understand or seem wrongheaded
You like the company's products or services	You've personally had bad experiences with the company
Record of executing well and performing at top levels	Record of performance problems or repeated negative "surprises"
Good prospects for sustained earnings and revenue growth	Questionable or poor prospects for sustained earnings and revenue growth
Excellent management of unquestioned integrity	Mediocre management or management bedeviled by ethical questions; high officials bailing out; company under investigation
Excellent labor relations	Perpetual labor problems
Great brand or brands	Unknown or disrespected brand
Unique, highly valued products and services	Commodity products or services, with little competitive differentiation other than price, *unless* company has a clear and sustainable advantage as low-cost producer
Highly respected, as shown, for example, by high rating on *Fortune*'s annual list of "Most Admired Companies"	Disrespected in the business community or by the public at large; low rating on *Fortune*'s annual list

GREAT COMPANIES TO INVEST IN	LOUSY COMPANIES TO INVEST IN
Financial strength	Weak (or teetering) financially; weak balance sheet, low profit margin, inconsistent earnings record, high debt, on the verge of bankruptcy
Keeps interests of shareholders in mind, perhaps as shown via history of dividend growth or stock buyback programs	Little or no record of keeping interests of shareholders in mind; seems to be run more for top management than for shareholders

Write It Down

The effort to articulate in writing why you want to buy or hold on to a stock is one of the most important disciplines in Sensible Stock Investing. You should be able to articulate clearly what makes a company attractive, hopefully in a way that a disinterested party could understand and certainly in a way that you yourself understand.

Make the Story brief and succinct. I like to stay within 200 words. The word limitation forces you to summarize the basic business of the company and what makes it investable. It stops you from just dumping data into your thinking. You must *interpret* that data, think conceptually, and understand the company from a macro level.

An essential part of being able to articulate a stock's Story is that you can understand how its business works. It is generally better to omit from your candidate list companies that have businesses that you cannot understand or that change so rapidly that you cannot keep up with what's happening in the field. Many technology companies walk a thin line here. Take EMC, the world leader in network storage: Only experts in the field could begin to understand (or explain) exactly how EMC's products work and how they are integrated with other computer products. But anybody can understand, at a macro level, the explosion of data-storage needs that accompanies modern computing, the rise of the Internet, and so on.

The Story should be interpretive and analytical. It is more than a listing of what products the company makes or what divisions it is organized into. Rather, it tells what makes the company dominant, why it is likely to grow, and what makes it a good investment. An example of a Story can be found in Appendix I, where Form 1 is a sample Easy-Rate Stock Rating Sheet of a superb company, PepsiCo.

And if you are a reluctant writer, Form 2 is a Story Questionnaire. Answer the questions there, and you will have the information you need to prepare any company's Story.

If you purchase a stock, having written the Story lets you preserve why you bought it for later review and updating. Have doubts about the company crept in for any reason? Has anything changed? Are the reasons you thought this was (or would become) a dominant company still true and valid? Should you look a little more deeply into the company's business and prospects?

Finally, writing out the Story gives you a basis to assign points to the stock in a scorekeeping system. Stocks with positive characteristics will get 6–10 points. Stocks with unattractive prospects will get 0–4 points. The latter would probably be enough, by itself, to knock such a company completely off your candidate list. Why own a "4" company when you can get an "8"?

CHAPTER C-6

Inherently Unplayable and Risky Companies

There are more than 6500 public companies traded on U.S. stock markets. Some of them are great companies, many are good, a lot are just OK, and more than you would think are lousy—as companies and as investments. So in addition to identifying great companies through their Stories and other methods, it is also important to understand which companies display factors that make them risky or questionable investments.

Consider all of the characteristics discussed in this chapter to be red flags when you are considering investments.

However, a note of common sense: If you have *particular or special knowledge* in a certain company or industry, some caveats in this chapter may not apply to you. I am certain that fortunes have been made in every one of the types of companies discussed here by people who really knew what they were doing in particular cases. But for the average individual investor without special knowledge, the factors in this chapter usually suggest that a company is either uninvestable or at best carries a high element of risk.

Bulletin-Board Companies

The bulletin board is the "over-the-counter" portion of the stock market where companies trade that are not large enough, or financially sound enough, to be accepted for listing on the NASDAQ, New York, or American Stock Exchanges. Bulletin-board stocks don't have the same reporting requirements as companies that trade on the major exchanges, so it is difficult or impossible to get reliable information about them. Bulletin-board companies may come to your attention because they hire people to advertise or send you e-mails telling you how great they are. Stay away from them.

Companies without Earnings…or, Concept Stocks

Don't invest in companies that have never made a profit.

In a start-up situation, even the most brilliant of investors cannot accurately predict *if* future earnings will emerge, *when* that might happen, or *how great* they will be, for an as-yet-unprofitable company. The most sensible approach is not to attempt to forecast earnings where there have never been any and not to try to pick the few winners that will emerge from a herd of unproven companies battling it out in a "bleeding edge" industry. The better play is to focus on more established companies where business surprises are less likely. There will still be plenty of unknowns to cope with.

In the short term, the stocks of companies without earnings (or even, sometimes, without *revenue*) can go up astoundingly in price, as investors bet on the *idea* or *concept* behind the company and forecast (sometimes astronomical) earnings for the future, often using dubious math to get there. This happened frequently during the late-1990s technology bubble. Some would say that investor behavior with respect to these stocks was characterized by irrational exuberance, mania, or idiocy.

As actual business performance made it clearer that these companies were not generating profits and were unlikely ever to do so, their shares became less desirable, owners turned into sellers, buyers fled, the share prices came down, and the bubble deflated in 2000–2002.

If you're a venture capitalist, assessing young unprofitable companies is your métier. You know how to value start-up companies and how to predict which ones will pay you back by becoming huge successes. You still make lots of mistakes, but you may be able to prosper with a 10 percent batting average, because the few spectacular successes overwhelm all the duds. But for the typical individual investor, this is gambling, not investing.

For short periods of time (say up to or around a year), so-called concept companies can be the market's biggest winners, even though they lack earnings. They may look really tempting because they are *narrowing their losses* steadily, quarter by quarter. Lots of dot-coms were like this in 1999. Nevertheless, the Sensible Stock Investor will resist the temptation. Sooner or later the market begins to demand profitability, and when that time comes, the companies without earnings plunge in price. Many dot-coms that flew high in 1999 lost virtually all of their value in 2000–2002. This is literally true, not just a figure of speech: 80 to 90 percent or more of their share price simply disappeared. Hundreds went out of business as their access to fresh capital dried up, and they could not generate internally the cash needed to finance continued life.

Sometimes, of course, investing in the "new new thing" turns out to be a superb long-term investment. But the odds are not with you in such endeavors. The smarter play is to wait until a company has turned the corner on earnings and is out of its developmental or cash-burning phase. Let the company prove that it has a business model that can turn a profit.

There are plenty of fortunes to be made in companies that have already shown they can operate profitably. Time is on your side when you own shares of proven superior companies. You can afford to be patient. Even if you missed Wal-Mart or Microsoft in their first five years, both were great stocks to own in the next five years, after their dominance was clearly visible. That is true of many dominant companies: They remain great investments for years after their dominance is clear.

If you just can't stand it, put aside a small amount of your investable cash for "fun money," and use that to invest in one or two favorite young concept companies. It'll be like buying a lottery ticket or going to Las Vegas—you'll have fun gambling, and who knows, you might strike it rich.

By the way, don't "cheat" on the "no earnings, no investment" rule by accepting "operating" earnings or "pro forma" earnings (both of which omit certain expense categories) in place of real, positive earnings calculated under Generally Accepted Accounting Principles (GAAP).

"Turnaround" Plays

A corporate turnaround is just what it sounds like: Management is trying to take a floundering company and make it healthy again. Occasionally, great money can be made in turnaround situations. It happens this way: The stock's price has been driven down (because the company has been floundering), it can be purchased on the cheap, and, if the turnaround is successful and captures the fancy of investors, the stock will be bid up, sometimes to astronomical levels if the renewed enthusiasm causes the price to overshoot its sustainable valuation. Apple Computer circa 1998–99 (after Steve Jobs returned to run it) would be a good example of that.

If you know exactly what you are doing—perhaps because it's your own company or a company in your industry—you too can profit from turnaround plays. But for the average individual investor, they are too risky. The risk is not knowing whether the turnaround will work. After all, if the company is floundering, it is doing so for *real reasons*—bad products, obsolete products, unsafe products, lousy marketing, inadequate distribution, accelerating competition, too much debt, high cost structure, bad credit rating. New management sometimes comes in and solves everything, but how do you know that will happen or, even if it happens, that the turnaround will be sustainable?

Rather than gamble on a turnaround, look for a company that has proven its success.

Companies That Primarily Depend on Advertising Revenue

Advertising revenue is plentiful when it's there. But ad revenue has a way of drying up suddenly when—well, when lots of things happen: TV or radio ratings go down; circulation declines; viewers (readers or "eyeballs") disappear; the economy slows or hints at recession; advertisers wander away to try out different media. As always, if you have special knowledge in this arena and can either foretell or time these things, and feel you can therefore identify dominant ad-based companies *with strong prospects for continued earnings growth,* go for it. Otherwise, be careful. Let dependence on ad revenues be a warning sign. It is no coincidence that many Internet companies' business models were originally dependent on ad revenues but have since been adjusted to subscription models, which are more predictable. More recently, on the flip side, "paid search" business models, which are ad-based, seem to be prevailing among Internet search services—such is the business model of the wildly successful Google. This flip-flopping of the apparent "winning model" just goes to illustrate the risk in predicting ad-based success.

Any Industry in Which You Can't Figure Out the Competitive Landscape

We are looking, in Sensible Stock Investing, for dominant companies. If a candidate company is in an industry in which you cannot ascertain the competitive environment, then you cannot judge your company's dominance characteristics (or lack of them). Look for knowledgeable statements from industry experts that your company is the "market leader" or that its market share is double that of its nearest competitor. The more specific information you can turn up, the better. If you cannot accurately place the company among its competitors, it is difficult to award it anything higher than a score of 4 or 5 on its Story.

Industries or Companies That Bother You Personally

Investing should be fun. Who wants to buy stock in—and therefore root for the success of—a company that makes a product or renders a service that he or she finds offensive? My personal prejudice in this regard is tobacco companies. Smoking killed both of my parents, and no matter how much money is to be made in tobacco, I will never invest in such a company. That lets out Altria (that is, Phillip Morris) and its ilk, no matter how "cheap" they are or how generous their dividends. Some people feel the same way about gun makers, industrial polluters, and the like.

Feel free to insert your own ethical belief here, and don't invest in companies that do things you do not admire. If Microsoft's proven anticompetitive practices truly offend you, and you don't believe that the company has turned over a new ethical leaf and now has a culture of playing hard but fair (rather than hard but dirty), don't invest in it.

Anything That Depends on Taste, Fashion, or Fads

How can you predict fashion?

Since the goal of Sensible Stock Investing is to purchase stocks of companies for which you can predict growing earnings for one to two years out, be very careful with—or just avoid—the stocks of companies whose success depends on taste or fashion. You will have to decide for yourself just what this describes, but in my book it includes companies involved in apparel and accessories (especially "designer" names); some footwear, including sports footwear and related workout clothes; teenager-focused companies; kid-focused companies; and the like.

This category may surprise you, especially when you figure that if you follow these proscriptions, many successful and well-known apparel companies like The Gap, Abercrombie & Fitch, Nike, Reebok, Jones of New York, Tommy Hilfiger, and Polo-Ralph Lauren fall under a cloud of suspicion.

You may convince yourself that some of these companies have developed products of "timeless" appeal. Of course, the same thing was thought to be true of The Gap a few years ago with its "classic" clothes. Then teenagers and other Gap shoppers suddenly got sick of khakis, and Gap ventured out of "classic" styles into the world of fashion. It suddenly became unfashionable to wear Gap clothes or even to be seen in a Gap store. The enterprise went into the tank as both a business and a stock.

While certainly fortunes have been made by investments in some of these companies, if you go back and look at their returns over the years, you will see a high degree of inconsistency, as taste and fashion wax and wane. Again, if you have special knowledge in these industries or think you know what teenage girls are going to favor in footwear next season, then have at it. But often the better course is to steer clear of all of them or to be ready to sell them at the drop of a hat (pun intended) if the stock starts to descend.

Technology Companies

This is just a warning.

This category refers to companies that make, install, or provide electronic/digital products, services, and technology consulting.

The stocks of technology companies are especially volatile. While sometimes in the late 1990s you heard that technology was "recession-proof," technology companies are in fact very sensitive to the overall business cycle. One doesn't hear much about recession-proof technology anymore, not after the sector was ravaged by the capital-spending downturn of 2000–2002. The fact is that the value of technology companies is greatly affected by how their products are used by *other* companies, including old-economy stalwarts like publishing or trucking. In 2000–2002, we saw how quickly companies of all stripes can slash capital spending during hard times, thus cutting off oxygen to many technology suppliers.

Not only do technology companies' prospects vary with macroeconomic conditions, they are also subject to

- the fast-changing competitive situation in technology itself;
- "sub-cycles" applicable to certain industry segments (chips come to mind);
- the danger of obsolescence—better, faster, cheaper products come along all the time, and hot products morph into commodities or yesterday's news with amazing speed.

All of that having been said, technology companies are often very tempting. Tremendous gains are often available from the tech sector, and in our efforts to beat the market, tech stocks can help enormously. That is one reason that we keep our prediction horizon relatively short (one to two years), so that we don't adopt a strategy that de facto prevents us from considering technology companies at all. Just be very careful with them. Sometimes they make great momentum plays.

Tracking Stocks

A tracking stock is a separate stock created by a company to "track" the financial results of a division of the company. Tracking stocks are real stocks, but they do not confer voting rights, they don't have a separate Board of Directors looking out for your interests, and they do not convey ownership in the parent company. That makes them difficult to evaluate, because what they represent is so nebulous. Tracking stocks are designed to provide an opportunity to buy into, say, a fast-growing part of a company without investing in the whole company. But since the unit (and the overhead charges assigned to it) is totally at the discretion of the parent company, it is difficult to determine just what you are investing in with a tracking stock. Be careful with them or stay away entirely.

CHAPTER C-7

The Company as a Financial "Black Box"

The real trouble with this world…is that it is nearly reasonable, but not quite. Life is not an illogicality; yet it is a trap for logicians. It looks just a little more mathematical and regular than it is; its exactitude is obvious, but its inexactitude is hidden; its wildness lies in wait.

—G. K. Chesterton

The Problem of Too Much Data

It is axiomatic that you should not invest in a company without understanding its finances. However, for individual investors, it is difficult or impossible to maintain a deep financial understanding of more than a very few companies. And many individuals simply do not understand the fundamental finances that make a corporation tick. We'll try to rectify that in this chapter.

Lack of understanding is not due to lack of information. Indeed, all of the necessary information is easily accessible on the Internet and elsewhere. Rather, the problems are that

- achieving a deep understanding of a company's finances is time-consuming,

- it is beyond the mathematical skills and financial acumen of many individuals, and

- for many people, it is no fun at all.

Fortunately, we can take advantage of the work of others to overcome these difficulties. Many information providers have already done most of the investigative work for us, and they make it readily available. On the Internet, the required information is easily found and usually free. Not only that, some of these sources add considerable value to the raw numbers by organizing them, analyzing them, computing ratios, and providing benchmarks for comparison.

There is so much information available, in fact, that one of the keys to successfully navigating the maze is being selective, using only information that truly adds to your knowledge of a company. For the busy Sensible Stock Investor, there are several goals in selecting the key information to use. He or she wants

- to employ multiple perspectives to arrive at a balanced understanding;
- to separate the wheat from the chaff and eliminate redundancies, so that he or she is not left simply with a confusing data dump;
- to logically weigh the various data and create a scoring system that sums it all up;
- to have a process that is relatively painless.

The Black Box

In order to achieve all of these goals, we need certain simplifying assumptions. Here is a great one: When thinking about a company *financially*, consider it to be a "black box." A black box is simply an unexplained mechanism, a device whose inner workings are invisible. The term comes from science, where sometimes it is not important to know how something happens, only that it does happen.

We already know generally about a company because we have written its Story. Now let's set that aside and, for financial analysis, use the simplifying assumption that the company is a black box. It has financial inputs and outputs that we need to deal with, so let's direct our energy to understanding those, without being too concerned for the moment with what happens inside the box.

Companies create profits by ingesting money, running it through their black box, and generating more money coming out than went in. This is called "value creation." For this part of our analysis, we don't need to see inside the black box—the company is just a money-processing machine.

So literally picture a black box (the company) with pipes protruding from the left and right sides. Each pipe has a flow of money going through it. Some of the pipes bring money into the box. These are the financial inputs, and they come in through the left side of the box. Out the right side go the pipes that take money out of the box—the financial outputs.

Financial Inputs

With the black box model, these are the most important financial *input* pipes—that is, the pipes carrying money *into* the box:

- *Revenues*: The money received from customers for products and services.
- *Borrowed money*: Almost every company borrows money, sometimes through simple short-term loans to have cash on hand, other times through long-term bank loans, and still other times from the proceeds

of bonds, which are long-term notes to the bondholders. Note that all borrowed money bears an obligation to pay it back with interest.

- *Equity*: The money received from shareholders when they purchase stock in the company. Early in
  a company's life, this money may be received from venture capitalists, investment "angels," family,
  friends, and the founders' credit cards. Later on, it comes from public offerings of stock.

Financial Outputs

These are the most important pipes coming *out* of the box:

- *Ongoing expenses*: Money paid by the company for such things as office supplies, consulting services,
  marketing and advertising campaigns, or whatever else the company spends to operate day to day.
  Some of this money goes to vendors and suppliers. For most companies, the largest ongoing expense by
  far is salaries.
- *Capital expenditures*: Money to buy things that have a useful life of over one year: computers, production
  machinery, buildings, and the like.
- *Acquisitions of other companies*: Money paid by the company to acquire other companies, in whole or in
  part.
- *Payments on debts*: Since there is no free lunch, this is the outflowing pipe of payments due on the
  "borrowed money" input pipe described above.
- *Taxes.*
- *Profits*. This pipe branches into three important sub-pipes:
  1. The *dividend* sub-pipe, through which the company sends a cut of its profits back to its shareholders.
     Not every company pays dividends (i.e., the sub-pipe is capped off).
  2. The *share-buyback* sub-pipe, through which the company buys shares of itself on the open market.
     It might do this because it needs those shares to pay off employees who have been compensated
     through stock options. Or it may buy back its own shares just to get the shares off the market.
     (Theoretically, this increases the value of each of the remaining shares, which becomes a slightly
     larger piece of the company pie than it was before.) Not every company buys back its own shares.
  3. The *retained-earnings* sub-pipe, through which the company recycles money back into itself for
     growth and expansion. The retained-earnings sub-pipe circles around from the right (outgoing)
     side and back into the left (incoming) side of the black box, where it becomes the fourth financial
     input pipe.

That's a pretty simple picture, isn't it? It's all you need to understand company finances sufficiently to
become a successful stock investor.

Cash versus GAAP

One final advantage of the black box view is that it makes it easy to picture the two principal ways that money inflows and outflows are accounted for.

It often comes as a surprise to new investors that cash flow is not the same thing as accounting earnings. Let's look at the difference.

First, look at the *cash* flowing through the pipes. Cash means just what you think it does: real-time green-backs (or their equivalents, like checks). Looking at the company on a cash flow basis gives you one view of the financial picture, and it is an important picture for this reason: If the cash flowing into the box does not at least equal the cash flowing out of it, the enterprise will die. Cash is the oxygen of a company. Payrolls have to be met. Vendors have to be paid. There simply has to be enough cash available on a *real-time* basis to keep the company afloat. If there is not, the company is kaput, no matter what its potential may be. Negative cash imbalances are what cause 70 percent or so of new companies to fail—even those with a great concept. On a much larger scale, cash problems can cripple even huge companies that become mired in a downward spiral of cash obligations exceeding cash inflows. Such companies end up in bankruptcy, their stock worthless.

The second way a company's finances are accounted for is through the myriad rules of Generally Accepted Accounting Principles (GAAP). The pipes are the same, but GAAP rules change what's flowing through them in two important ways:

- GAAP occasionally counts as "money" some things that are really theoretical and intangible. That is, GAAP recognizes some things as money that are not *cash*. A simple example is goodwill. Goodwill is a noncash item that must be accounted for under GAAP. If an acquiring company pays more than what is known as "book value" for an acquired company (and it almost always does), the difference is called goodwill—a way of expressing the value of the brands, expertise, and other intangibles that the company has acquired which do not show up as part of its book value. Goodwill has no cash equivalent; it is entirely an accounting construct. But its effect can be significant, since companies often pay tens or hundreds of millions of dollars more than book value for other companies (which, under GAAP's rules, must sooner or later be written off the books).

- Probably the more important impact of GAAP, however, is that it requires accountants to alter how they report the *timing* of money flowing through the pipes. Thus the money *reported* going in and out is time-shifted from the comings and goings of the actual cash. GAAP does this in order to follow a basic accounting principle called "matching": Money inflows and outflows are "recognized" not at the time of the actual movement of cash but instead when the events that brought those dollars in or caused them to be used up actually take place. The matching principle requires accountants to move dollars across the calendar in both directions. For example, revenue dollars can move "down" the calendar, which effectively hurts current profits: If you own a subscription business—a magazine, say—you collect for a year's subscription up front. But your customer receives the magazines during the ensuing year, the last magazine getting to him or her about a year after it was paid for. From a cash flow point of view, you got the money when the subscriber paid. But from GAAP's point of view, the time when you can *book* that revenue is when the subscriber gets the magazines. So the accountants must spread the cash out over 12 months. Some of that revenue slips right into next year, and this year's profits look worse than they "really are." Similar timing alterations can apply to expenditures. Say your business buys a piece of capital equipment—a new PC for you. Under GAAP, your accountants must match the expense of the computer to the time when you are going to benefit from it. For a PC, that's typically three years. So the expense of the computer is "depreciated" over three years, even though you paid cash for it now. This has the effect of pushing out an expense for which you've already expended cash, and that makes this year's profits look better than they "really are."

The WorldCom debacle of 2002 was based on exactly this disconnect: The company misclassified (that is, it lied about) $3.8 *billion* in routine expenses, calling them capital expenditures, which allowed them under GAAP to push out most of the expense into future years. The result was to make the current year's profits look much better that they "really were." This sort of accounting shenanigan just delays the inevitable, because those expenditures must be booked eventually. Expenses that have been pushed down the calendar will depress future years' earnings, when the delayed charge finally is booked. In WorldCom's case, the day of reckoning came when it announced that it had filed for Chapter 11 bankruptcy protection—the largest in U.S. history.

Significantly, it is GAAP's rules that apply when the company reports its revenues, expenses, and earnings to the SEC, so it is GAAP numbers that are the "official" ones, even though they can vary significantly from the flow of cash. In many companies, most of the time, the effects of these cash/GAAP disconnects tend to be about equal in both directions, and the end result is not much different whichever way you look at it. Therefore, over time, increases in a company's cash flow should roughly equal its increases in reported net income. Sometimes, though, unusual circumstances—or outright fraud—can make the cash flow view quite different from the GAAP-profit view.

For the Sensible Stock Investor, the GAAP picture is the more important one, because it is the one that research has linked to stock prices. However, keep an eye out for situations where GAAP's "official" profits exceed a company's cash flow. That's a huge red flag.

It is interesting to note that both of the following can (and do) exist:

• Companies may be cash-rich but unprofitable under GAAP.
• Companies may be profitable under GAAP but reeling from insufficient cash flow.

Both of these situations present tenuous investing possibilities. The Sensible Investor wants to put his money into companies that are *both* cash-solid and GAAP-profitable. Cash flow is readily available on most financial Web sites, the numbers being derived from the companies' official SEC filings.

Keep the black box model in mind as we now explore the various financial factors that are important in discovering excellent companies with good investment possibilities. After the Story, financial factors are the second major category in which a company can earn "points" under our Easy-Rate™ company scoring system.

CHAPTER C-8

Financial Evaluation Factors

If you have 70 percent of the information, have done 70 percent of the analysis, and feel 70 percent confident, then move.

—Marine Corps' "70 Percent Solution"

Overview

On our Easy-Rate™ company scoring system, we have already seen that the company's Story is worth up to 10 points.

As important as the Story is, the finances of the company are even more significant. Therefore many more points are available to award a company for its financial condition.

In this chapter, we will develop the scoring system used to award "financial" points to companies. Under the approach described here, a company scoring every point possible would amass 48 points for its financial condition and prospects. In Appendix I, Form 1, you will find a sample filled-out Easy-Rate Stock Rating Sheet that shows you where to put the numbers discussed in this chapter.

There are five financial factors that we consider.

1 and 2.   Earnings and Cash Flow

Earnings Generally

Earnings are the profits of a company, after taxes. The simple equation is, revenue minus expenses equals earnings. When we use "earnings" here, we are referring to the "official" profits of the company, calculated according to the Generally Accepted Accounting Principles (GAAP) discussed in the previous chapter, reported to the SEC every quarter by all publicly traded companies, and audited once per year.

Earnings are the gold standard for assessing companies financially, because of their proven correlation to stock prices. That makes them our most logical starting point. As we have seen earlier (Chapter B-3), a stock's price at any *point* in time is a result of many transient factors, but *over long time periods* stock prices tend to track earnings. Thus it is obvious that for you to get sustained price increases in your stocks, you need to buy companies with the ability to achieve *sustained earnings growth*.

Each word in "sustained earnings growth" is significant:

- **Sustained:** One-time profit gains do not represent long-term value creation in a company or in its stock, although they are sometimes responsible for spurts in either. We want investment gains that keep going, so we need earnings that keep growing.

- **Earnings:** Over the long haul, *profits* are what investors are looking for. Profitless "concept" companies may do well in the market for a while, but they usually suffer price pullbacks (or crashes) if they go for long periods without reaching profitability. The same fate befalls profitable companies if they drop into a money-losing mode for any length of time or even if they remain profitable but suffer declines in their rates of profit growth (perhaps as they mature). In the latter case, their stock prices tend to contract in about the same proportion as their earnings growth rate contracts.

- **Growth:** The market favors companies with earnings *growth*. In other words, a company that has earnings of, say, $5,000,000 every year is certainly making profits, but it is not *growing* them, and therefore the market will look less favorably on its stock than one that displays earnings *growth*. Higher stock market multiples tend to be awarded to companies with *higher rates* of growth, *consistency* in that growth, and/or *accelerating* earnings growth. If a company can put two or three of these factors together—for example, consistency *and* a high growth rate—investors will usually value that company more highly than others.

A quick but important semantic note: In talking about earnings, we're always interested in earnings *per share* (universally abbreviated EPS). If we buy a share of stock in a company, EPS will show what our cut is. (The number of shares outstanding for most companies changes constantly because of new share offerings, share buybacks, the exercise of stock options, and other factors. The number of shares available to the public is called the "float.")

Ultimately, to rate companies on their earnings, we need to try to predict what the future EPS growth pattern is likely to be. We'll do this by looking at two items of information:

- the company's track record of past earnings; and
- the consensus of analysts' projected future earnings estimates.

Earnings History

Past earnings are significant because they show the company's track record: If we could have everything, we would want a company that has been able to produce profits, grow them from year to year, do it consistently, and accelerate the growth rate.

Consider these two companies:

Company A

Year	1	2	3	4	5	6	7	8	9	10
Increase in EPS	17%	18%	17%	19%	20%	18%	18%	19%	16%	20%

Company B

Year	1	2	3	4	5	6	7	8	9	10
Increase in EPS	7%	9%	12%	12%	15%	19%	22%	25%	27%	30%

Company A has a fantastic record as a growing company. It has been building its value year in and year out, and at an average rate which far exceeds the growth record of most companies and certainly of the economy in general. If in Year 1 its earnings were $1M, in Year 10 its earnings would be over $5.3M. This company is a terrific financial performer.

As good a track record as Company A has, Company B's is better, because the *growth rate is increasing*. That is, its growth is *accelerating*. Very few companies can compile a record like this one. At the end of 10 years, its profits would have grown from $1M to over $5M, and if the pattern continues, its profits in actual dollars would pass Company A's in the next year. All else being equal, the *stock* of Company B would probably have done better over the ten years than the stock of Company A, because of the acceleration in the profit growth rate. While the total profits in Year 10 are about equal for both companies, an investor looking at Company B can reasonably project better *future* results in the years going forward. (This is an inference, of course.)

With this as background, we can devise a scoring system for past EPS growth. The multitude of different financial data sources supply past earnings growth rates covering different time periods. The data source used throughout this book, Morningstar.com, supplies precomputed annual growth rates going back three years. This is sufficient for our purposes.

We want our scoring system to reward profit growth itself, consistency in achieving that growth, and accelerating rates of growth. Here is an approach which does that: First look at the company's average annual EPS growth rate for the past three years. Award the company points as follows:

3-year EPS growth rate < 4%:	-0-
3-year EPS growth rate 4% to 8%:	+1
3-year EPS growth rate 9% to 14%:	+2
3-year EPS growth rate 15% to 21%:	+3
3-year EPS growth rate 22% to 30%:	+4
3-year EPS growth rate 31% to 39%:	+5
3-year EPS growth rate 40% to 50%:	+6
3-year EPS growth rate >50%:	+7

This scoring system embodies several important ideas.

- First, we are looking for companies with above-average annual EPS growth. So the scoring system doesn't even award points unless the company's earnings have been growing at least 4 percent per year, which is about the rate of the whole economy's growth.

- Second, the sheer number of points available for the highest growth rates shows how important we consider this factor. The +7 points for exceedingly high growth rates is nearly equal to the number of points available for the company's Story, and you know how important we consider the Story to be. The S&P 500's average annual EPS growth rate tends to be in the 10 to 20 percent range when the economy is doing well.

- Third, remember that we are using real GAAP earnings, not "pro-forma," "operating," or other fake varieties of earnings.

In addition to the three-year average growth rate, we need to add scoring factors that reward a company's turning the corner to profitability and recent acceleration in earnings growth:

- *Company turning the corner to profitability*: If the three-year EPS growth rate is shown as NMF (not meaningful), but the company is profitable *now*, that means that the company has gone from unprofitable to profitable during the preceding three years. That is a very good sign, so award that company +4 points (instead of using the scale above).

- *Company whose growth is accelerating*: If the company's most recent one-year growth rate *significantly* exceeds its three-year growth rate, add 1 point. If the one-year growth rate is significantly lower than the three-year rate, subtract a point.

Taking everything into account, the company's score for its past earnings record will range between −1 and +8. An unprofitable company or one with an average annual EPS growth rate of less than 4 percent would get no points. A company with a three-year growth rate of more than 50 percent, *and* whose most recent year was significantly higher than that, would get +8 points.

Cash Flow

In considering a company's past earnings record, one should not ignore the relationship between reported earnings and cash flow. Typically we would not buy a company that did not have at least as much cash flow as it has reported earnings. As previously covered in the black box discussion, in a given year earnings can differ from cash flow. But over the course of time, the variations between earnings and cash flow essentially wash out, so that over, say, three to five years the total cash flow of the company should equal the total earnings.

But if, in a given year, the company's reported earnings significantly exceed its cash flow (say by more than 5 percent), that is a big red flag. So is a condition where the company's cash flow is negative while the reported earnings are positive. If you see either condition for the past 12 months, subtract 4 points from the company's past earnings score. In fact, under such a situation, you may just want to save yourself some work and delete the company from further consideration.

Future Earnings Estimates

Future earnings estimates are important because, in the final analysis, we are trying to predict how the company is going to do in the future. Most individual investors do not have the time or knowledge to project earnings themselves, but we can take advantage of the widely distributed estimates made by Wall Street stock analysts of how the company is likely to do going forward. These projections are really the best information that the average individual investor has freely available, even though they are often too optimistic and are perpetually being adjusted.

For our scoring, we'll use the three- to five-year "consensus" estimates—averages of several analysts following a company. These estimates are collected by financial information consolidators and are a standard data item displayed on financial Web sites. The scoring system is the same as that used for past EPS growth rates, with the exception that there are no "extra" points possible, because these estimates do not show acceleration or deceleration. The consensus growth rate will be a single number, like 14 percent. Award 0 to +7 points using the same scoring scale as for Past Earnings.

Summary Example of Scoring for Company's Earnings and Cash Flow

Let's look again at Companies A and B. Company A has the earnings record shown earlier and, say, a consensus forward projection of 15 percent growth per year. Here's how we would award points for past and future earnings:

- +3 for the most recent three-year average growth rate (about 18 percent).
- No points added or subtracted for the one-year rate being significantly higher or lower than the three-year rate. Company A's growth rate has been steady but not accelerating.
- +3 for the projected future EPS growth rate (15 percent).
- No subtractions based on cash flow problems.

Company A gets a very good (but not great) total of 6 points for its historical and its projected EPS growth. There is nothing wrong with this company's record; in fact, it is a solidly growing company. But it really doesn't get big scores for either past or projected future earnings growth. This result reflects that our standards are pretty tough, as they should be if our goal is to beat the market.

Let's say that Company B's consensus forward projection is for 35 percent earnings growth over the next three to five years. Here's how it would rate:

- +4 for the past three-year average growth rate of about 27 percent.

- No points added for the one-year rate being significantly higher than the three-year rate. Even though the growth rate has been accelerating, the most recent year's rate of 30 percent is not significantly higher than the three-year average. (One might argue that Company B's record of accelerating growth over 10 years entitles it to an "acceleration credit" of some kind, but it would be extremely speculative to think that this is going to go on indefinitely without some study to back up the conclusion.)

- +5 for the projected future EPS growth rate. The company does get credit here for likely future acceleration, since the projected three- to five-year rate is appreciably higher than the rate in recent years. (Presumably the stock analysts have done the requisite studies and calculations to support such a high projected growth rate.)

- No subtractions based on cash flow problems.

So whereas Company A got a total of 6 points for its past and projected future EPS record, Company B gets 9 points. As we said earlier, all other things being equal, Company B's stock price is likely to be more highly rewarded in the marketplace than Company A's, and the earnings scores reflect that.

3. Revenue Growth

The third area of interest is revenue growth. A company whose revenue is growing must be churning out products or services that customers really want. Not only that, the company probably has some degree of pricing power for those products or services. That is the kind of company we want to invest in.

Revenue growth is a precursor of earnings growth. However, revenue growth is several degrees removed from earnings growth. Revenues coming into the black box must be turned into earnings by means of a high-performance operation.

It is clear that a company cannot achieve long-term earnings growth without consistent sales growth. In fact, some studies show that revenue growth correlates better with stock performance than earnings growth itself. According to the April 2002 issue of *SmartMoney* magazine, five-year revenue growth correlated more strongly with the performance of their ten-year stock picks than any other factor.

A company generates sales growth via several avenues:

- Selling more "units" of its goods or services. This can mean selling more "old" products (by taking market share from competitors or holding its own in a growing market), or introducing successful new products (which sometimes means creating an entirely new market).
- Raising prices. It usually takes a highly sustainable competitive advantage to be able to do this consistently.
- Buying another company, thus gobbling up that company's revenues for itself.

The average three-year revenue growth rate of the S&P 500's companies tends to be around 6 to 9 percent.

For scoring a company's revenue growth, we'll use the same scale as for past earnings growth. This accords revenue growth the high degree of importance it deserves. So if Company X has compiled an average annual revenue growth rate of 31 percent for the past three years, we would award it +5 points. If the most recent year's growth rate is significantly greater or smaller, we add or subtract a point accordingly.

4. Return on Equity

The next area for scoring a company's financials is return on equity, or ROE.

Return on equity shows how much profit a company produces as a percentage of the total equity that shareholders own in the company. It is calculated by dividing net income for the year by the average shareholders' equity for the year and then multiplying that number by 100 to turn the ratio into a percentage.

"Shareholders' equity" is the company's assets minus its liabilities. It represents the shareholders' stake in the net assets of the company.

ROE example: If a company earns $10M in a year, starting the year with $25M in shareholders' equity and ending the year with $35M in shareholders' equity, its ROE for that year would be 10/([25+35]/2) = 33%. Now that you've seen that calculation, don't worry about ever needing to do one yourself. Precalculated ROEs are readily available on most financial Web sites.

Current ROE

One important financial mission of any company—perhaps the most important—is to earn a high ROE. ROE is widely utilized as a thumbnail indicator of management's efficiency in utilizing the assets at its disposal—the value-creating activities inside the black box. When a company posts a high ROE, it is efficiently using its assets to create profits. Company achievements that increase its efficiency and/or eliminate waste improve ROE. If one were to look inside the black box, one would find that ROE is driven upward by improved profit margins, strong earnings growth, better productivity, non-buildup of inventory, cost reductions, share buybacks, and revenue gains. ROE can also be increased by high debt, which reduces the denominator in the equation.

Traits like high profit margins and efficient productivity are highly desirable, but the last factor—debt—is a two-edged sword. In our company scoring system, we will reward companies for producing superior ROEs, but (as seen in the next section) we will penalize them if they do it by borrowing too much. High debt levels are not *necessary* for high ROEs. Many companies are able to produce high ROEs without taking on any debt at all.

ROEs can range from negative numbers (reflecting negative earnings) to 100 percent or more. The ROE for S&P 500 companies averaged between 10 and 15 percent for most of the twentieth century, but it rose sharply in the 1990s, past 20 percent by the end of the decade. Historically, an ROE above 15 percent is considered to be good performance, indicating that management is doing a decent job producing returns from the assets at its disposal. Recently (early 2006), the S&P 500's average ROE was 20 percent.

Here is the Easy-Rate scoring scale for current ROE:

ROE < 8%: -0-
ROE 8%-11%: +1
ROE 12%-15%: +2
ROE 16%-20%: +3
ROE 21%-26%: +4
ROE 27%-33%: +5
ROE > 33%: +6

ROE Consistency

In addition to rewarding a company for its current ROE, we want to reward companies who have proved that they can achieve consistently high ROEs. Some companies post wildly varying ROEs from year to year. However, the best companies put up decent ROEs even when the economy makes conditions tough. We want to reward this kind of ability. Using 15 percent as the historical benchmark for a high-performing company, we will award +1 point for every consecutive year that a company's ROE has been 15 percent or above, up to a total of +5 points representing five consecutive years.

Adding the two categories together, you can see that a company can earn up to 11 rating points for the combination of a very high current ROE plus an ROE above 15 percent for five years running.

5.   *Debt-to-Equity Ratio*

You will recall from the discussion of the financial black box that debt—borrowed money—flows into the box and therefore increases the company's assets. Long-term debt and shareholders' equity are the two main components of the "capital structure" of a company, and different companies have different mixes of the two. Some firms operate with a high proportion of debt, perhaps because they are so confident of their success that they want to take advantage of the leverage that debt provides. But other times, a company takes on high debt because it is constantly in cash-flow hell and needs the borrowed money just to keep going.

A company gets into debt by borrowing money from banks or by issuing bonds. Whichever road it selects, the company owes the money back (with interest) until the debts are paid off. In other words, debt—particularly the interest obligation—is a drag on a company's operations and on its earnings. Debt increases the risk to a company. The endgame for a company that cannot service its debt load is bankruptcy.

Therefore, we want to reward companies that carry a low debt load. All else being equal, such companies will be more likely to generate sustained earnings growth. We also need a check and balance on our use of ROE, since increasing debt also increases ROE. Our preference is for companies which can generate high ROEs *without* taking on massive debt loads.

Obviously, the larger the company, the more debt it can carry comfortably. So we cannot rate a company's debt position merely on the sheer dollar amount of debt that it has. We need to compare that dollar amount to the size of the company.

A common measure, and the one we use here, is the ratio of the company's debt to its equity, or the D/E ratio. For example, if a company has total long-term debt of $1 billion and equity capitalization of $1 billion, its D/E ratio would be 1, or 100 percent. This, in fact, is about the average D/E ratio of the S&P 500's companies.

In our scoring system, we will award more points to companies with lower D/E ratios and award the maximum points to companies with zero or little long-term debt. The reason is obvious: Low-D/E companies sidestep entirely the corrosive effects of paying interest.

Here is how to score the D/E ratio:

D/E > 80%: -0-
D/E 61% to 80%: +1
D/E 41% to 60%: +2
D/E 21% to 40%: +3
D/E 0% to 20%: +4

As with other elements of our system, this is a demanding rating scale. The median D/E ratio for the companies in the S&P 500 tends to hover around 100 percent. That high a ratio would garner no points from our system. A totally or nearly debt-free company gets the most rating points.

Some investment pundits believe that debt ratios should be compared only within an industry, on the theory that it is unfair or misleading to compare debt ratios of companies which, by their very nature, are likely to operate with or without high levels of debt. To the Sensible Stock Investor, however, this does not pass a basic smell test: If a company is in an industry that typically uses a business model that requires lots of debt, and the company also adopts that model, it is saddled with a built-in financial disadvantage compared to companies with debt-free business models. Companies choose their capital structure. You should not grant a "free pass" to a highly indebted company just because everyone else in its industry carries high debt too.

We do make a special exception for banks. By the very nature of their business, banks invariably bear enormous debt (they owe money to their depositors). When you're scoring a bank, just give it a middling +2 points on this factor. The bank's ROE score will be more insightful.

Financial Indicators That Are Not Used

There are a host of other numbers that might be used in evaluating a company's financial soundness and future prospects. In developing our Easy-Rate scoring system, we need to strike a proper balance between using plenty of information and different measures, on the one hand, and not wasting time with redundancy, on the other hand.

The following is a discussion of financial indicators that are not currently employed in our scoring system, along with a brief explanation of why they are not used. The individual reader, of course, is free to pick and choose from among these (or others), devise point values for them, and use them if he or she thinks they add vital information about a company of interest.

Cash Flow

Other than the subtraction of 4 points for insufficient cash flow to justify reported earnings, we do not make an independent judgment of a company based on its cash flow. You will recall from the financial black box that cash flow is a company's net earnings *before* depreciation, amortization, and other noncash charges are subtracted under GAAP's rules. You will also recall that a company's cash flow can sometimes paint a significantly different picture from its GAAP earnings, that sufficient cash flow is essential to a company's very survival, and that a company can be "GAAP-profitable" but running out of cash.

Despite all this, we do not score a company based on its cash flow. This goes against the approach of many investment analysts who believe that it is *better* to focus on cash flow when investigating a company. They argue, for example, that cash flow is a better measure of a firm's ability to translate revenues into profits through superiority over the competition, pricing power, or management's ability to control costs. They also point out that statements of cash flow, while not immune to manipulation, are more difficult to "manage" than the GAAP rules for profits. They particularly take this view as to capital-intensive businesses, because such businesses tend to incur lots of depreciation, which "distorts" their GAAP profits. They also believe that writing off goodwill under GAAP completely misconstrues how a company is "really doing."

In Sensible Stock Investing, we respectfully disagree. Although there are instances where cash flow is a valuable indicator, nevertheless common sense suggests giving primary emphasis to reported profits. Cash flow, by ignoring interest obligations, amortization, and depreciation, ignores obligations that the company has paid or still has to pay. As Warren Buffett has said, the tooth fairy does not make these payments—the company does. To ignore them is to ignore very real obligations. If these obligations were not accounted for when the cash actually went out the pipe, the company got a "free cheat" that year but still has to pay the piper in later years.

We hold to this reasoning even when it comes to goodwill, which has no cash equivalent at all. The fact of the matter is that goodwill *does* have value to the acquiring company. After all, the brands, expertise, and existing customers—which are important reasons the acquiring company bought the acquired company—are of very real value. They must be paid for (that's why the acquiring company usually pays more than book value). The mechanism by which this is done is through the concept of goodwill, which must be accounted for. If the acquiring company way overpaid for its acquisition (which happens all the time, especially when companies are auctioned off), then the acquiring company has truly diluted its value to its shareholders, and the write-off of this overpayment over time reflects economic reality better than ignoring it by looking only at cash flow.

"Quality" of Earnings

In the awarding of points for past earnings, we use official reported earnings as reflected in companies' SEC filings and reported on virtually all financial Web sites. Using reasoning similar to that which they apply to cash flow, many market analysts try to "look behind" the official earnings on the theory that some kinds of earnings are "better" than others. The term "quality of earnings" refers to "how good" different earnings types are, with some sources of earnings being thought superior in sizing up a company.

A sort of hierarchy of earnings quality has emerged:

- The "best" earnings come from the continuing operations of the core business of the company. The reason these are seen as of the highest quality is because they come from what the company actually *does*. Therefore, operating earnings growth comes from increases in core revenues, implying that there is a growing demand for the company's products and services. There is no question that this is a good thing.

- Down a slot on the pecking order are earnings increases that come via acquisitions. There are several reasons for viewing acquired earnings skeptically, including (1) acquiring companies can paper over troubles in the company's core business, (2) the accounting rules for mergers and acquisitions leave plenty of loopholes for manipulating numbers, and (3) acquired companies can range from strategically sound to ego-driven off-the-wall distractions. Some companies rarely, if ever, make acquisitions, while others are serial acquirers, generating hardly any growth from their own R&D or organic ideas. The success of an acquisition almost always depends on how well the acquired company is integrated into the new parent or combined entity. Some integrations go beautifully, while others are totally botched and can damage the acquiring company for years. In mid-2003, for example, Gillette acknowledged that its acquisition of Duracell years before had never been properly integrated and had been damaging Gillette's overall performance ever since. (In 2005 Gillette itself was acquired by Procter & Gamble—we'll see whether that integration goes any better.)

- Down another notch are earnings generated by cost-cutting measures. Let's say a company's revenue is flat or declining. The company can still generate profit growth by cost-cutting measures such as layoffs, cutbacks in capital spending, reductions in day-to-day spending (like travel and three-martini lunches), cutbacks in R&D, freezing or reducing raises for a year or two, and so on. These profits are thought to be of low quality, because there is a limit to how much you can cut costs. For many companies, after two or three rounds of cost cutting, there is no more to cut. Not only that, while cost cutting may increase earnings in the near term, it may harm the company in the long term. This can be especially true with research and development cuts, which can cripple a company for years to come. Of course, every company should always be looking for ways to keep its costs low through re-engineering efforts, productivity-enhancing technology, and the like. But ultimately, to be of any use to long-term investors, rising earnings *must* originate with rising revenues.

- Still lower on the earnings totem pole are gains from one-time events. Examples would be the selling of a business or plant, a restructuring, a windfall from the rise in stock price of a partially owned company, or similar events that are not ongoing. Such events may help raise earnings once (during the quarter they are booked), but they are not sustainable and give no insight into the company's long-term earnings prospects. This can also work in reverse: Companies in the midst of big changes will often take a huge one-time charge *against* earnings, using that charge to create a "restructuring reserve." That lowers their reported earnings for that year. But in later years, the company dips into the reserve for money related to the restructuring, thereby helping its operational results in the later year. Usually, these helpings don't amount to a lot of money, but they can be the difference between meeting and missing the all-important consensus earnings number expected by Wall Street.

- Finally, at the absolute low end of the scale are earnings that have been pumped up by aggressive accounting or even fraudulently concocted via accounting measures that violate GAAP principles. Companies that are caught doing this often have to go back and restate earnings for prior years or announce that future earnings will be affected by the installation of new accounting procedures or safeguards. Their stock usually craters immediately.

Sensible Stock Investors will keep their eyes and ears open for earnings-quality factors that may apply to stocks of interest. But most individual investors do not have the time or knowledge to effectively "adjust" officially reported numbers, which requires extensive analysis and many subjective judgments. We have other rules (particularly the one that steers us clear of any company in the news for financial shenanigans) to protect us. Our preference for consistency helps shield us from one-time events. And our separate rating of revenue growth in addition to earnings growth helps to eliminate companies that are potentially harmful to us. Finally, remember that in the many studies that have examined the relationship between earnings and stock prices, stock market returns have been correlated with officially reported earnings, not with earnings as adjusted for their perceived "quality."

Growth in Book Value per Share

The annual percentage change in a company's book value is simply another measure of the company's growth. We've already covered growth thoroughly by looking at Earnings Growth (Past and Future) and at Revenue Growth. So to use growth in book value would be unhelpfully redundant.

Book value can also be misleading. A company's assets are subject to GAAP treatments that often leave lots of room for subjectivity. For example, while typically general manufacturers list most of their assets on the balance sheet, software companies frequently do not show software as a balance sheet item, even though it is in fact the company's largest actual asset. There's too much slipperiness around book value to rely on it as a company-quality indicator.

Return on Assets or Return on Capital

Clearly, when a company is considered as a financial black box, its reason for existence is to create positive returns. There are various returns that can be measured:

- Return on equity (ROE), which we do use in rating the company.
- Return on assets. This is the percentage a company earns on all of its assets in a year: earnings divided by its total assets.
- Return on capital (also called return on investment). This is the profit generated on the company's total capital. Total capital is made up of the equity owned by its shareholders (the E in ROE) plus the capital coming from long-term debt (that is, debt with a term greater than one year). A business may borrow money rather than issue stock if it believes it will generate greater returns on the borrowed money than the costs of borrowing it. As noted earlier, capital coming in via borrowing raises the company's ROE. So a company will have a higher ROE if it capitalizes itself partly through debt rather than entirely by issuing stock. (Remember that we protected ourselves against becoming overly impressed by highly leveraged companies by penalizing high debt levels.)

These measures are obviously somewhat redundant. While it is a tenet of Sensible Stock Investing to come at issues from multiple angles, we do not want unhelpful redundancy. So we have chosen ROE as *the* return margin that we will measure, with the check and balance being that we penalize companies that carry too much debt. This combination works well in identifying promising companies.

Profit Margins

Some stock-picking approaches place great emphasis on gross or net profit margins. Gross margin is the "intermediate" profit after *some* of the company's costs have been accounted for, while net margin is the profit after *all* of the company's costs have been accounted for. Both are expressed as a percentage of sales (as in, Company X's gross profit margin is 50 percent).

While it may seem intuitive that it is better to have high profit margins, the fact is that there are successful businesses that have low margins (grocery chains), high margins (software companies), and everything in between. Either a low-margin or high-margin business can produce sustained earnings growth. There is no direct relationship between profit margins and sustained earnings growth. In fact, some actions that companies take to improve their margins—cutting R&D or business investments, for example—may cause long-term harm to their businesses.

Therefore, Sensible Stock Investing does not demand, say, that there be a 50 percent (or some other) level of gross margin from every sale. We *do* demand that the business be profitable (which obviously requires positive margins), but beyond that, our main interest is in the probability of sustained earnings growth.

Another reason not to use margins as a separate evaluation factor is that net margin is implicit in the calculation of ROE, which we do use as an evaluation factor. It turns out that the equation for calculating ROE breaks down into the product of three other ratios. Net margin is one of them. Therefore, using the net margin ratio as a separate evaluation factor would be redundant with our use of ROE.

Asset Turnover

Asset turnover is another of the three component ratios embodied in ROE, so its separate use would also be redundant with our use of ROE. Asset turnover, which is also a measure of efficiency, represents how many dollars in revenue a company generates for each dollar of assets, that is, total revenue divided by total assets. The higher the ratio, the more efficiently the company's black box is processing the assets at its disposal.

Meeting or Not Meeting Consensus Expectations

Some stock-picking methods place great emphasis on a company's history in missing, meeting, or exceeding the quarterly earnings expectations of Wall Street analysts. There are some studies that show this to be an effective predictive factor.

There is no question that the market itself reacts swiftly to companies that miss, meet, or beat expectations. It is not unusual to see a company's share price rise or fall 5 percent or even 10 percent in a single day after its earnings are announced, based on either an earnings "miss" or "hit." Stock prices often gyrate as well based on management's "guidance," which is typically announced at the same time as quarterly earnings and which can provide a negative or positive outlook about the future.

But really these are transient reactions based on a questionable foundation:

• Analysts are changing their earnings estimates constantly.

• Companies regularly attempt to influence the analysts' numbers with press releases, conference calls, "analysts' days" (dog and pony shows), and the like.

- Estimating earnings is just plain hard (involving, as it does, speculation about the future). The company itself often doesn't know until a few days before they report just what the number is going to be.

- There are enough loopholes and subjective elements in GAAP accounting that companies can often "manage" their earnings to the expected number or, better yet, beat it by a penny or two every time.

In the final analysis, what does it mean if Intel (for example) beats by a penny earnings expectations that have themselves been adjusted downward by 20 percent earlier in the quarter because of information that Intel itself put out? Whatever it means (which may be nothing at all), it seems a slender reed on which to base a long-term evaluation of the company.

One corollary: There has been shown to be some correlation between stock price performance and *consistent upward earnings revisions* by analysts. This makes sense, because it implies a continuing flow of good news about the company (and its industry). However, we presently do not use this in the company scoring system.

CHAPTER C-9

Dividends as a
Company Evaluation Factor

Dividends (and Share Repurchases) Explained

We have reserved dividends for separate discussion, because strictly speaking, dividends are not a part of a company's financial structure or performance. Rather dividends are the result of a decision by management and the Board of Directors about what to do with the profits of the company.

What Are Dividends?

Dividends are portions of a company's earnings paid out (usually quarterly) to the company's shareholders. They are transfers of cash by the corporation to its owners.

As we saw in the black box discussion, after all expenses and taxes have been paid, what's left is the company's earnings. A company has decisions to make as to what to do with those earnings:

• It may choose to plow back all of its earnings into the company to fund growth, acquisitions, special projects, and company improvements.

• It may siphon off some of those earnings and send them in the form of dividends to shareholders.

• It may use some of its earnings to buy back shares of itself on the open market. (Share repurchase programs are discussed in the next subsection.)

Thus, dividends are discretionary with each company. No company *has* to pay dividends. Dividend programs (or the lack thereof) reflect the company's philosophy and strategy regarding the proper balance between sharing profits with shareholders *now* versus using that money for reinvestment in the company, leading (presumably) to enhanced value in the *future*.

Once begun, dividend programs tend to persist. A company that pays a dividend does all it can to keep doing it. Investors count on dividend-paying companies to keep paying them. Most management teams are loath to cut dividends, because of the negative signal it sends to the investment community. Stable and increasing dividends usually indicate that the company's management has confidence in the company's prospects. It is a newsworthy event when a company cuts or eliminates its dividend, because that is usually interpreted as a sign that management lacks confidence in its future earnings capabilities. A stock usually falls back when a company cuts or eliminates its dividend.

As a general rule, dividend-paying companies tend to be larger and older than their non-dividend-paying brethren. Many of them have been paying dividends uninterruptedly for decades. Often, the dividend pay-out is raised annually.

Investor sentiment tends to wax and wane with regard to dividends and the companies that pay them. In the early part of the 20th century, stocks were *expected* to pay dividends. In their classic *Security Analysis* (1934), Benjamin Graham and David Dodd wrote, "The prime purpose of a business corporation is to pay dividends to its owners." Those companies that didn't were considered to be second-class investments, definitely inferior to bonds. In fact, stocks were expected to yield *more* than bonds (that is, pay a higher percentage return) to make up for their riskier nature.

But by the time of the bull market of 1982–1999, there was far less interest in dividends than in share price growth. The humongous rise in share prices during the long bull market dwarfed dividends' contribution to total return. Many investors flocked to the fast-growing companies of the "New Economy." With the S&P 500 going up 20 percent plus per year, there was nothing exciting about the 1 to 2 percent dividend yield of slower-growing stocks. According to *Fortune*, the percentage of companies in the S&P 500 paying dividends fell from 94 percent in 1980 to 74 percent by the end of 2001. People who first got involved in stock investing during this time may therefore have received a misleadingly low impression of the importance of dividends to total stock returns over the long haul.

But when the bubble started to deflate in 2000, with stock prices going backward, investors' interest was rekindled in dividend-paying stocks. So while it is true that during the inflation of the bubble dividend-payers did not go up as much, it is also true that during the deflation they did not lose as much. A study by Smith Barney showed that non-dividend-paying stocks fell an average of 60 percent in the first 15 months following the market's peak in early 2000, while dividend-paying stocks fell an average of 20 percent. That follows a general historical pattern of dividend-paying stocks providing a "cushion" in a down market while also participating (but not as greatly) in market upswings.

Most studies show that 45 to 50 percent of the total return of the stock market during the twentieth century was made up of dividends, despite the significant decline in contribution during the final twenty years. The result of the major downshift in dividend policies in the 1980s and 1990s was that the bulk of most stocks' total return came from the increasing *price* of the stock, not from its dividend. According to T. Rowe Price, from 1995 to 1999 (the peak of the bull market), dividends accounted for only 8 percent of the stock market's total return.

In 2003 the federal tax laws were changed to cap the income tax on dividends at 15 percent, making them the least-taxed component of total return, and this has helped spur recent increases in both the number of companies paying dividends and the payout rates. Perhaps not surprisingly, according to T. Rowe Price,

2003 saw the reversal of a twenty-year decline in the number of S&P 500 companies paying a dividend, and the number of dividend-paying companies continued to increase in 2004–2005.

What Are Share Repurchases?

Share repurchases—or buybacks—are another way a company can use its profits to benefit shareholders, although the benefit is indirect and "virtual" compared to the real dollars-in-pockets you get from dividends. Stock buybacks were hardly in the picture prior to about 1980. But according to *Fortune,* money spent on share repurchases increased at an annual rate of 26 percent between 1980 and 2000.

In theory, share repurchases reward shareholders by taking some of the shares of the company out of circulation, thereby making each remaining share represent a larger piece of the pie, worth more than before. Stock prices often get a short-term bump when a company announces a share buyback. On the surface, that makes sense, not only because each share will (after the buyback) represent a larger piece of the pie but also because dividends are taxed, whereas "paper" gains from increased share prices are not. Thus, many investors would rather see a company use excess cash to repurchase shares.

The following should be noted, however:

- Many stock buyback programs are announced but not implemented or are started but not completed. Unlike dividend programs, which tend to be watched closely, it is rarely reported when an announced share repurchase plan is failed to be implemented or completed.

- Most stock buyback programs are one-time or irregular events. Once a share repurchase program is announced, no implied promise arises that there will be more of them. Rather, each program is a finite event, with a finite number of dollars allocated to it over a finite time frame.

- Share repurchase programs are often announced when a company is doing well—that is why it has excess cash to purchase the shares. Unfortunately, that is precisely the time when share prices are likely to be at their highest. Thus, companies often "buy high," exactly what you'd rather not see them do. They also tend to stop buying shares during periods of trouble—precisely the time when their share price may be lowest.

- When repurchases are made, the shareholder must have faith that the market will be savvy enough to reprice the remaining shares to account for the fact that some of them are gone.

Finally, many share repurchase programs are primarily motivated by the need for the company to get shares "in house" to award to employees exercising stock options. This circumstance arises in companies that use stock options as a significant element in employee compensation. The shares of stock that are purchased by the company are then given to employees exercising stock options. Most of the time, these shares are *not* taken out of circulation, because the recipients sell their stock the moment they get it (to get cash). Therefore the shares go right back into the market, they do not make other shares represent a larger piece of the pie, and there is no proportionate increase in the value of outstanding shares. In essence, the stock repurchase is simply a compensation expense to the company, and the buyback program does shareholders no good at all (other than keeping employees happy).

Pros and Cons of Using Dividends to Evaluate Companies

Some companies pay dividends; others do not. Some of the greatest companies of our time (such as Warren Buffett's Berkshire Hathaway) have *never* paid a dividend. During its heyday, Microsoft, one of the all-time great wealth producers, never returned any of its earnings to shareholders. It kept all of it. (Microsoft eventually built a cash hoard in the tens of billions of dollars and finally began a dividend program in 2003.)

So there are certainly examples of superior companies that pay no dividends, and there are also examples of bad companies that do pay dividends. Reasonable minds differ on whether a company's dividend policies tell you anything useful about how good the company is. Let's look at the pros and cons and make up our own minds.

Here are the principal reasons for believing that a company's payment of dividends is a good sign about the company:

- A company that pays dividends—especially rising dividends—must be financially solid; otherwise the Board of Directors would not pay out the money. The dividend's payment suggests that cash flow is above and beyond what is needed to reinvest in the business to grow and improve it. A dividend payout probably indicates management's confidence in the stability and growth of future earnings, quite possibly based on information that is not publicly available.
- Dividends are "proof" of profits. A company paying dividends has no issues with quality of earnings: It must have cash to make the payments. Unlike earnings figures, dividends cannot be manipulated because they are actual dollars paid to shareholders. Studies have shown that, as a group, dividend-paying companies tend to have cleaner accounting, with fewer one-time charges and things of that ilk.
- Such a company, because of its strong financial position, does not need to return to the capital markets often, if at all, to fund its growth. It is self-funding, with cash left over.
- A company that pays dividends will probably invest the earnings it does retain more carefully. The dividend program imposes discipline upon management. Companies with less retained earnings make better decisions about what to do with the remaining money. Managers who must make regular dividend payments to shareholders will tend to treat cash as a precious commodity and will invest retained earnings only in the best ideas.
- Conversely, a company that retains all of its earnings may waste or do stupid things with the money. For example, a company with "too much cash around" may make ego-driven acquisitions, overpaying for them and then compounding the error by failing to integrate them properly. Or the company may fund development projects of dubious value (again, these are often ego-driven), make high levels of capital expenditures, become lax about controlling costs, spend more and more on perks for executives, "trophy" headquarters buildings, and the like. They may allow their hypercompetitive vice presidents or division heads to waste money on empire building.
- A company that pays no dividends and that bases much of its executives' compensation on stock options can have managers who are too motivated to get the price of the stock up in the short term (so they can

exercise their options at a handsome profit). This can lead them to do crazy things that are not in the best long-term interests of the company. The managers in question, of course, are often not long-term shareholders—they own the stock only long enough to sell it, because it is part of their compensation package.

- Dividends, because they are almost always the result of continuing programs, tend to put a "floor" under the price of a stock.

- Several studies suggest that companies that pay dividends tend to perform better over the long haul. For example, a 2003 study by Standard & Poor's found that a basket of U.S. stocks with the best history of boosting dividends and profits had an annual compounded return of 12.3 percent (vs. 10.8 percent for the S&P 500) over the prior 17 years. The report built on academic studies going back to 1956. Similarly, Jeremy Siegel reports in *The Future for Investors* (2005) that the 100 highest-yielding stocks in the S&P 500 have performed better (in total return) than the index as a whole over the past 50 years.

In contrast, these are the reasons most often given that companies which are better investment opportunities do not pay dividends:

- Companies that are on a growth track need all the money they can to make acquisitions and fund good internal projects. Therefore, it is in the long-term interest of shareholders that the company not pay dividends but rather that it reinvest in the company's growth and improvement. Retained earnings are the easiest source of fresh capital for fast-growing companies.

- The payment of dividends suggests that the company does not have enough good reinvestment ideas—i.e., it is a maturing, mature, or stagnating business.

- If the company wishes to distribute earnings to benefit shareholders immediately, share buyback programs are a more tax-efficient way of accomplishing that end. That is, taxes must be paid by stockholders on dividends received, but shares whose values have increased as the result of buyback programs are not taxed on the increased value unless and until the shares are sold.

So it is debatable how useful a company's record of paying dividends, or of increasing its dividends year by year, is to the question of its prospects for sustained earnings growth. What should our conclusion be?

The Sensible Stock Investor finds the first set of arguments to be the more compelling. That is, the payment of dividends, especially a long history of paying increasing dividends, probably points to superior companies with a higher probability of sustained earnings growth. In particular, a company with a strong dividend record suggests that it can hold up the "sustained" part of the bargain in terms of earnings growth.

In the last chapter, when we examined financial factors in rating companies, we looked mostly at the "growth" element, scoring more points the faster a company's earnings and revenue were growing. Unfortunately, the vast majority of dividend-paying companies are comparatively slow growers. This makes sense: If management saw a lot of high-probability, low-risk ways to grow faster, they would direct more of their earnings toward those opportunities than toward paying dividends. But that said, there is little doubt that a past history of paying and increasing dividends is usually a sign that management has confidence in the company's continued earnings power.

Therefore, we do award Easy-Rate points to companies that pay dividends. This also helps to balance our rating system—which is designed for all companies—between fast-growing companies and slower-growing but reliable companies. Each scores points for their particular strength, and neither has a systematic bias or edge in the rating system. And of course, companies that can do well along both dimensions end up racking up the most points.

Point System for Evaluating Companies Based on Dividends

We can now devise a simple scoring system for companies based on their dividend policies and practices. Our goal is to reward companies that pay and increase dividends consistently.

To avoid companies that pay only a minuscule dividend, we only award points to companies whose current dividend yield is at least 0.6 percent. Assuming a company clears that hurdle:

- The company gets +1 point for each consecutive year that it has paid a dividend without lowering it from the year before. The nonpayment of a dividend in a year, or the lowering of a dividend, breaks the string, and you can only count backward from the current year to that year. Maximum points available is +5 (meaning only look at the last five years of dividend payments).

- The company also gets +1 point for each year that it has *increased* its dividend during the past five years. It does not matter whether the increases were in consecutive years or there were breaks in between.

So a company that has paid and increased its dividend every year over the past five years would get a total of +10 points (+5 for the uninterrupted string of dividends and another +5 for raising the dividend each year). A company which has paid a dividend each of those five years and increased it in two would get +7 points. A company that paid a dividend for 45 straight years but lowered it this year would get 0 points, because the streak would have been broken.

Note: In applying these rules, watch out for the following:

- A dividend "increase" refers to the actual dollars-per-share paid out, not to the "yield" (which is a percentage and varies daily with the stock's price). Both numbers are almost universally reported in the financial media. Be sure to use the dollars-per-share figure.

- If the dividend per share suddenly drops by a half or a third one year, make sure it was not because the stock split 2-to-1 or 3-to-1. Such would not count as a decline in the dividend, and it would not break the string of consecutive years of nondeclining dividend payouts. (Most financial Web sites automatically adjust their numbers for stock splits.)

CHAPTER C-10

Bonus Points

What Are Bonus Points?

In our Easy-Rate™ company scoring system for individual investors, there should be a place for third-party opinions. Unlike the managers of mutual funds, the individual investor cannot visit each company personally and take the measure of its executive team and of the company. So we have a few bonus points available to enable us to slip in a little knowledge and opinions from people who may be in a better position to know some salient facts.

In our rating system, we utilize two such factors:

- Whether the company scores highly on *Fortune* magazine's annual list of the country's most admired companies
- How well the company scores on Wall Street's stock analysts' consensus ratings

America's Most Admired Companies

Each year, *Fortune* conducts a detailed survey to determine which companies are the "most admired." The way *Fortune* does it, companies are scored on eight dimensions, such as innovation, people management, quality of products and services, and financial soundness. The scores on the individual factors are then combined into a composite score that can run from 0 to 10. *Fortune* publishes the results of their survey in March every year, and the results are also available to subscribers on Fortune.com.

We use this list as an opportunity to award bonus points because it reinforces our search for excellent companies. A company must score 7 points or more on *Fortune*'s scale to hit our radar screen:

>8.0 on *Fortune*'s scale: +2

7.0–7.9: +1

<7.0: -0-

Analyst Recommendations

It is well known that the buy-hold-sell recommendations of analysts are often rife with overoptimism, conflicts of interest, and occasional outright fraud (although not so much lately). Nevertheless, even before the reforms of the past few years, studies showed a correlation between the consensus of analyst recommendations and stock performance. The recent highly publicized reforms—especially those designed to separate investment-banking influence from the recommendations of analysts—have gone a long way to eliminate the most egregious abuses of the past.

The phrase "consensus recommendations" refers to the average recommendations by analysts as compiled by financial information consolidators. The banks and other companies that analysts work for have a myriad of rating schemes, but it is pretty much standard for the consolidators to reduce these schemes to a simple scale of 1 through 5, where 1 indicates "strong buy" (the best rating) and 5 indicates "strong sell" (the worst rating). The consensus ratings are available on almost every financial Web site. A stock's consensus rating is a simple average of the individual ratings assigned by the different analysts covering the company.

The Sensible Stock Investor *never* takes these ratings literally, knowing that ratings tend to be overly optimistic and may be influenced by conflicts of interest. But we can compensate by utilizing only the upper end of their scale to create our own scale. That allows us to award helpful bonus points:

Consensus rating 1.0–1.3: +3

Consensus rating 1.4–1.8: +2

Consensus rating 1.9–2.2: +1

Consensus rating >2.2: -0-

As it should be, this scale is tough. A stock whose consensus rating is not at least a "Buy" gets no points at all from us. Since the reforms of recent years took full hold, the average consensus rating for S&P 500 stocks has tended to be about 2.5, which would not score any points for us.

CHAPTER C-11

Putting It All Together:
A Company Scoring System

Building a Company Scoring System

Now let's pull together the discussions in earlier chapters and summarize the Easy-Rate™ scoring system for evaluating companies. Remember, rating companies is just the first step in our three-step process. The second step—stock valuation—will be discussed in Part D. The third step—managing the portfolio—will be discussed in Part E.

Our company scoring system has been designed to identify investable companies. It allocates points to each predictive factor that we have decided to use. It is designed to identify companies with the best prospects for *sustained earnings growth*.

In our system, a variety of factors are considered, so that no one factor dominates. This is consistent with our basic Sensible Stock Investing tenet that a multi-pronged, comprehensive approach is best, and it is an important safeguard against becoming overly focused on one or two characteristics while blinding yourself to other factors. The system here uses financial strength, growth, "business dominance," and several miscellaneous factors to create a comprehensive system for identifying companies that might be good investment prospects. The total number of points available is 63, in three categories:

- The company's Story—up to 10 points
- Financial factors—up to 48 points
- Bonus factors—up to 5 points

Use of the system has shown that the best companies score in the high 30s and the 40s.

Working with this kind of system for several years has made one thing abundantly clear: No matter how you tweak it—bring certain factors in and out, adjust the point-ranking values, and so on—the same good companies keep rising toward the top and the same bad ones keep sinking toward the bottom.

The Scoring System Summarized

The following table summarizes the factors and point values that have been developed in the previous chapters. Keep it by your side for quick reference when you are scoring companies.

See Appendix I, Form 1, for a filled-out Easy-Rate Sheet that illustrates the full system in action.

The Company Scoring System Summarized

Rating Factor	Description and How It Works	Points Available
EPS (Earnings per Share) Growth Rate (Historical)	Award points based on the company's past 3 years' EPS growth rate (annualized), using the scale at right. If the 3-year rate is shown as NMF, but the company is profitable now, that means that the company has gone from unprofitable to profitable—award it +4 points. Add a point if the most recent 12 month's EPS growth rate is significantly higher than the 3-year figure, or subtract a point if it is significantly lower. Score in this category will range from zero to +8.	<4%: -0- 4% to 8%: +1 9% to 14%: +2 15% to 21%: +3 22% to 30%: +4 31% to 39%: +5 40% to 50%: +6 >50%: +7 Also: NMF = +4. One-year rate meaningfully higher than 3-year rate = +1, or meaningfully lower =-1.
EPS Growth Rate (Future)	Based on consensus estimates of analysts for future earnings growth rates (3 to 5 years out). Use same scale as above. Total points available is +7.	Use same scale as EPS Growth Rate (Historical)
Revenue Growth Rate	Based on past 3 years' average revenue growth rate. Use same scoring system as for EPS Growth Rate, including point adjustments if the past year's growth rate is significantly higher or lower than the 3-year average. Score will range from 0 to +8.	Same scale as EPS Growth Rate (Historical)
ROE (Return on Equity)	Based on most recent year's or current ROE. Also add +1 point for each consecutive year (up to 5) that ROE has exceeded 15%. Total points possible is +11.	ROE < 8%: -0- ROE 8% to 11%: +1 ROE 12% to 15%: +2 ROE 16% to 20%: +3 ROE 21% to 26%: +4 ROE 27% to 33%: +5 ROE > 33%: +6 Also: +1 for each consecutive year of ROE >15% (up to 5 years).

D/E (Debt-to-Equity ratio)	Based on current ratio of long-term debt to equity. Maximum score is +4. For banks, *D/E* ratio is a non-indicator (all banks have high debt). Give banks +2.	>80%: -0- 61% to 80%: +1 41% to 60%: +2 21% to 40%: +3 0% to 20%: +4
Cash Flow	Subtract 4 points if most recent year's cash flow is less than 95% of earnings.	Cash flow negative or trails EPS by 5%: -4
Admiration Rating	Based on *Fortune*'s annual survey of America's Most Admired Corporations. *Fortune* rates companies on a 1–10 admiration scale. Up to +2 points available.	>8.0: +2 7.0 to 7.9: +1 <7.0: -0-
Analysts' Consensus Rating	Based on average of analysts' recommendations, discounted for their well-known optimism and other problems. Based on common 1 to 5 scale, where 1 indicates "Strong Buy" and 5 indicates "Strong Sell." Up to +3 points available.	1.0 to 1.3: +3 1.4 to 1.8: +2 1.9 to 2.2: +1 >2.2: -0-
Dividends	Based on most recent 5 years' dividend performance, both consistency and growth. Minimum current yield must be 0.6% to score points in this category, to eliminate giving credit to companies that pay only a minuscule portion of their earnings out as dividends. Maximum score is +10.	+1 for each year (up to 5) that company has paid dividend without reducing it. Also, +1 for each year that company has raised its dividend.

PART D. VALUING STOCKS

Chapter D-1.   What Is Valuation and Why Do You Need It?

Chapter D-2.   Common Ways to Value Stocks

Chapter D-3.   Valuation Ratios

Chapter D-4.   Dividends as a Valuation Tool

Chapter D-5.   Putting It All Together: Valuing a Stock

CHAPTER D-1

What Is Valuation and Why Do You Need It?

Price is what you pay. Value is what you get.
—Warren Buffett

Overview: A Valuation System for Stocks

Valuation—which means whether a stock is worth its price—will be explained in a second.

But first, let's take a quick look at where we are going with it. Just as we did with scoring companies in Part C, here we are going to develop a simplified valuation system for the companies' *stocks*.

Using the same Easy-Rate™ Stock Rating Sheet already introduced (see the sample in Appendix I, Form 1), we will assign valuation "grades" to stocks based on how they stack up against several criteria. As is our wont in Sensible Stock Investing, the criteria attack the problem from several angles:

- **Valuation Ratios.** These will be explained in Chapter D-3. Basically we are looking for stocks that are reasonably priced when compared to several benchmarks.
- **Dividends**. The company's payment or nonpayment of dividends can have a bearing on whether it is fairly priced.

Those of you who do not wish to read the detailed explanations of how the Easy-Rate valuation factors have been derived—who just wish to begin valuing stocks—can skip right now to the summary in Chapter D-5. However, the following three chapters are short, and therefore I suggest that all readers look them over before diving into the techniques themselves. A decent understanding of valuation is an important fundamental to becoming a Sensible Stock Investor.

Valuation is the second step in Sensible Stock Investing's three-step process. The first step, as we saw in Part C, is to identify great companies whose stocks are *candidates* for investment. The second step, discussed

153

here, is to determine whether any of the candidate stocks can be bought at a favorable price. The final step—portfolio management—will be discussed in Part E.

Basic Valuation Explained

Valuation refers to the assigning of a "proper" value, or price, to a stock. We put the quote marks around "proper" to draw attention to the fact that while the word implies that there is a single correct answer, in fact a stock's "proper" price is a theoretical notion, not a physical property of the stock.

You will see many terms for a stock's "proper" price:

- Intrinsic value
- Real value
- True value
- Correct value
- Fair value

Valuation is a guide as to when—that is, at what price—to buy and sell a stock. When the question is whether to *buy* a stock, the goal obviously is to identify whether the stock's price is likely to go *up*. Such a conclusion would be based on a belief that the market has presently *under*priced the stock and that investors in the future are likely to bid up the price. Conversely, when the question is whether to *hold or sell* a stock, the goal is to identify when the stock's price is likely to *drop*, based on evidence that the market has *over*priced it—meaning that investors in the future are likely to bid its price down.

Of course, the market determines the actual price of a stock at any time. Whether that price is "proper" or not is, as stated earlier, a theoretical construct. A multitude of mathematical models have been invented over the years to estimate "proper" values. Many mutual funds, brokerages, analysts, money managers, and commentators have their own proprietary models. These can be quite complex and sophisticated. (Unfortunately, from the investor's point of view, many of these valuation methods are proprietary and not transparent, so it is hard to evaluate them.)

Beyond those who have models for estimating "proper" value, in Chapter B-4 we met the Efficient Market Hypothesists, who believe that the current actual market price *is always* the "correct" price. If that hypothesis were correct, there would be no need to be discussing valuation. We rejected the hypothesis.

With all the models and methods around, just remember that ultimately any valuation method amounts to an *appraisal*, an educated calculation—an opinion—of what a stock "ought" to be worth.

In the next four chapters, we will explain valuation, examine the most common financial tools to estimate fair prices for individual stocks, and show you how to use them in reaching your own intelligent valuation appraisals. Following a by-now-familiar Sensible Stock Investing theme, we will employ several perspectives to create a multidimensional valuation approach that we can use to help us make good investment decisions. Happily, high-level mathematics is not necessary, which is good news for the average individual investor. Our ultimate goal is to improve the odds of buying stocks at favorable valuations—that is, at prices that maximize our chances of making a profit.

Why Valuation Is Important

It is a basic tenet of Sensible Stock Investing that there is a difference between the *excellence of a company* and the *potential of its stock as an investment.*

The excellence of a company has been discussed in Part C. Boiled down, company excellence is based on a company's high probability to sustain earnings growth over a meaningful period of time.

Assuming that an excellent company has been found, the next step in Sensible Stock Investing is to determine *whether* and *when* to buy it. Every stock's price changes from day to day, meaning that opportunities to make investments in great companies at favorable valuations come and go regularly.

While it is rare that a lousy company can make a great investment, it is often true that *a great company can be a lousy investment.* That's because if you pay too much, you get too few shares for your money, and the stock's overall return is likely—if not doomed—to be subpar. That's why we have to carry our analysis beyond simply identifying excellent companies.

If you pay too much for a stock, it's as if the stock has a steel ball chained to it. Sad to say, for the rest of the time you own that stock, your returns will suffer because you paid too much for it. Sooner or later, unless a bubble or other improbable market phenomenon bails you out, the inexorable grinding rationality of the market will cause that price to come down. This unfortunate result is practically foreordained at the time you overpay for the stock. The truth is that valuation will play as much a role in the returns you generate as the performance of the companies whose stocks you buy.

Of course, the same logic works in reverse. If you are fortunate enough to be able to grab some stock in a great company at a price that is beneath what the market will eventually decide is its true value, the relentless logic of the market will work in your favor. Buyers will come to the stock, pushing its price up.

So some sort of concept of "proper" value is necessary as a benchmark for good investment decisions. Despite their imperfections and unknowns, valuation models are worthwhile because they provide that benchmark.

CHAPTER D-2

Common Ways to Value Stocks

Two Methodologies

While there are countless variations in detail, there are basically two approaches to stock valuation:

- By the mathematical calculation of a "proper"(intrinsic, fair, correct) price for the stock
- By using what are known as valuation ratios and comparing them to historical norms

The goal of each approach is the same, namely to determine whether the current actual price of the stock is under, over, or about equal to what it "should" be.

Intrinsic Value Calculations

In their seminal book *Security Analysis* (1934), Benjamin Graham and David Dodd proposed a method of calculation that would result in a precise dollar value that a stock was worth. That classic textbook (often referred to simply as "Graham & Dodd") is considered to be the beginning of modern stock analysis and the first clear expostulation of what has come to be known as "value investing." Graham followed it up in 1949 with *The Intelligent Investor*, a book written for laymen, which has been updated through several editions, most recently in 2003. Warren Buffett studied under Graham, so the lineage of value investing extends over decades from Graham and Dodd to Buffett today.

In a nutshell, Graham and Dodd proposed that the present "real" value of a share of stock—no matter what it was actually selling for on the open market—was the net present value of the company's future stream of profits. ("Net present value" simply refers to the amount that the company's future stream of profits is mathematically worth today.) Since in those days companies paid so much of their profits out as dividends, Graham and Dodd based their calculations on future streams of dividends. Using a common mathematical technique called "discounting" to convert a future stream of money into what it is worth right now, they were able to estimate what they called the stock's "intrinsic value."

On top of that, to be extra safe and guard against possible calculation mistakes, they recommended that no stock be purchased unless it was selling for considerably less than the calculated intrinsic value. They called this the "margin of safety."

Over the years, this approach to valuing stocks has gained many disciples, Buffett being the most famous. Also with the passage of time, many changes and embellishments have been made to the original hypotheses. As stated earlier, there probably exist nowadays hundreds of variations on the original approach.

But essentially all calculations of intrinsic value share these common elements:

- They are based on the thesis that the true value of a company is measured by the stream of profits it will generate in the future. The more profits the company is expected to make, the more its stock should be worth today.

- They utilize some measure of these profits, such as dividends, earnings, or cash flow, to express the expected monetary output of the company for the future life of the business. The most common measure these days is cash flow. Cash flow has supplanted reported earnings *and* Graham and Dodd's use of dividends. Cash flow is favored because it is less manipulable by accountants than reported earnings. And dividend payouts are so much smaller than they were in 1934 that dividends no longer reflect profits reliably. (That said, you might still reason that Graham and Dodd's focus on dividends was the best approach, because dividends are what you actually get in your pocket, with any gain from the stock's price being based on market events and therefore inherently speculative.)

- Since the future is unknowable, sensible estimates must be made about factors that will influence the company's ability to generate future cash flow. Thus, calculations of intrinsic value depend on estimates or presumptions about future market share, sales, growth rates, costs, profit margins, debt, inventory levels, lease obligations, capital expenditures, and all the other hundreds of factors inside the black box that will affect the company's performance. Therefore, the bottom-line future estimates are projections based on (1) past performance combined with (2) reasonable suppositions about the future.

- Because the far future becomes harder and harder to predict, there is usually some cutoff point (often 5 or 10 years) beyond which the company's future performance is presumed to revert to "average" or some reasonable constant. To account for the cash streams that will be generated in the years beyond the cutoff point, the analyst will add a perpetuity value, which is an estimate of all the cash flows beyond the cutoff point.

- Taking all this data into account, the estimated future cash flows are added up. Needless to say, this sum is a very important number. Any misestimate or botched prediction that throws it off ruins the calculation.

- The sum of future cash flows is adjusted to its "net present" value using a common mathematical technique called "discounting." This calculation, in turn, depends upon estimates of the company's cost of capital over the calculation period. This "discount rate" estimate is also extremely important, because the final result is very sensitive to even slight changes in the rate(s) used.

- Finally, the company's net present total value is divided by the number of shares to yield the intrinsic value per share. This then becomes the "proper" value, the benchmark to determine whether the company's actual market price is overvalued (too high), undervalued (too low), or about right.

A company's intrinsic value is easy to conceptualize, but as you can see, it is hard to calculate. The whole process just described is called "discounted cash flow" analysis.

Problems with Intrinsic Value

We said earlier that the investor needs some benchmark by which to be able to judge whether a stock's actual market price is too high, too low, or about right. The calculation of intrinsic value certainly provides such a benchmark.

But the calculation is fraught with problems. First, while it yields a precise number, any calculation of intrinsic value is not "accurate" in a scientific sense. You may recall from high school math that a number can be precise (carried out, say, to five decimal places) but *wrong*. Precision and accuracy are not the same thing. Thus one danger to the investor is that the precision of a discounted cash flow analysis implies correctness, generating a false sense that the "proper" value is now known.

A second problem is that many judgments and guesses go into calculating intrinsic value. Intrinsic value is referred to so often without qualification that it begins to sound like a physical property of the stock itself. But it is not that at all; it is a calculated appraisal based on many estimates. Anyone who has ever bought a house or car or watched an auction knows that the actual value of anything exists in the minds of the buyer and seller. Value is not a physical property but a result of human behavior. "Right price" is an amorphous concept that changes from person to person, time to time, and situation to situation. It has many subjective elements.

A third reason that we know that a calculated intrinsic value is suspect is that the future is unknowable. The intrinsic value calculation is an estimate built upon estimates, presumptions, and conjecture. Misestimating a company's projected growth rate, profit margin, or cost of capital can have a significant effect on the final calculated intrinsic value. Some companies have volatile earnings that rise or fall dramatically in response to news about the economy or other factors. And of course, the farther into the future that estimates are made, the more likely they are to be wrong, even if the company has a long track record from which to extrapolate. If we *could* see any company's future earnings over the next 100 years, or until the business ends, and if we *could* discount them back at a known interest rate, then we *would* know its intrinsic value, to the penny. But we can't.

Finally, even if by some miracle the calculation were totally accurate, there is another problem with intrinsic value based on discounted cash flow analysis. It requires a logical leap that each dollar per share of a company's cash flow (or earnings) really is returned to you as a shareholder. The logical leap is actually two jumps chained together:

- The first is a (usually unstated) premise that the future cash flows will somehow end up in your pocket as a part owner of the company. But, of course, shareholders do not receive all the profits of a company, because most companies retain most or all of their profits for reinvestment in the company.

- The second part of the logical leap is that profits not paid out as dividends—but instead retained to grow the value of the company—will cause the price of the company's stock to rise over time. In other words, that growth in the company's intrinsic value will be mirrored by corresponding growth in the price of its stock.

You can see that Graham and Dodd's original concept of intrinsic value—based on the *dividend*s that actually ended up in shareholders' hands—required far less of a logical leap than under today's conditions, where most earnings are *not* paid out as dividends, cash flow is used as a proxy for earnings, and earnings growth is used as a proxy for stock-price growth.

So the fact is that there is no such thing as a "correct" price for a stock at any given moment. Instead, what exist simultaneously are the actual market price plus a debatable "intrinsic value"—an educated appraisal—of the stock's worth.

That's OK, you say, this is only a benchmark. And you are right. But there is another, easier way for the average investor to create that benchmark, and it works just as well if not better.

Another Method: Valuation Ratios

There is a second way that many investors approach stock valuation: They use "valuation ratios." These common tools are simple mathematical ratios that compare the stock's current price to quantifiable aspects of its business: its earnings, its revenue, its book value, and so on. Over the years, experience has taught that such ratios fall into typical ranges for overvalued, undervalued, and fairly valued stocks.

Valuation ratios have several advantages over discounted cash flow calculations for the individual investor:

- They are readily available.
- They are free, precalculated, from a multitude of sources.
- They result in a multidimensional appraisal of the company, since they come at the question from multiple points of view.
- They are transparent, not the outcome of any proprietary cash flow model with its required assumptions and estimates.

Valuation ratios do not yield a single "proper" price for a stock, but rather they produce an opinion (such as fair, underpriced, or overpriced) of the stock's current market price.

The lack of a single price benchmark might lead some to say that valuation ratios result in an appraisal that is less *precise* than discounted cash flow calculations, and that is true. But of course that does not mean that it is less *accurate*. And the multidimensionality of valuation ratios is a big plus. Whereas in the calculation of intrinsic value mistaken assumptions and projections are all integrated together into the single result, the use of valuation ratios produces several points of view. If one is greatly at variance with the others, it can be isolated, making it available for further study or dismissed as an anomaly.

So in Sensible Stock Investing we will use valuation ratios to make our appraisals of whether stocks are fairly priced, underpriced, or overpriced.

Let's get started.

CHAPTER D-3

Valuation Ratios

What Are Valuation Ratios?

"Valuation ratio" means *any ratio of the stock's current price (P) to one of its fundamental financial numbers.* That is, the price per share, P, is always divided by another number derived from the business. The resulting ratio is then compared to historical norms to help assess whether the stock is fairly valued at its current price P.

Valuation ratios might be said to reflect the market's expectations for a stock. They represent investor sentiment. The higher the ratio, the more the market expects from the stock, hence investors' increased willingness to "pay up" to buy it. But remember, the price component of the return you experience as a shareholder is a function of the stock's price change *relative to what you paid for it,* not simply to its price change in the abstract. Therefore, *your* willingness to "pay up" should be based on an appraisal of whether the market's expectations are reasonable or not.

The following are examples of valuation ratios (all of which will be discussed in more detail below):

* P/E, or price-to-earnings ratio, which compares the stock's price to the company's reported earnings. This is the famous "multiple" that we have seen before.
* P/S, or price-to-sales ratio, which compares the stock's price to the company's revenue.
* P/B, or price-to-book ratio, which compares the stock's price to its formal accounting book value.

All of the valuation ratios we use in Sensible Stock Investing are available for free on virtually all financial Web sites. They are usually updated to the day (they change daily as stock prices change and as other data—such as reported earnings or revenue—become available quarterly).

In this chapter, we will go over each valuation ratio, describe what it means, and comment on how to use it. In the next chapter, we will discuss the special subject of dividends as a tool in rounding out our appraisal of a stock's price. And in the final chapter of this Part D, we will pull all the information together into a Sensible Stock Investor's method for valuing stocks. If you want to peek ahead to see how it all comes together, look at the sample Easy-Rate™ Stock Rating Sheet in Appendix I, Form 1. As is common in Sensible Stock Investing, our use of a combination of perspectives will allow us to assemble a valuation mosaic, discern the dominant patterns, and not worry too much about whether any single method gets it exactly right.

At the end of our valuation approach, we will have a simple rating scale for stock valuation:

- Excellent (meaning the stock looks cheap compared to its company's prospects)
- Good
- Fair (meaning the stock's price seems about right)
- Poor
- Bubble (meaning the stock is probably *way* overvalued, perhaps because it is caught up in a mania of some kind)

In the valuation summary Chapter D-5 at the end of this Part D, we will present a table that shows how to translate different valuation scores into ratings of Excellent, Good, etc. on the Easy-Rate Sheets. Now let's look at the valuation ratios themselves.

Price-to-Earnings Ratio (P/E)

The price to earnings (P/E) ratio is the granddaddy of all stock valuation ratios. It is by far the most common expression of valuation, so ubiquitous that it regularly appears in newspaper stock tables, where space is precious. We have seen the P/E ratio before, in Chapter B-3, when we were talking about what determines stock prices. The P/E ratio is the famous "multiple" discussed there.

Mathematically, the P/E ratio is simple: It is the company's price per share (P) divided by its earnings per share (E). So if a stock's P is $100 and its E is $5, its P/E is $100 divided by $5, or 20. Note that the P/E ratio is a unitless number: Dollars divided by dollars yields just a number. It is not a percentage, nor is it expressed in dollars. It is just a simple ratio.

The P/E ratio is helpful evidence of a stock's valuation. Various studies have shown that stocks purchased when they have low P/E ratios tend to outperform, over time, stocks with high P/E ratios. The studies agree that valuation ratios are "directionally helpful": The lower the valuation ratio at time of purchase, the better the likely performance over time.

There are two cautionary notes about the P/E ratio.

- The first is that earnings (the E in P/E) are legally manipulable. As we have seen, many elements of earnings are the product of subjective decisions. While the earnings of every public company are audited annually and must conform to Generally Accepted Accounting Principles, there is a lot of play in the joints, and not every company treats every situation the same way.

- A second caution is that there is no standard time period for the earnings (E) used in the P/E ratio. The two time periods that we use are:

    Trailing P/E: This uses the company's earnings over the past twelve months (or TTM, which stands for "trailing twelve months"). These earnings have been officially reported, so there are no estimates involved, but of course it is old news.

    Forward P/E: This uses present-year earnings (that is, the company's current fiscal year). Note that these may include *estimated* earnings for at least part of the year if the current fiscal year is not yet over. That eliminates the old-news aspect, but it introduces the risk that the estimates are wrong.

It is important to be sure, when comparing the P/E ratio of one stock to another (or of the stock to itself over different time frames), that they have been calculated using the same time period. The financial media are not consistent on what E they are using, but most Web sites and other sources are *internally* consistent, and they identify (somewhere) which time period they are using. If you get all your P/E's from the same source, that more or less guarantees that they have all been calculated the same way. For that reason, I highly recommend the consistent use of one source.

Arithmetically, it is easy to see that a stock's actual price (P) is a multiplication of its earnings (E) times its multiple (E times P/E equals P). As investors, we want the stock's P to go up. There are two ways for this to happen. The first, discussed earlier, is that the company is an excellent one which is able to generate *sustained earnings growth*. That makes E go up, and therefore P should go up with it (assuming that the market reacts rationally to the fact that E is going up).

The second is for the P/E ratio itself to go up. This is a function of investor sentiment about the stock. What causes investors to "award" a higher P/E ratio to one stock over another? These are the principal reasons:

- *Predictability.* Investors like companies that have consistent earnings growth rates. Remember the old Wall Street saying that uncertainty is an investor's enemy. A company that is steady, even if not spectacular, overcomes the uncertainty objection. So demonstrated consistent success is often rewarded with favorable sentiment and a higher P/E ratio. Conversely, volatile (less predictable) earnings may get stuck with a lower P/E ratio to compensate for the perceived higher risk.

- *Sustainability.* Investors tend to more highly value a stock that looks like it will be able to sustain its earnings momentum over long periods of time. That might be because of its competitive advantages or the fact that it is in a healthy industry, is riding a megatrend, has a fine management team, etc.

- *High expected rates of profit growth.* High growth expectations are usually based on factors such as the company's past history of high growth rates, leading position in its industry, the riding of a megatrend, sustainable competitive advantages, pricing power, sheer excitement, and the like. The higher P/E ratios reflect investor belief (or hope) that the faster-growing companies are worth more because of their growth. Thus, premium P/E ratios tend to be awarded to stocks that have a very high probability of superior long-term growth. Conversely, the market usually views low-growth companies as worth less than high-growth companies, and so typically assigns them lower P/E ratios.

- *Small size*: A small company experiencing success in a new and emerging industry can generate hyper-growth, which in turn triggers investor sentiments of unlimited promise and greed, leading to higher P/E ratios. In addition, smaller (newer) companies have an easier time sustaining high growth rates, before the law of large numbers sets in.

- *Participation in an industry that seems to have perpetually high P/E ratios.* Technology companies, for example, always seem to have high P/E ratios, even when the technology sector as a whole is faltering. There is something about technology that seems to capture investors' fancy over and over again. The same seems to be true of telecommunications, biotechnology, and a few other industries. It turns out that the market often tends to overvalue high-growth-rate companies and to undervalue low-growth-rate companies. This is what Jeremy Siegel calls the "growth trap" in his book *The Future for Investors* (2005), the trap being that despite their high rates of growth, it is hard to make money on stocks of companies that the market has way overvalued.

Since before the Great Depression, the average trailing multiple for the Dow stocks has been around 17. According to data compiled by Robert Shiller (author of *Irrational Exuberance,* which in a stroke of great timing was published just before the crash of 2000), the P/E ratio for the S&P 500 has varied from a low of about 5 (in 1920) to a high of about 44 (at the peak of the market bubble in 1999). In recent years, P/E's for the market as a whole have tended to hover a few points higher than the long-term 17 average. This may be a residue of the late-1990s bubble, it could signal a long-lasting change in investor sentiment and behavior, or it could mean that the bubble has not yet fully deflated. The range of multiples for individual stocks, of course, is very wide, varying from 0 up to over 100.

If a stock has no earnings, its P/E ratio is usually considered to be not meaningful (commonly designated "NMF").

Price-to-Earnings-Growth Ratio (PEG)

The PEG ratio is calculated by dividing the P/E ratio by the earnings growth rate of the company. Arithmetically, that would be (P/E)/G, which is commonly shortened to "PEG." For example, imagine that Company A has a P/E ratio of 50 and a (phenomenal) earnings growth rate of 60 percent per year. Its PEG would be 50 divided by 60, or 0.8. The *G* in PEG, the earnings growth rate, is normally the three-to-five-year consensus figure of analysts covering the company. That consensus estimate of G is available on most financial Web sites, as are precomputed PEG ratios.

The purpose of the PEG ratio is to add context to the P/E ratio by relating it to the company's growth rate. The idea is that a high P/E ratio by itself (such as the 50 in the above example) may not be so bad when viewed in the context of a company's fast-growing earnings. Higher-growth businesses *should* have higher P/E's, because they are likely to have a larger stream of future profits than slow growers. That makes their present value higher.

Let's see how this works in practice. Consider Company A again, with its high P/E of 50. Under some "value" investment systems, Company A would be thrown out as a candidate *on that basis alone.* But recall that the underlying company has been growing its earnings at 60 percent per year. That company is clearly creating value at a rapid rate. Might it not be exactly the kind of company that we want to invest in? The PEG ratio allows us to see that. If the 60 percent growth rate is projected to continue, the PEG ratio here would be 50/60, or 0.8. That is considered to be a very good PEG ratio. So we see the mosaic of valuation building: The "bad" P/E of 50 looks better when we see it in the context of a company building its earnings 60 percent per year.

For comparison, let's imagine that Company B, which has been growing its earnings at 8 percent per year, is expected to maintain that growth rate and is trading at a P/E of just 16. Under some systems, the second stock would be considered attractive on the basis of its "reasonable" 16 P/E ratio. But the PEG ratio tells a different tale and allows us to see that it may be unwise to favor Company B over Company A. The PEG of the first stock is 0.8. The PEG of the second stock is 2.0 (16 divided by 8). As with all valuation ratios, lower is better. Here, Company A's PEG ratio is less than half Company B's. All other things being equal, as measured by the PEG ratio, Company A is a better value, despite its high P/E ratio of 50.

Even better would be Company C, with a P/E ratio of 10 and an earnings growth rate G of 20 percent per year. Such a stock has a PEG of 0.5 (10 divided by 20). This would normally be considered a very good value. If it's a great company, Company C would be a very tempting candidate, especially considering that an earnings growth rate of 20 percent per year is probably more sustainable than Company A's stratospheric 60 percent.

PEG ratios typically fall in the range of about 0.5 to 4, with any ratio of 1.0 or below considered to be excellent. Some investment "systems" refuse to consider any stock unless its PEG ratio is 1.0 or less. As usual, we won't be that rigid. We'll use the PEG ratio as but one of several building blocks in our valuation assessment.

Price-to-Cash-Flow Ratio (P/CF)

A company's earned cash flow, over time, should equal its reported earnings. (This was discussed in the black box example in Chapter C-7.) However, in any given year, there may be a significant (and legitimate) difference between the numbers, because of accounting rules and interpretations that affect the timing of the recognition of revenue, the booking of costs, the use of reserves, and things like that.

Cash flow is thought by many commentators to be a better indicator of a company's financial health than its officially reported profits, because cash flow is less manipulable by the accountants than reported earnings are.

Since cash flow is less manipulable than earnings, some would argue that the P/CF ratio is a better valuation indicator than the P/E ratio. As Sensible Stock Investors, we can be agnostic on this argument by using both. Over time, the two ratios should converge anyway. For a point of reference, the S&P's average P/CF ratio tends to be in the 15–22 range, the same as its historical P/E ratio. (That makes sense, because over time earnings and cash flow should be about equal.) The cash flow number typically used in the P/CF ratio is for the trailing 12 months. P/CF ratios, like all the valuation ratios discussed here, are readily available on practically every financial Web site. And as with all valuation ratios, lower is better.

Price-to-Sales Ratio (P/S)

Our next valuation ratio is the price-to-sales, or P/S, ratio. It is the price per share of the stock (P) divided by its sales (revenue) per share (S). So if a stock is selling for $100 per share and racking up $25 in revenue per share, its P/S ratio is 4 (100 divided by 25). As with the P/E ratio, it is important to define the time period over which the revenue-per-share number is measured. It is pretty standard to use revenue for the past 12 months. P/S ratios are easy to find on virtually all stock Web sites. If you get your numbers from a single source, you can be confident that all the P/S ratios have been calculated the same way.

The P/S ratio is useful for several reasons. Strong and steady revenue growth is desirable for any company. Good sales are required to drive growth, so for most companies there is a strong relationship between its sales growth levels and its ultimate value as an enterprise. Sales growth (or shrinkage) is often an early indicator of a company's later earnings performance. And companies can't fiddle as much with revenues as they can with earnings. Virtually the only accounting rules affecting sales relate to when they are recognized on the books. Thus the P/S ratio is less subject to distortion than the P/E ratio.

The big shortcoming of the P/S ratio is that companies vary widely in their ability to convert revenue into earnings. For example, retailers typically operate with low profit margins, and therefore they tend to have low P/S ratios. That's OK. Our multipronged use of a variety of valuation ratios will help us guard against any one being misleading.

As a point of reference, the P/S ratio of the S&P 500 tends to hover in the 3–4 range.

Price-to-Book-Value Ratio (P/B)

The book value of a company is the accounting value of the enterprise—its assets minus its liabilities. Assets include "hard" assets—such as buildings, machinery, and money—plus some "soft" assets, such as goodwill and patents. Liabilities are financial obligations (debt). The book value theoretically approximates what the owners would receive if the company were liquidated.

The valuation ratio known as price to book value of the company is its price per share (P) divided by book value per share (B), abbreviated P/B. As with other valuation ratios, the lower the better. Of course, if the ratio is below 1 (price less than book value), the market is, in a sense, suggesting that the company is worth more dead than alive, which would cause one to wonder about its worth as an investment (or the quality of its current management).

As with most accounting concepts, book value is malleable, and sometimes its usefulness seems dubious. For example, land may be carried on the books at the price paid when it was acquired decades ago, even though its real market worth is much higher now. On the other hand, many so-called new-economy businesses are "asset light," meaning that much of their value is not based on tangible assets like land and buildings but rather on intangibles like the value of a brand name, the knowledge inside the heads of its employees, the company's ability to innovate, pricing power, or the expertise of its management. Some would argue that the book value of tangible assets is therefore a less important metric than it used to be when the economy was dominated by firms that owned factories, land, heavy equipment, and the like.

Nevertheless, the P/B ratio continues to be used, and there is little question that it gives us some useful information about a company's stock price, perhaps more for brick-and-mortar companies than for asset-light companies. Several academic studies suggest that stocks with low P/B ratios tend to outperform stocks with high P/B ratios. Once again, because we come at the valuation question from a variety of angles, we have a built-in system of checks and balances as we make our appraisals. The average P/B ratio in recent years has been around 2 to 3.5. Older industrial companies tend to be nearer to 1 (their B is higher), while newer technology companies sometimes hit 20 or more (reflecting their comparative lack of "hard" assets).

In Summary

We will use six ratios to rate stock valuations in Sensible Stock Investing:

*   Price-to-earnings—P/E—for the trailing 12 months
*   Price-to-earnings—forward P/E—for the current fiscal year
*   Price-to-earnings-growth—PEG
*   Price-to-cash-flow—P/CF
*   Price-to-sales—P/S
*   Price-to-book-value—P/B

We will assign each stock a valuation rating of Excellent, Good, etc. based on the composite picture painted by the above six ratios, combined with a consideration of the company's dividend situation. The scoring system is revealed in the summary Chapter D-5. Dividends are the subject of the next chapter.

CHAPTER D-4

Dividends as a Valuation Tool

Historical Perspective on Dividends

Some companies pay dividends; others do not. In Part C on rating companies, we granted significant importance to steady payments and increases in dividends. The idea was that dividend-paying companies not only generate free cash each year but also are confident that they can continue to fund both reinvestment in the company and the payment of dividends every year.

Now, let's consider a separate question: Is a company's payment of dividends a positive sign when it comes to appraising the company's stock price? Clearly, since the whole idea of valuation is to appraise a stock's likelihood of paying back a good return on our investment, the answer will be found when we consider dividends' effects on total stock returns.

To get started, we need to consider a bit of history about stock dividends.

A century and more ago, investing in stocks was far less common than it is today. Then, as now, stocks were considered riskier than bonds, for two reasons:

- There is the *risk of the principal diminishing or being lost,* which is far more likely with stocks than with most bonds.
- Stocks display a *variability in return* compared to the fixed contractual interest stated on every bond.

Thus stock investors then—as now—expected to be compensated for the extra risk by receiving a higher *potential* rate of return. This has become known as the "equity risk premium"—the shot you get at greater returns because you are willing to risk your money in a stock rather than put it into a safer bond.

A century ago, most of the return from the average stock came from dividends. Changes in the stock's price—being considered speculative—were not the main attraction for most investors. Stock dividends were therefore sort of a bond-interest substitute, with a hoped-for potential price "kicker" attached. Many companies paid out the bulk of their profits in dividends. The dividend yield on the typical stock exceeded the interest rate on the typical bond. The investor could compare the likely dividends from a stock to the much-less-risky interest from a bond and decide whether higher dividend returns made up for the extra risk of the stock.

At that time, unlike today, it was taken for granted that a stock should pay out a higher yield than a bond, to make up for the stock's risks. Under these conditions, the still-common phrase "how much an investor should be willing to pay for x level of earnings" made complete sense, because investors *actually received* the earnings in the form of dividends. A stock investor, as part owner of the company, truly *was* buying the earnings stream, which would be paid to him or her in the form of dividends. The company mailed out the money every quarter. Companies that didn't pay dividends were considered second-class investments, mere speculations. We saw earlier that Graham and Dodd, in their famous *Security Analysis* (1934), looked *only* to dividends in valuing companies.

As recently as the late 1950s, the prevailing dividend yield on stocks almost always exceeded the prevailing interest yield on bonds. But by the 1980s and 1990s, company practices and investor expectations had changed. With the bull market that began in 1982, dividends began to drift downward, and that trend accelerated in the 1990s. Companies kept more of their cash to reinvest in themselves, while investors began to take for granted not only that bonds would yield more than stocks, but also that stocks' predominant returns would come from *price changes* rather than dividend payouts. An investor who was counting on making money from the rising price of a stock was no longer automatically derided as a "speculator."

Today, the average dividend yield of S&P 500 stocks hovers in the 1 to 2 percent range, not much of a return by itself. Many of the highest total-return stocks of the past couple decades *never* paid a dividend, and nobody thought twice about it.

Dividends as a Valuation Tool

What has all this got to do with valuation?

Well, remember that the goal of valuation is to determine whether a stock is selling at a bargain. Because companies that pay dividends rarely lower them, a stock that pays a dividend already is "guaranteeing" a certain return on your investment. Common sense therefore suggests that a stock's dividend yield ought to be considered as a potential "plus factor" in valuing the stock. Sometimes one hears the phrase that a decent dividend yield "places a floor" under the price of a stock. While this is an overstatement (sometimes companies do cut or even eliminate their dividends), it conveys the general idea: If all the valuation ratios are equal, a dividend-paying company is a better buy than a non-dividend-paying one.

Note that in adopting this point of view, we are rejecting a notion sometimes heard that an investor should not care whether a stock pays a dividend, because he or she should be indifferent as to whether a company pays a dividend to its shareholders or the company keeps that money—to reinvest in itself to fund expansions, to buy back its own stock, to buy other companies, or whatever.

We do not think that the Sensible Stock Investor should be indifferent on this issue. As was explained in Part C, too much cash on a company's hands is often not a good thing, because the company's executives frequently lose discipline about what to do with it. Paying a regular dividend is a good discipline for a company—it helps keeps the interests of the shareholders in the foreground (as opposed to, say, funding low-potential projects or wasting money on empire-building). Dividends also are a sign that the company has real cash behind its earnings to pay the dividend and that its earnings are not the result of accounting legerdemain. That is the kind of company a Sensible Stock Investor wants to own.

Besides, it seems logically inconsistent to demand that a company generate positive cash from its operations (as we do insist) but then be indifferent as to whether *we* generate cash from our own investment "business." When you get a dividend, you get real money. During a period where there is no significant price appreciation (as in a sideways or bear market), dividends are real income that provides a return on your investment. So the Sensible Stock Investor considers good old cash dividends to be a plus factor—not the only standard for measuring a company's worth, certainly, but one with a role to play in the appraisal.

What level of dividend yield is enough to make a difference in assessments of valuation? It would not be unreasonable to suggest that a company paying more than the S&P 500's average yield (about 1.7 percent) is providing a decent head start on total return and that a 2 to 4 percent yield is a significant head start.

As usual, we will utilize a point-scoring system for evaluating dividend yields in our Easy-Rate system. The complete point scale for dividends will be shown in the next chapter, along with the point system for all the valuation ratios that we use.

CHAPTER D-5

Putting It All Together:
Valuing a Stock

This chapter ties up the preceding chapters and depicts the Sensible Stock Investing valuation system. The total valuation for a stock is based on a scoring system that is similar to the one we used to rate companies in Part C.

We use the Easy-Rate™ Stock Rating Sheet system for recording and evaluating each of the valuation factors. See the sample filled-out Easy-Rate Sheet at Form 1 in Appendix I.

All of the following ratios are readily available for free on most financial Web sites.

P/E Ratio (Trailing)

Look up the stock's trailing price-to-earnings (P/E) ratio, which is based on the stock's last 12 months of reported earnings (i.e., no estimates are involved). Note that the most recent "trailing twelve months" may not coincide with the company's fiscal year—that's OK.

Use the following scale to rate the "fairness" of the stock's price.

P/E < 11	Excellent	+5 points
P/E 11–15	Good	+4 points
P/E 16–32	Fair	+3 points
P/E 33–80	Poor	+1 point
P/E > 80	Bubble	-0- points

This scale attempts to provide a universal rating system that can be used for all stocks in all industries under all market conditions. Again, in Sensible Stock Investing we blend many approaches, so any "mistake" made here is not fatal, because this rating scale is only one of several we will use.

Note that the "Fair" category includes P/E's of up to 32—many experts would consider this to be unacceptably high. However, there is justification for having "fair" go that high. In *The Future for Investors* (2005), Jeremy Siegel explored the characteristics of the highest-performing S&P 500 stocks since the index was created. Many of them had P/E ratios that were higher than the market's long-term average of about 17—ranging all the way up to 27. So a P/E of, say, 27 historically has not necessarily meant that a firm is "pricey." It simply means that investors have higher expectations for earnings growth for this firm than they do for a firm with a P/E ratio of, say, 17. The most successful firms consistently exceed the market's expectations, and that is why they become the long-term best performers. Siegel's high-end level of acceptability has been adjusted upward from 27 to 32 in our system to account for the fact that during the past several years P/E ratios have run higher across the board—around 20—than their long-term historical average (about 17). That difference of 20/17 (or about 17 percent) has been added to Siegel's high end of 27 to reach the adjusted figure of 32 used here.

However, if you feel this scale is too liberal, you can change it to suit your own notions. For example, you might feel a "Fair" rating should be given only to a stock with a P/E ratio of 15 or 20. Fine, use that, and recalibrate the other categories accordingly. The important point is to *have* a scale that is supported by some logic.

Some investors may wish to create different scales for "growth" companies with fast-growing earnings (which tend to have higher P/E ratios), "value" companies with slower-growing earnings (lower P/E ratios), and so on. You might wish to maintain a separate scale for certain industries that traditionally have higher P/E ratios (like technology).

Here, to keep it simple, we'll stick with the single universal scale. For comparison, the S&P 500's long-term historical average P/E has been around 17, while in more recent years it has usually been a little higher than that, around 20.

P/E Ratio (Forward)

This uses the P/E ratio for the current fiscal year, where the E is constructed from actual results for quarters already completed, plus the mean of analyst estimates for the remaining quarters of the year.

For simplicity, use the same scale as above to rate the forward P/E ratio. This provides a different point of view on the stock's valuation, and it comports with the approach in much of the literature to value stocks on their "upcoming" P/E. Normally, any company we are interested in will have a lower forward P/E than current P/E, since its earnings per share would be expected to go up (thus raising E, the denominator, and lowering the ratio itself).

PEG Ratio

PEG, you will recall, stands for price-to-earnings-growth ratio. It is the company's P/E ratio divided by its estimated earnings growth rate for the coming three to five years. PEG ratios are available precomputed on many stock-data Web sites. Record the company's PEG ratio and rate it as follows:

PEG up to 1.0	Excellent	+5 points
PEG 1.1–1.5	Good	+4 points
PEG 1.6–2.0	Fair	+3 points
PEG 2.1–3.0	Poor	+1 point
PEG > 3.0	Bubble	-0- points

For comparison, the S&P 500's PEG tends to hover around 1.7.

P/CF Ratio

The price-to-cash-flow ratio should, over time, be similar to the P/E ratio, so use the same scale as for the P/E ratios. Historically, as would be expected, the P/CF ratio for the S&P 500 has been about 17, a little higher in recent years.

Watch out for one potential big red flag here. The P/CF ratio should be no higher than the P/E ratio, because the company should have earned *at least* as much cash as the profits it is reporting. If the P/CF ratio is higher than the P/E, stop and find out why. If there is no legitimate explanation, the stock should probably not be a candidate for further consideration, because the company is using accounting adjustments to raise its reported earnings beyond what it pulled in cash, which is unsustainable.

P/S Ratio

As explained earlier, the price-to-sales ratio is useful because it looks at a company's sales, which are a necessary precursor to earnings. Record the company's P/S ratio and rate it on the following scale:

P/S up to 1	Excellent	+5 points
P/S 1–2	Good	+4 points
P/S 3–5	Fair	+3 points
P/S 6–9	Poor	+1 point
P/S > 9	Bubble	-0- point

For comparison, the P/S ratio of the S&P 500 tends to be around 3.3.

P/B Ratio

The Price-to-Book ratio of the S&P 500 is usually around 5–6. Use the following scale to rate your stock:

P/B up to 2	Excellent	+5 points
P/B 3–4	Good	+4 points
P/B 5–6	Fair	+3 points
P/B 7–9	Poor	+1 point
P/B > 9	Bubble	-0- points

Dividend Yield

For dividends, the rating points are based on the stock's current yield:

Yield >8%	Excellent	+5 points
Yield 6%–8%	Good	+4 points
Yield 2%-4%	Fair	+3 points
Yield 1%-2%	Poor	+1 point
Yield <1%	No credit	-0- points

Notice that we don't call the lowest category "Bubble," since the dividend yield on a stock does not really indicate whether it is in a bubble or not. In recent years, the dividend yield of the S&P 500 stocks has averaged about 1.5 to 1.7 percent.

Adding It Up to Arrive at a Total Valuation

Normally, the Total Valuation of a stock is derived simply by summing the points from the individual categories. Then we convert that sum to a word characterization by using the following table:

Stock Valuation Table

Total Valuation Points	Valuation in Words
32 to 35	Excellent
28 to31	Good+
23 to 27	Good
18 to 22	Fair+
14 to 17	Fair
10 to13	Poor+
6 to 9	Poor
< 6	Bubble

There will be times when you wish to adjust the valuation method to account for factors we have seen. For example, you may wish to ignore the P/B ratio for an "asset-light" company or to put more emphasis on PEG for a fast-growing company.

Examples of Valuing a Stock

To close out our discussion of valuation, here is a look at two valuations of eBay. No adjustments were made; we have just applied the Easy-Rate point system in its base form.

Example 1: eBay (June, 2004)

P/E Trailing	133	Bubble	-0- points
P/E Forward	77	Poor	+1
PEG	2.0	Fair	+3
P/S	27	Bubble	-0-
P/CF	12	Bubble	-0-
P/B	12	Bubble	-0-
Dividends	0%	No credit	-0-
Total Valuation		**Bubble**	**+4 points**

There is little escaping the fact that eBay was highly overvalued, riding along on a wave of Internet euphoria. That said, the price of eBay was nevertheless rising steadily, and because of that, we purchased the stock for one of our sample portfolios discussed in Part F. The stock's price was rising *because* it was in a bubble (and because it is a great business), but not on the basis of any rational assessment of the company's "true" current value. Later in the book, we will see that bubbles, for all the derision they receive, are not always bad for the individual investor. In fact, at the time eBay was tied for the highest-rated *company* using our

Easy-Rate system. It was and is a superb company. But its economic fundamentals did not justify its price, and from this actual price, there was virtually no hope of long-term market-beating price appreciation. A few weeks later, its price started to free-fall, and we got out of the stock just 10 percent off its high. In the meantime, we had ridden the bubble to some nice gains. Later in the year, we bought it again and made another burst of profits from it. That is called "momentum" investing, and it is discussed in Chapter E-4.

Example 2: eBay (April 2005)

P/E Trailing	55	Poor	+1 point
P/E Forward	42	Poor	+1
PEG	1.3	Good	+4
P/S	13	Bubble	-0-
P/CF	33	Poor	+1
P/B	6	Fair	+3
Dividends	0%	No credit	+0
Total Valuation		**Poor+**	**+10 points**

At this point (ten months later), eBay's price had been cut nearly in half. Three reasons: (1) They ran into the law of large numbers—formerly incredible growth rates had dropped to merely fabulous. (2) They announced a price increase which was very poorly received by their customers, generating some of the only bad publicity the company had ever received. (3) The stock had been "priced for perfection." When perfection (or the perception of it) stopped with the negative reaction to the price increase, nervous investors sold the stock. In the meantime (between June 2004 and January 2005, when the stock began to tumble), we had yet again repurchased the stock as a momentum play and made a nice short-term gain on it.

Note that the *halving* of eBay's price did not bring it into decent valuation territory. Under our precepts, it remained a candidate only for momentum speculation. Note also, however, that a single one of the valuation ratios—the PEG ratio—graded as "Good," which is sometimes the case with a fast-growing company like eBay, even when all the other ratios look bad.

Now, to show you what a stock with a nice valuation looks like, let's look at ExxonMobil in June 2004:

Example 3: Exxon Mobil (June 2004)

P/E Trailing	15	Good	+4 points
P/E Forward	15	Good	+4
PEG	2.1	Poor	+1
P/S	1	Good	+4
P/CF	10	Excellent	+5
P/B	3	Fair	+3
Dividends	2.3%	Fair	+3
Total Valuation		**Good**	**+24 points**

Exxon Mobil was and is an excellent company, the highest-rated energy company in our system at the time. It was also one of our holdings. Its price was completely justified by its financials, and in fact the overall "Good" rating suggests that it was underpriced. At the time, the company was being helped along by record-high oil prices and burgeoning worldwide demand for oil, which was just fine with us (as owners of the stock, not as purchasers of gas). The 2.3 percent dividend yield was a nice bonus on top of the stock's steady gains in the market. In the next ten months after this valuation was determined, Exxon Mobil's price had risen 34 percent. Add in the dividend, and the total return was about 36 percent.

The Valuation Rating System Summarized

Use the following table as a quick reference when you are valuing stocks. If any ratio is unavailable, award an average score of +3.

The Stock Valuation System Summarized

Valuation Factor	Description and How It Works	Point Scale	
P/E Ratio (Trailing)	P/E means price-to-earnings ratio. Use TTM (most recent 12 months) *officially reported* earnings. The single scale is built around S&P 500's historical values. A more sophisticated system would use different scales for slow-growth, moderate-growth, and fast-growth companies.	P/E < 11 P/E 11 to 15 P/E 16 to 32 P/E 33 to 80 P/E > 80	Excellent +5 Good +4 Fair +3 Poor +1 Bubble -0-
P/E Ratio (Forward)	Scale is same as above, but for the *current fiscal year's* earnings, which may include a combination of officially reported earnings and estimates for unreported quarters.	Same scale as P/E Ratio (Trailing)	

Valuation Factor	Description and How It Works	Point Scale	
PEG Ratio	PEG means price-to-earnings-growth ratio, which is the P/E ratio divided by consensus estimates for future earnings growth. Anything up to 1.0 is considered excellent.	PEG < 1.0 PEG 1.1 to 1.5 PEG 1.6 to 2.0 PEG 2.1 to 3.0 PEG > 3.0	Excellent +5 Good +4 Fair +3 Poor +1 Bubble -0-
P/CF Ratio	P/CF means price-to-cash-flow ratio. This should always be equal to or lower than the P/E ratio, because the company should be generating at least as much cash as it is reporting profits. Because over time the two ratios should converge, use the same scale as for the P/E ratio.	Same scale as P/E Ratio (Trailing)	
P/S Ratio	P/S means price-to-sales ratio, using TTM (trailing 12 months) revenues.	P/S < 1 P/S 1 to 2 P/S 3 to 5 P/S 6 to 9 P/S > 9	Excellent +5 Good +4 Fair +3 Poor +1 Bubble -0-
Dividend Yield	Dividend score is based on the stock's current yield.	Yield > 8% Yield 4% to 8% Yield 2% to 4% Yield 1% to 2% Yield <1%	Excellent +5 Good +4 Fair +3 Poor +1 No credit -0-

To complete the valuation, add up the points from the table above and characterize the total as in this table. Record all information on the Easy-Rate Sheet for the stock. See the example in Appendix I, Form 1.

Stock Valuation Table

Total Valuation Points	Valuation in Words
32 to 35	Excellent
28 to 31	Good+
23 to 27	Good
18 to 22	Fair+
14 to 17	Fair
10 to 13	Poor+
6 to 9	Poor
<6	Bubble

PART E. MANAGING YOUR PORTFOLIO

Chapter E-1.   Managing a Portfolio Is Different from Picking Stocks

Chapter E-2.   Managing Risk

Chapter E-3.   Types of Stocks

Chapter E-4.   Momentum

Chapter E-5.   Timing

Chapter E-6.   Concentration and Diversification

Chapter E-7.   Articulating Your Stock Investment Strategy

Chapter E-8.   When to Buy

Chapter E-9.   When to Sell

Chapter E-10.   Summary of Portfolio Management

CHAPTER E-1

Managing a Portfolio Is Different from Picking Stocks

The best players win the most with their good hands and lose the least with their bad hands.
—Poker maxim

The Sensible Stock Investor seeks to allocate money to stocks that are likely to generate the highest return—price appreciation plus dividends. Most of the investment media focus on stock selection. You will find it easier to get suggestions about what stocks to pick than about any other aspect of stock investing.

But picking stocks—which we divided into two steps, identifying great companies in Part C and valuing their stocks in Part D—is only part of what you need to do to be a successful stock investor. The third step is *managing your portfolio.*

As important as stock picking is, portfolio management probably has more impact on your total returns. Portfolio management—an ongoing process—does not necessarily mean that you will do a lot of trading. It does mean that you will monitor your portfolio to protect your assets against loss and maximize the potential for gains.

Portfolio management requires a strategic outlook. To do it well, you need a philosophy that guides you toward reaching your investment goals. That philosophy embodies principles such as:

- managing risk;
- picking suitable types of stocks;
- being appropriately active or passive in managing and trading them;
- deciding how many stocks to own and how diversified they should be; and
- deciding how much time and desire you have to spend looking after your investments.

The most successful stock portfolios consist of stocks that have been selected with specific goals in mind and then managed with strategies that suit those goals.

The Four Basic Decisions of Portfolio Management

There are four actions which you can take in relation to a stock:

- *Do not buy* it (which equates to a decision that you'd rather have the cash than the stock)
- *Buy* it (because you believe that the stock's price is going to rise)
- *Sell it short* (because you believe that the stock's price is going to fall)
- *Sell* it (when you already own it but believe that the price is going to fall)

That last decision—whether to sell a stock you already own—is what makes portfolio management complex. That is because (1) your money is tied up in the stock (and therefore not available to invest elsewhere); (2) you must weigh the wisdom of selling the stock against the consequences of hanging on to it; (3) if you sell, you will incur transaction costs and probably trigger a taxable event; and (4) if you sell, you get cash back, which means you have to decide what to do with the money, bringing the other three decisions back into play.

Is Selling Compatible with the Buy-to-Hold Philosophy?

Just holding on to a stock is simple, but it is not always sensible. Although you will often hear otherwise, a rigid Buy-and-Hold approach has *not* been proven to be the best overall strategy for stock investing. Quite the contrary, many of the most famous and best stock investors over the past century have traded their portfolios quite actively. Even Warren Buffett, who is reflexively associated with the Buy-and-Hold philosophy, has sold many of his positions over the years. There are only a few famous stocks that Buffett has held for years and years (like Gillette and Coca-Cola). Many others have appeared in and then disappeared from his portfolios, meaning he bought them and then sold them.

Of course, the overall investing goal is to maximize your total returns over time. Achieving that goal requires combining the best opportunities for price and dividend gains with guarding against loss. To accomplish these goals, you will design your portfolio management "style" to:

- pick likely winners;
- time their purchases well;
- get the most out of each successful pick that you can;
- sell when it is time; and
- cut losses early.

When you think about it, each of these elements is a form of managing risk. You "pick likely winners" to increase the chance of making money and decrease the chance of losing it. You "time purchases well" for the same reasons. And so on. So let's take a closer look at risk management.

CHAPTER E-2

Managing Risk

The first rule is not to lose. The second rule is not to forget the first rule.
—Warren Buffett

Managing Risk, Generally

Portfolio management is largely about managing risk.

"Managing risk" has a broad definition: It means doing things that safeguard your money from the possibility that any investment decision may be wrong.

Therefore, risk management includes any practice that:

- lowers what we have called the "inherent risk" in investing in stocks;
- increases the probability that your stock investments will profit (or, stated another way, lowers the risk that you will miss out on making money from good opportunities);
- takes you out of harm's way by exiting individual stocks or the entire market when conditions warrant.

Risk management is not a prediction that things are going to go bad, but it is a defense against the possibility that they might go bad. As we will see, avoiding outsize losses is the most important factor in beating the market. The simple techniques we describe here will help you do that.

Every risk management maneuver, itself being an investment decision, carries *its* own risk. The risk in risk management is that it will make you so cautious that you will not make as much money as you would if you accepted more risk. For example:

- Easing into a stock position through multiple purchases—a common risk management technique—will *cost* you money if the stock goes straight up after your initial purchase. It is not money you *lose*, per se, but money you *fail to make* by not buying the stock all at once in the first place.

- Selling a stock because of a *short-term* price drop will stop your losses in the short term, but if the stock reverses itself and goes back up and beyond the price at which you sold it, the decision to sell will cost you the profit you would have made if you'd simply hung on to the stock.

- Diversifying will cost you money compared to what you would have made if only you'd known which single stock in the universe was going to do the best and just bought that.

So why practice risk management? To protect against *devastating* losses. In the long run, your returns are most likely to beat the market if you avoid outsize losses.

Risk management techniques range from the extremely simple—like easing your way slowly into the market—to highly complex activities utilizing sophisticated investment products and strategies that are beyond the ken of the average individual investor. In this regard, one often hears the term "hedging." Hedging is a subset of risk management. The term usually means buying (or selling) something—like another security, an "option," or your own stock short—which theoretically offsets the risk of what you already own. We will manage risk using simpler techniques.

In this chapter, we will give a general overview of risk management and introduce the individual investor's major tool for sidestepping risk: the sell-stop order. In subsequent chapters, we will focus on several risk management techniques that will improve the quality of your investment decisions. As usual, we will follow the Sensible Stock Investing practice of looking at things from different angles and setting up a system of checks and balances.

Note: This book is only about *stock* investing. It does not cover other asset classes such as cash and bonds. Probably the most fundamental risk management technique for *all* your investment money is to allocate it sensibly across asset classes. Some studies have shown that a very high proportion of your total return on all your money will be determined more by how you allocate it among asset classes than it will be by which stocks you buy with your stock money. Take this with a grain of salt (it is based on indexes, averages, and Buy-and-Hold passivity), but nevertheless it is considered axiomatic to successful overall investing that you spread your money intelligently among the basic asset classes. For example, a basic allocation of 60 percent stocks, 30 percent bonds, and 10 percent cash is not uncommon. To repeat: This book is not about asset allocation; it is about stock investing.

Why Controlling Losses Is So Important

Central to the objective of beating the market is the mathematical reality that large losses must be avoided. If you don't avoid them, it is very hard to make up for them. Consider the following table, which shows what percentage *increase* you need to make up for a *loss* in a stock.

Make-Up Calls

If You Lose This Much in a Stock...	You Need to Gain This Much to Break Even...
5%	5%
10%	11%
15%	17%
20%	25%
25%	33%
30%	43%
35%	54%
40%	66%
45%	82%
50%	100%
55%	122%
60%	150%
65%	186%
70%	233%
75%	300%
80%	400%
85%	567%
90%	900%
95%	1900%

Observation #1: Look at how the "makeup" percentage starts to diverge from the percentage lost when you get up to 10 percent lost. It really accelerates at around the 20 to 25 percent loss mark. If you take a 40 percent loss in a stock, it must reverse itself and go up 66 percent to get back to your purchase price. Sometimes that happens, but often it does not, even after years. This strongly suggests that the Sensible Stock Investor *never* undergo that large an actual loss in a stock: Your chances of making it up are not attractive. In fact, our baseline recommendation is to hold any loss to 10 or 15 percent—no more.

Observation #2: If you glance through the stock tables in any newspaper, you will observe that the difference between many stocks' fifty-two-week highs and lows is often 50 percent or more. Stated another way, about 25 percent up or down is "normal volatility" for many stocks over the course of a year. If you're unfortunate enough to purchase a stock near the highest point it will attain in the year (despite all the safeguards we have against that happening), and it goes *down* 50 percent, it will need to reverse itself and *double* in price to get back to where you started. That is a very difficult hurdle. Normally, you should sell before it ever gets that far.

The sensible conclusions from this should be obvious. You should never take a loss of more than 10 to 15 percent or so in a stock, because it is just too difficult to make up. This is not a psychological inquiry into your "tolerance for risk." It is simply a mathematical observation. So under most circumstances, stick to the shaded areas of the table above. Sell before you lose more than 10 to 15 percent. Anything more is unacceptable.

Simple Disciplines for Lowering the Inherent Risk in Stock Investing

Early in this book, we defined a Sensible Stock Investor as someone who follows common sense, best practices, and sensible risk avoidance, and who devotes a reasonable degree of attention to his or her investments. To put these principles into practice, you must consider whether you will utilize or avoid three common stock investing techniques: Should you "short" stocks? Should you use margin? Should you use options?

The following portfolio management styles are listed from the least risky to the most risky.

Buy Long Only, without Shorting, Margin, or Options

"Long" means that you own a stock. If you are long 500 shares of McDonald's, that means you own 500 shares of McDonald's stock.

A "long only" strategy is the most conservative approach to stock investing. You either own shares of stock or hold your money in cash. You do not attempt to magnify your results by using margin, bet against stocks by shorting them, or hedge your bets by using options. If you own a stock, you hope it goes up. In the words of an old Wall Street saying, you "let your winners run and sell your losers."

This is the strategy that we follow in the real-life portfolios discussed in Part F.

Buy Long and Sell Short, Without Margin

A "long and short" strategy involves both buying stocks long (as just described) and selling them short. In a short sale, you sell stocks that you don't own. Your broker borrows shares (from another investor) and sells them for you. The proceeds from the sale go into your account. At some point, you must buy those shares back and return them to their original owner (this is called "covering" the short).

Selling short is a bet that a stock will go *down* in price. The idea is that you'll make a profit by later purchasing the borrowed shares at a lower price, giving them back to the investor you borrowed them from, and profit on the drop in price. You "buy low and sell high," but in reverse order.

The attraction of short selling is that you can profit when a stock's price *falls*. But shorting stocks increases risk on several fronts:

- While you hold the short position—meaning that you have borrowed and sold the shares but have not yet bought them back and replaced them—you owe the investor from whom the shares were borrowed any dividends that the stock pays.

- Over history, the market has risen, so when you short a stock, the overall market odds are against you from the beginning. You probably would choose to short a stock because you believe it is vastly overvalued. Well, stocks can stay overvalued for years. That's how bubbles happen.

- Your potential losses are unlimited. A stock held long can only go down to zero, meaning you would lose all the money you put into it but no more. A stock sold short can rise in price "infinitely," and you are responsible for the difference, no matter how high it goes.

- You can get caught in a "short squeeze." That is what happens when someone with a short position *is forced* to buy back shares of the stock he's shorted, either because the position has turned against him (the stock's price is going up) or because the original owner of the shares demands them back. In either case, the "squeeze" is that the short position must be covered by buying the shares now, whatever their price.

Shorting stocks is at the very outer edge of acceptable risk for the Sensible Stock Investor. The tools we use (such as rating companies and valuing their stocks) could probably be used for identifying short candidates as well as long candidates. In the end, though, we recommend against shorting altogether.

For one thing, some investors find it problematic to bet against a company rather than root for it—remember, in the company there are probably lots of very smart people trying to make their company great. But the main reason not to use this tool is that while you may be absolutely correct in the long term that the stock is going to decline in value, you can lose lots of money in the short term. Taking a short position exposes you to unlimited losses, while the maximum gain is the cost of the shares sold.

So short sellers get squeezed in all the situations that are normally considered good for investors: The stock's price rising is usually good news, but not if you shorted it. Market rallies and bull markets—which bring most stocks along upward with them—hurt short sellers. An extended bull market or bubble creams short sellers, who must liquidate their positions.

In our real-life portfolios described in Part F, we do not short stocks.

Buy Long Using Margin

This is a more aggressive and risky strategy than the first one. "Using margin" means that when you purchase stocks, you borrow part of the price from your broker. The margin acts as a multiplier of your investment's performance. The multiplication effect works in either direction.

- For example, if you borrow 50 percent of the cost of buying the stocks, the magnification factor is 50 percent if the stock goes up. The math goes like this: You invest $1000 and borrow $500, so your $1000 gets you $1500 worth of shares. If the stock price doubles, you own $3000 worth of shares.

Subtract out the $500 owed the broker and the original $1000 you put in, and your profit is $1500. That is $500 more (or 50 percent more) than if you hadn't used margin.

- The magnification factor works similarly if the stock goes down, but not in your favor. Your $1000 plus the broker's $500 buys $1500 in stock. If the price falls in half—to $750—you're down $500 to the broker plus $250 to yourself, a total of $750, which again is 50 percent more than if you had not used margin.

The use of margin magnifies the risk of stock ownership in other ways. For example, in a margin purchase, the stocks purchased are used as collateral for the loan, and by law or brokerage policy, that collateral must be maintained at certain levels. If the stocks in your account decline in value, so does your collateral, and the brokerage can take actions such as issuing a margin call (i.e., you have to send them money) or selling your stocks out from under you to reconcile the collateral situation. And because margin is a loan, interest must be paid to the broker, thus raising the cost of ownership and making it harder to come out ahead.

For the average individual investor, we recommend staying away from the use of margin. None of the transactions in the demonstration portfolios have been made on margin.

Long and Short Using Margin

This is a combination of approaches #2 and #3. Using the two strategies in conjunction compounds the risks. Therefore we do not recommend this approach for the Sensible Stock Investor.

Using Options

Options are a legitimate way to "hedge" (try to reduce the risk of) stock investing. However, the use of options is a whole different subject, and it is beyond the scope of this book. Therefore, we do not use options.

Sidestepping Losses by Using Trailing Sell-Stop Orders

We said earlier that the Sensible Stock Investor uses a variety of tools to reduce risk and improve his or her probabilities of success. Probably the most important is one that protects you from losses when positions turn against you, allowing you to sidestep the risk entirely.

There is a very effective tool for doing that: the standing, trailing sell-stop order. That is a mouthful, and it is usually shortened to "trailing stop," "sell-stop," or "stop-loss" order. But all the words in the full name contribute to understanding it, so let's use the long version for now and see why each word is significant:

- "Standing" means the order stays in place until you cancel it. Technically the order is referred to as "good until canceled." The standing order—available from every brokerage—is perfect for most individual investors, who are not watching the market every minute. You can go on vacation and your standing order will be ready to protect you while you relax. Another advantage of standing orders is that you decide *in advance* the price at which to trigger the order. That's when you are at your most rational, not in the heat of a quickly moving market.

- "Trailing" means that you reset the order as your stock goes up. You might do this every couple of days, once a week, or at longer intervals. Just do it regularly. Say you have chosen to set a sell-stop order at 10 percent below the stock's current price. If, the next time you look, the stock has gone up 5 percent, you reset the sell-stop order at 10 percent below the new higher price. You have locked in the 5 percent increase in the stock's price. Your order thus "trails" along behind your stock as its price goes up. This is one of the more enjoyable parts of stock investing, resetting sell-stop orders as your stocks go up. (Of course if the stock's price has gone down, you leave the former stop price alone, since it is there to protect you against losses.) It does not take long to review and reset all the sell-stops in a small portfolio—maybe a minute per stock online.

- "Sell" means the order is an order to sell the stock.

- "Stop" means the order is designed to *stop losses*. A "stop" order is an order that sits there doing nothing until the stock's price falls to (or through) the price that you selected. Then the order converts to a market order, meaning it is executed at the next available price. Most stop orders, in practice, are executed at the exact price you designated.

So trailing sell-stop orders are used to limit losses from your purchase price or to lock in the gains of stocks as they advance. By using orders of this type, the Sensible Stock Investor protects himself or herself against backslides by entering stop-loss orders at some percentage or dollar amount below each stock's current price. He or she "trails" the price of the stock as it moves up by increasing the stop price from time to time. Those trailing stops will get you out if the stock suddenly starts to tumble.

Stop-loss orders work like ratchets. Just like a Craftsman wrench that you can set to turn one way but not the other, trailing stop-loss orders allow your stocks freely to go up but lock your profits in when they start to go down.

Setting Stop-Loss Trigger Points

There are several ways to set sensible stop-loss values. Remember, the goal always is to give the stock enough room for volatility (so you don't sell yourself out of a good stock that is just going through normal gyrations), while at the same time being restrictive enough so as not to let any more profits escape than absolutely necessary when an unfavorable trend is forming. You want to neither overreact nor underreact to normal price volatility.

Percentage Below Current Price

This approach is simple: Set your stop-loss order at some percentage below the stock's current price.

Stocks fluctuate all the time. You want to be able to distinguish a clear trend (which should influence your investment decisions) from the "noise" of normal price fluctuations (which should not). That, in brief, is the hold-or-sell challenge for a stock investor:

- On the one hand, you bought the stock with hope of holding it for a long time and in the belief that it represents a leading company that will produce market-beating returns. You bought it fully aware that there would be short-term price swings, which reflect nothing about the stock's long-term performance.

- On the other hand, nothing lasts forever, and there will be times that a falling price reflects the market's recognition that the company's prospects are deteriorating, that its stock is way overvalued, or that the market itself is turning bearish. In each case, the stock's price may have reached an important tipping point, and its drop therefore might be an absolutely valid reason to sell.

How do you know whether weakness in your stock is just temporary or the start of a long-term serious decline? Simply put, you don't. Nobody does until later. If you employ stop-loss orders, you will find from time to time that you are "stopped out" of a stock that, as things turn out, would have been profitable just to hang on to. But that's OK. Cutting losses and preserving gains are so important to overall success that the risk of getting stopped out is preferable to the risk of taking a large loss. And, if a stop-out proves to be a mistake, you can reverse it. As the situation clarifies, nothing prevents you from repurchasing the stock if you decide that the declines were in fact short-lived trading spasms. Plus, you can further manage the risk of mistaken selling by using two or three sell-stops to ease out of your position gradually rather than giving all your shares a single stop price.

In setting sell-stop percentages, it is useful to divide stocks into two categories: Those just purchased, and those that have started to go up since you bought them.

Special rules apply just after you have purchased a stock. We put newly purchased stocks "on probation." As soon as the purchase transaction goes through, set up a stop-loss order at 5 to 10 percent below your purchase price. I usually use 8 percent.

Never stubbornly hold on to a stock just because of the psychological difficulty of admitting you made a bad purchase. Mistaken purchases are just part of the game. The stock may never get back to even. The far better approach is to get rid of an initial loser early. The relatively tight probationary stop-loss orders will do this for you automatically and unemotionally.

Once a stock rises above your purchase price, you should set the stop-loss percentage in accordance with all the information at your disposal. This includes the market timing indicators that will be discussed in Chapter E-5 and the reasons to sell in Chapter E-9. As we will see, there will be times when you want to really tighten up the sell-stops (thus making it more likely that the stock will in fact be sold), and other times when you want to loosen things up (thus making it more likely that the stock will be held).

Dollar Value Based on Stock's Chart

Another way to set the stop-loss trigger value is to examine the stock's chart for the past year or so. (Charts are available from brokerage and financial Web sites.) You may see that while overall the stock has been rising over that time, some significant rises and falls are a normal part of its behavior pattern. The price dips may exceed any reasonable percentage sell-stop that you might normally set. But you don't want to sell the stock based on such dips, because you really believe that the overall trend will be continue to be upward.

In that case, see if you can draw a line on the chart for the past few months connecting the stock's highs and another line connecting its lows. Often, you will find that drawing these lines creates an upward-sloping "channel" that has higher highs and higher lows as you move along in time. The channel represents the stock's overall trend—upward. Its price is volatile within that channel, but it has not escaped it. Typically, the price will seem to "bounce" off the lower edge of the channel, never going lower. It will also occasionally "break through" its highs, going higher and perhaps establishing a new channel at a higher level. Other times, it will "bounce" off the upper trendline, going lower for a while but remaining in the channel.

In using charts, look for trends that extend at least a month, with several months being better. In drawing the "trendlines," try to find at least three days where the highs and lows exactly touch the lines that you are drawing. Extend the lines past the data to the right of the chart. This shows you what may happen if current trends continue, which is what you are hoping for (if the channel is sloping upward).

What you want to do here is to set the sell-stop at the price indicated by the lower edge of the channel. Perhaps provide a tiny cushion by setting the stop price 1 or 2 percent below that lower trendline. What you are looking for is the stock's price to remain within the upward-sloping channel that it has established. If the channel itself is wide, the stop price set in this way may be a higher percentage below the current price than you would normally use (say 20 percent vs. 15 percent), so you are taking more risk with this method. But you do it because the stock has established a recent pattern that you believe is predictive of future behavior. That is, you think that the overall price trend will be upward despite occasional significant dips.

You still "trail" the sell-stop. But instead of trailing it as a set percentage below its current price, you reexamine the chart periodically (say weekly or biweekly), confirm that the channel has not been violated, and reset the stop price at the new lower edge of the channel (again, perhaps with a small cushion). This will be a higher price than the previous one, because there will be one or two more weeks' worth of data, and the trendline itself is upwardly sloping.

Using the Moving Average

This is a variation on the channeling method just described. Most charts allow you to superimpose the 50-day (or some other number of days) moving average line over the stock's price line. For a stock in a long-term uptrend, its price will usually be above the moving-average line (because the price, despite daily volatility, is overall going up, pulling the moving average line with it). The moving average line moves along underneath the stock's actual price. Here's what you are looking for: When the stock has a short-term dip, it seems to "bounce" off the moving average line, always staying at or above it.

Using the same criteria as above (namely, you believe that the overall trend will continue upward), set the stop-loss at the value of the moving average (again perhaps with a 1 or 2 percent cushion to allow for slight variations). This represents the value below which you do not expect the stock's price to go. Reset it weekly or biweekly.

As with the channel approach, you may be taking on more risk here, because the moving average may be 20 percent or even 30 percent below the stock's actual price, a wider margin than you would normally set a stop-loss percentage. So only use this method for stocks in which you have the most confidence.

CHAPTER E-3

Types of Stocks

Stocks Have Personalities

The investment media tend to divide stocks into two principal types: "growth" and "value." This is a crude division. *Growth* stocks are considered the hares of the stock kingdom, fast but frequently changing directions and not necessarily having long-distance stamina. *Value* stocks are the tortoises, steady plodders that can go on forever.

The traditional rule of thumb for telling one from the other is that growth stocks have high valuation ratios, while value stocks have low ratios. For example, some leading sources of information about growth and value stocks distinguish the two by one simple measure: the P/B (price-to-book) ratio, which we explored in Chapter D-3. When analyzing a large group of stocks, such as the S&P 500, they call the half with the highest P/B's the "growth" stocks and the half with the lowest P/B's the "value" stocks.

Dividing the stock kingdom into two broad species—growth and value—can be helpful, but it has too often led pundits into the trap of extrapolating dubious conclusions from this relatively blunt distinction. For example, it leads advisers into recommendations as to how much money an investor "should" have in the two categories (value and growth); studies and stories about which type has done better over the long or short term; which type is doing better right now; and so on.

From a Sensible Stock Investing point of view, all of this must be taken with a grain of salt, for at least three reasons. First, the original measuring stick, the P/B ratio, is one-dimensional. Second, advice about how much money one "should" have in growth and value stocks is based on extrapolations of future performance from historical performance, and as we all know, "past performance does not guarantee future results." And third, the conclusions tend to be based on the (usually unstated) presumption that the investor will passively Buy-and-Hold the stocks by way of index mutual funds—as distinguished from investing in individual stocks and actively managing them.

As Sensible Stock Investors, let us be a little more discerning when characterizing stock types. The proposition suggested here is that companies and their stocks tend to exhibit certain "personality" traits, like humans, and therefore tend to behave in somewhat predictable ways, according to type. That makes sense, because we know that the stock market is really a social system anyway. As with humans, it is rare for a company/stock to be a pure type in all characteristics. But stocks, like people, usually have predominant traits.

Type A Stocks

Type A stocks correspond most closely to growth stocks in the conventional way of thinking. The *A* stands for things like *Alpha male, Aggressive,* or *Attention Required.* Like Type A people, they are characterized by loudness, pushiness, moodiness, volatility, and quick reactions to the environment around them.

Type A stocks tend to have the following characteristics:

* Fast-rising (or fast-plunging) revenues and earnings, well in excess of the economy's (say >20% per year or so)
* High valuation ratios (P/B, P/E, etc.) compared to the overall market
* Youth (say within ten years of first having gone public), or a dynamic "youthful outlook" no matter what their chronological age; in some cases, this translates into immature behavior
* Sensitivity to news, which contributes to volatility
* Tendency to be in "hot" businesses or in "breakout" industries or fields
* No or very low dividends (because their earnings are plowed back into the aggressive pursuit of growth)
* Comparatively heavy debt (they run themselves "on margin")
* Highly acquisitive, with aggressive acquisition programs
* Revolutionary hype (they often like to portray themselves as changing the world)
* Cutting-edge product(s)
* Highly cyclical: Type A's tend to be very sensitive to economic cycles, market trends, and cycles peculiar to their own industry
* Wider price volatility than the market as a whole
* One-trick ponies: Dependent on one or a few products or technologies, maybe a single "revolutionary" product

Because of these characteristics, Type A stocks tend to mesh well with an active trading pattern and least well with a Buy-and-Hold approach.

Type A stocks are often aggressive, risky, speculative investments. They do their best when they are benefiting from powerful secular trends *and* have a strong and growing economy propelling them along. They do their worst when either of those elements is missing. Normally, it is not the best idea to own Type A stocks during the contraction phase of the business cycle. On the other hand, they may be the *best* stocks to own when economic growth is strongest. Stocks like this are often the market leaders when the market is on a roll.

Type B Stocks

Type B stocks (standing for *Big, Buy-and-Hold, Buy on Dips,* maybe *Blue Chips,* sometimes *Boring*) are similar to the value stocks of conventional terminology. They share many characteristics with their Type B human counterparts. They tend to recede into the publicity background (which does not mean they cannot be industry leaders), make less noise, attract less attention, be calmer and steadier, and take a longer view of things. Type B companies and stocks tend to have:

- Steadier earnings and revenue growth (<15 percent or so), probably coupled with a long history of such growth
- Lower valuation ratios
- Less price volatility
- Lower sensitivity to news; they make less news themselves
- Less sensitivity to macroeconomic conditions and business cycles
- Dividends (because not all earnings are recycled to drive growth)
- A well-established history, often decades old
- Significant internally generated growth (sometimes combined with acquisition-driven growth)
- Diversified revenue streams that complement each other
- Low debt; they don't run themselves "on margin"
- A culture that does not always approach things as if there is a revolution to be led; this does not mean that they cannot be the source of important changes, discoveries, or patents, but they don't approach everything in a frenzy to lead the world
- A business model which is not necessarily dependent on important societal change but could also fill perpetual human needs, like beer, bread, razors, diapers, cola, basic materials, cosmetics, industrial goods, energy, and real estate

Because of these characteristics, Type B stocks lend themselves to a more relaxed trading philosophy. For the stockholder, there is less volatility, news, and risk to react to. Because of their long history, successful Type B companies are the kind that you can usually be sure are still going to be around 5, 10, maybe even 25 years from now. They are better suited to the Buy-and-Hold end of the trading spectrum.

Type C

Type C is actually a ringer. It does not stand for a type of stock or company at all but rather for *Cash.*

This is not a trick. To manage a stock portfolio sensibly, cash is a legitimate parking place for "stock money" when:

- You're in a generally declining or sideways market—nothing seems to be doing well
- You're in a deflating bubble, like the 2000–2002 deflation of the late-1990s bubble
- No great stock investment opportunities are apparent
- You are in a protection mode

It is an unfortunate myth of the stock-investment industry—especially the mutual fund end of it—that the smartest investors are "fully invested" at all times. This myth is an obvious corollary of the Buy-and-Hold dogma. It is unfortunate because it is the reason why so many investors who were fully invested when the market peaked in early 2000 stubbornly (or ignorantly) stayed paralyzed in the market all the way down. It's also why many of them will stay fully invested the next time a bubble pops or a bear market claws them up.

The Sensible Stock Investing approach is to try to apply a little more intelligence than that. As we will see in Chapter E-5, "timing" is not a crime. If, for whatever reason, you sell a stock, you may not want to reinvest the money right away. Rather, you may want to hold it in cash for a while, until conditions change for the better. Don't be afraid to be uninvested. If you cannot find enough good places for your "stock money," let it sit in cash until valuations improve, market conditions change, or you discover a promising new investment opportunity. As Warren Buffett said in his 2003 annual letter to Berkshire Hathaway shareholders, "Sitting it out is no fun. But occasionally, successful investing requires inactivity."

Type D Stocks

In Type D stocks, the *D* stands for *Dividends*. Type D stocks are those that have unusually high dividend yields (say 3 to 5 percent or more) and that are often purchased for the very purpose of getting those dividends. The investor is focused at least as much on receiving dividends as he or she is on price gains. Type D's are the high-dividend subset of Type B stocks.

Companies that pay significant dividends tend to be:

- Large
- Well-established, older, mature companies
- Pretty low risk; they are very likely to be around 5, 10, or 25 years from now
- Stable (if not fast-growing) cash generators; many of them are cash machines that easily generate enough cash to fund both internal reinvestment and the payment of the dividends
- Less volatile (because the dividend payout puts a "floor" under their stock price)

High-dividend stocks are intriguing. For one thing, the good ones are fully capable of providing growth in share price in addition to their dividend payout, so total return comes from two significant sources (share price increases plus dividends). For another, not only do they pay real cash back to their shareholders every quarter, but also in most cases those dividend payouts are close to sacrosanct. Paying the dividend is part of the company's culture. Company executives are aware of the dividend history/policy and work actively to maintain it. Not only are dividends not cut, but also many Type D companies have a history—an implicit policy—of *increasing* the dividend regularly. Companies such as Johnson & Johnson, General Electric, and many others have increased their dividends every year for decades.

Because of these increasing dividends—meaning that the actual payout per share goes up—a very interesting phenomenon takes place: Your *percentage yield* as a shareholder will also go up over time. This can happen even though the current dividend yield quoted in the newspaper (say 3 percent) stays more or less the same (because the stock's price is climbing at about the same rate as the dividend payout).

This aspect of dividends is not well understood, so let's see how it happens. Say you purchase a stock when its dividend yield is exactly 3 percent, so for example you invest $1000 and the stock pays you $30 that year. No matter how the stock's price changes over the coming years, *your* yield will always be based on the $1000 that *you* invested in the stock. Let's further say that the company's long-standing practice is to increase its dividend in line with its increasing earnings and that your company—an excellent one, naturally—increases its earnings 10 percent per year. That means in Year 2 the company pays out 10 percent more to you, or $33, so *your* yield that year is 3.3 percent. (It no longer matters what the *current* yield printed in the newspaper is. If the stock's price rises exactly in line with the company's increased earnings, the stock's price next year is also 10 percent higher, so the newspaper will still list the *current* yield as 3 percent. But that only applies to new buyers, not you.) The next year, the company does it again—increases earnings by 10 percent—and pays you a little over $36. Your yield—still based on your $1000 investment—has jumped to 3.6 percent. In this example, it would take about eight years for your stock to be yielding *you* 6 percent, or twice what it was when you bought it. In another eight years, it will be yielding you 12 percent on your original investment, or more than the long-term average *total* return of the stock market itself.

This is the most powerful aspect of Type D companies. It is why investors expect less actual growth in the stock price itself. It is why retirees (looking for income) become attracted to dividend-paying stocks. It is why many income-seeking investors consider dividend-yielding stocks to be more attractive than bonds (whose yields never change). It is why more companies are initiating or increasing dividends in light of the 2003 tax cut on dividends, which renders dividends fully as tax-advantaged as long-term capital gains.

There is risk, of course, that your Type D stock's price will drop, perhaps by an amount equaling the dividend it pays or even more. This risk tends to be relatively small for most well-selected companies, but it still dictates that you keep an eye on how the stock itself is actually doing. That said, most investors will have little reason to trade heavily in their high-dividend stocks. The major attraction is not to make money from price increases, although that is delightful. The major attraction is the dividend itself.

Certain Type D stocks represent companies that are organized specially to be dividend-payers.

- *Real Estate Investment Trusts (REITs).* REITs were created by Congress in 1960. To qualify as a REIT, a company must distribute at least 90 percent of its taxable income annually in the form of dividends. Historically, most of the return from REITs has come from these dividends, although there are periods when they provide an above-average price return to boot. REITs are the only practical way for most individual investors to invest in residential and commercial real estate developments. REITs are liquid, have ticker symbols, and trade just like stocks. Real estate is often recognized as a distinct asset class (beyond the "big three" of stocks, bonds, and cash), so they offer the investor some diversification benefits. Current dividend yields often are 5 to 8 percent or more, right out of the gate for new buyers. Note, REIT dividends do not qualify for the 15 percent federal income tax rate on most dividends; they are taxed as ordinary income.

- *Master Limited Partnerships (MLPs).* These appear mostly in the oil and gas industry. Shares are traded like stocks and are liquid, providing small investors a way to participate in partnerships that otherwise would not be possible. Shareholders become limited partners in the enterprise, meaning that they own an interest in the assets of the business, which in turn entitles them to dividends and other distributions from the business. For example, Kinder Morgan Energy Partners, a long-time holding in this book's portfolios (see Part F), is an MLP. Because the shares trade, there is also the usual potential for capital gain or loss.

Type E—Exchange-Traded Funds

An exchange-traded fund (ETF) is a mutual fund that trades like a stock—it has its own ticker symbol, trades throughout the day, and so on. (Contrast with traditional mutual funds, which are priced only once per day, are bought from and sold back to the mutual fund company, and sometimes have restrictions on how frequently they can be traded.) Each ETF is composed of bundles of stocks that reflect the composition of an underlying portfolio, usually an index. The ETF's value is based on the value of the underlying stocks that it holds. ETFs offer the features of a mutual fund in an instrument that trades like a stock.

Being baskets or indexes of stocks, ETFs do not fit the normal stock-picking criteria of Sensible Stock Investing, and they cannot be rated on our Easy-Rate Sheets. However, since they trade as stocks, they can display momentum and can therefore be purchased on that basis. See "Type M Stocks" in the next section.

Type M Stocks

We will reserve full discussion for the next chapter, but for completeness we list Type M stocks here. *M* stands for *Momentum,* meaning upward velocity of price. As we will see, sometimes it makes sense to invest in a stock exhibiting strong momentum, for no other reason, really, than that it is going up. These tend to be short-term propositions, and not every Sensible Stock Investor will want to get involved with them. Traditional investment advisers generally deride momentum investing, but when done carefully, it can be quite profitable.

Summary

In this chapter, we have created a new, sensible categorization system for companies and their stocks that goes well beyond the "growth" and "value" approach in common use. Our categories are based on how companies and their stocks usually behave, what characteristics they have, what level of risk they present, and what level of potential reward they offer.

To review, these are the categories:

- *Type A.* The alpha males of the stock world. Often move fast. Very sensitive to general economic conditions and news of any sort. Often at the cutting (or bleeding) edge of technological or other kinds of development. High risk/reward profile. High P/E and other valuation ratios. Usually volatile. Issue no dividends. Can be risky to Buy-and-Hold. Better suited to active watching and management.

- *Type B.* More sedate, mature, well-established. Generally steady results. Slower to either grow or shrink. Usually have diverse revenue streams that can cover for each other. Usually issue dividends, sometimes of significant amount. Have more moderate P/E's and other valuation ratios. Usually less volatile than Type A's. Suited to moderately active attention.

- *Type C.* Not a company or stock at all, but rather standing for *cash*. The savvy investor will park at least some of his or her "stock money" away from the market when investment conditions are not favorable.

- *Type D.* Companies/stocks purchased primarily for their dividends. Usually have high yields, plus a long record of disbursing dividends and raising them regularly.

- *Type E.* Exchange-traded funds.

- *Type M.* Momentum stocks.

CHAPTER E-4

Momentum

The trend is your friend.
—Wall Street adage

What Is Momentum?

In stock investing, momentum refers to a persistent change in an important financial number. The number could be earnings, revenue, or the stock's price, to give three examples.

We are going to limit our use of momentum to refer to just the stock's price. Therefore, when we say that a stock "has momentum," that means that its price is showing a persistent change upward—it is trending up and rising steadily.

We are taking the time to talk about price momentum here, because it plays a role in several of the portfolio management topics that will be dealt with further on.

One use of momentum is to spot stocks that might be investment opportunities simply because they *have* momentum. Let's discuss that first.

Momentum Investing

A momentum investor seeks to take advantage of a persistent upward trend in stock prices. The thinking behind momentum investing is that such a trend, once established, will continue until something happens that slows, halts, or reverses the trend. In physics, a body traveling in a certain direction at a certain speed will continue to do so until some force causes it to change direction or speed. Here, the "body" traveling is the stock's price, and the direction of travel is up. The momentum investor believes that the stock's price will continue to go up until some force causes it to slow down, stop, or reverse. That belief finds support in several academic studies, which suggest that recent stock "winners" tend to continue their winning ways.

So a price-momentum investor looks for stocks that are currently "winning," as demonstrated by their recent record of upward price movement, and simply attempts to ride the upward movement. Unlike the methods of picking excellent companies and valuing their stocks discussed earlier in Parts C and D, the pure momentum investor does not worry about earnings or revenue growth rates, the Story behind the company, valuation ratios, or any other fundamental factors. He or she may not necessarily believe that the stock will do well in the long run, but that doesn't matter—the belief is that the trend will continue at least a little while longer.

A pure momentum investor may not know anything about the company or stock other than its ticker symbol and the charts that show that it has momentum. We will improve upon that approach.

While momentum investing may sound like gambling, there are at least four sensible propositions that give it foundation:

- First, the commonsense notion that there may be a bandwagon effect: Many investors are looking for stocks that are "hot," and their collective action creates buying pressure, which leads to increases in the price of the stock. We know that the market is a social/behavioral system, and this is just an example of that system in action. If a stock keeps outperforming the market, more investors discover it and jump on board, sending it even further ahead and attracting more buyers. Thus there is a certain self-fulfilling dimension to momentum investing. The momentum investor figures it will work until it doesn't, at which time he or she will exit gracefully, profits in hand. Momentum reversal can happen quite abruptly and unpredictably, just on a bit of bad news—as when a brokerage house lowers its rating on the stock, or the company misses its consensus earnings number or issues a tepid outlook. But the momentum investor is ready for it, prepared to sell instantly (through the use of tight trailing sell-stops). It should be obvious that momentum investing has nothing to do with Buy-and-Holding.

- Second, because the market is not perfectly efficient, investors sometimes underreact to good news and positive fundamentals. In other words, there are times when the market takes a while to appreciate the full implications of positive news. The market is trying to be rational and efficient, but it can require time for stock prices to catch up to more "proper" values. During this reaction period, the stock's price will generally move upward, creating a trend that the momentum investor can ride. In fact, during the ride, more good news may come in, keeping the buying pressure going and the price rising. Again, the momentum investor—who is, in a way, "front-running" the crowd—rides the trend until it stops or slows down, at which time he or she hops off, profits in hand.

- Third, a generally upward price trend for a stock often indicates that institutions are buying it. Mutual funds, banks, pension plans, college endowments, and hedge funds make up the majority of trading volume each day, so it is likely that persistent buying pressure (leading to rising prices) is largely caused by institutional activity. Might as well follow the money and go where they are going.

- Some research has shown that winners generally keep winning, and losers generally keep losing. Each of the stock-advice newsletters atop the performance rankings of *The Hulbert Financial Digest* for the 5,

10, and 15 years through 1999 used a momentum-based strategy, with "momentum" generally meaning that a stock had outperformed the market over the previous 6 to 12 months.

Distinguish momentum investing from, say, a roulette player who is betting on red because black has come up 10 times in a row. Surely, the gambler thinks, black can't possibly come up an 11th straight time. But the gambler is wrong, because in roulette each spin is totally independent from all previous spins: The probability of red or black is *always* 47 percent on every spin. (The probability is not 50 percent because of the green 0 and 00 slots on the wheel.) In momentum investing, on the other hand, trends—such as ten straight weeks of generally rising prices—are *not* independent from each other. Rather, they are a product of the sentiment in the marketplace, which has a certain continuity to it. The eleventh week is *not* independent from what has gone before.

Does Momentum Investing Have a Place in Sensible Stock Investing?

Because it involves no fundamental analysis of companies and no valuation disciplines, momentum investing is usually criticized in the financial media. Sarcastic terms like "momo players" have arisen to describe creatures like momentum investors. Fundamentalists hate momentum analysis (they would be unlikely to dignify it with terms like "analysis" or "investing"), because it ignores both the actual economics of a company's operations and valuation.

But, in a Sensible Stock Investor sort of way, let's be careful here. Common sense suggests that we can pick out at least one idea from momentum investing that can help us make better investing decisions ourselves: Stocks that are displaying price momentum are likely to continue to go up.

Price trends—the relatively steady movement of a stock's price either up or down—often demonstrably exist. The time frames may be short or long. Trends not only exist but also often persist: A stock that has been strong for a period of time will tend to remain strong, while weak stocks tend to remain weak. Usually, the steady upward price movement of a momentum stock takes place within a band. The stock's price may not go up *every day*, but its price movements occur within a range that is tilting upward. Normal "noise" (day-to-day price volatility) takes place within the band, but the band itself is going up.

Simple examination of price charts shows that many times trend lines or channels can be quite persistent. A general upward trend may last for weeks, months, or years. Even for someone who has no knowledge about what is *causing* the trend, its very existence is there to see. Trends are a graphic representation of investor sentiment. How long a positive upward trend will continue is unknown, but they often last long enough to make us some money.

When we invest on the basis of trends, we must protect ourselves on the downside. But we do that anyway. Some readers may balk at the notion of momentum investing, especially after all the time we spent discussing how to identify excellent companies in Part C and how to value them in Part D. Those points are all still valid. But remember the underlying goal of those discussions was to improve the chances of making successful investing decisions. We have the same goal here: to tilt the playing field in our direction by applying our knowledge about how the stock market works. We tilt it by recognizing the possibilities inherent in the persistence of trends, *combined with* sell-stops to limit our downside risk.

Some pundits say that momentum investing works only in bull markets. Well, that's true (by definition) if you're buying the whole market. But it's not true with individual stocks—some can show strong upward momentum even when the market as a whole is flailing. In the same vein, some pundits say that last year's winners are this year's losers. That's also often true, but so what? For one thing, we're not committed to yearlong holding periods. For another, we use sell-stops to protect ourselves when a stock that was going up starts to go down. The fact that stocks are inconsistent from year to year only matters if you are buying and holding through thick and thin. We generally try to hold only through thick.

How Long Makes a Trend?

We noted earlier the importance of time frames in investing. The time frame of interest here is how long a history of upward price momentum we consider to be sufficient to define a trend. The answer depends on where we lie along the spectrum of day traders to Buy-and-Holders. As usual, we look for a sensible middle ground. Day traders may be satisfied with trends that appear for as little as a few minutes. Buy-and-Holders probably never look at momentum at all, since their intent is to hold their purchases "forever," so any price movement of shorter duration is irrelevant.

For our middle ground, I suggest a minimum period of at least three to four weeks. That is, when we are looking for a stock on the basis of momentum, we will require that the stock have displayed steady upward price movement for at least that long. Longer periods (such as two or three months) are fine too.

In our stock-typing system introduced in the last chapter, stocks purchased on the basis of momentum form a category of their own, called Type M.

How Do You Find Type M Stocks?

There are several ways to find Type M stocks. One way is to simply look up the chart of any stock that comes to your attention as a "tip." You might see that the stock has obvious price momentum, which has persisted for some time.

Another method is to use a simple screen. (Screening tools are available widely on the Internet. They work by scanning all stocks for characteristics you specify.) Here is a Type M screen that I have used:

- Four-week price change at least +10%
- Thirteen-week price change at least +15%
- Twenty-six-week price change at least +20%

- Revenue growth rate at least +10%
- EPS (earnings per share) growth rate at least +15%

Notice that the last two factors are not price-related at all but rather are fundamental company financial factors. I include these in the screen to be sure there's a successful company behind the momentum. It also cuts down on the number of stocks picked up by the screen. Depending on market conditions, this screen usually yields anywhere from 5 to 75 stock candidates (more in a bull market, fewer in a bear market).

Before purchasing any stock identified as a Type M candidate, typically I do a workup on the company using the Easy-Rate system (just as I would with any other candidate). If the company seems good enough, I might purchase its stock without regard to its valuation—making it a true Type M stock. Or I might require a decent valuation—value plus momentum can be a powerful stock-finding technique.

Does it work? It sure does. Here's a great example, taken from the demonstration portfolios discussed in Part F. The stock is eBay. We purchased it three times in 2004. Each time, eBay the company was the highest-rated *company* we had, but the stock carried a Bubble *valuation*, making it ineligible for purchase based on our normal requirements.

But it was hard not to notice that eBay almost always seemed to have good price momentum. To make a long story short, here are the results of the purchases and subsequent sales. (In each case, the sale was triggered by eBay's hitting a 10 percent sell-stop):

- #1: Bought 1/7/04 for $6520, sold 7/8/04 for $8205, 26% increase (52% annualized).
- #2: Bought 8/25/04 for $5129, sold 1/6/05 for $6347, 24% increase (78% annualized).
- #3: Bought 11/4/04 for $5009, sold 1/6/05 for $5288, 6% increase (36% annualized).

To Buy-and-Holders, this kind of trading (three "round trips" in one year!) is crazy. But the trades cost little ($10 apiece), and the profits overwhelm the taxes. Do you think we minded paying the capital gains taxes on these holdings? Not a bit.

Summary Diagram—The Sensible Stock Opportunities Map™

We finish this chapter with a diagram that sums up the Sensible Stock Investor's approach to selecting stocks. We call this diagram the Sensible Stock Opportunities Map™.

SENSIBLE STOCK OPPORTUNITIES MAP

	BUBBLE	POOR	FAIR	GOOD	EXCELLENT
HIGH	POSSIBLE MOMENTUM PLAYS (GROWTH TRAPS)		BEST CANDIDATES (ALL TYPES)		
	NON-CANDIDATES		UNLIKELY CANDIDATES (VALUE TRAPS)		
LOW					

Company's Score (y axis)   **Stock's Valuation** (x axis)

The Map is a type of illustration beloved by consultants, a "two-by-two" diagram that shows the relationship between two variables. The left-hand (or *y*) axis represents the company's score, discussed in Part C. There we saw that under our Easy-Rate system, a company can garner anywhere from 0 to 63 points and that we are usually interested only in higher-rated companies that score in the 30s and 40s.

The bottom (or *x*) axis presents the stock's valuation, discussed in Part D. There we saw that valuations can range from worst ("Bubble") to best ("Excellent"), and again we are normally interested in the better valuations.

The four quadrants of the Stock Opportunities Map are as follows:

Upper Right

This is where all the planets align, and we find excellent companies bearing attractive valuations. This quadrant yields the best candidates no matter the type of stock: A, B, D, or M. If the map were in color, this quadrant would be green, as on a traffic light, meaning that it is safe to proceed.

Lower Right

This quadrant has good valuations going for it but not good companies. Therefore it is a yellow quadrant, meaning exercise caution. It will not yield many legitimate investment candidates. In fact, it is the home of so-called "value traps," stocks that appear attractive because of favorable valuations but can trap the unwary who do not understand that the valuation may be low because the company is a dog.

Upper Left

This quadrant, also a yellow cautionary one, is the home of great companies with unattractive valuations. Normally such stocks are not candidates for the Sensible Stock Investor. In fact, they are "growth traps," stocks that look good because of the company's excellent growth characteristics, but often have no upside, because they are already fully valued (or overvalued) by the market.

However, this quadrant is sometimes also the home of excellent momentum plays, as many Type M stocks are of just this nature—excellent companies with poor valuations. Despite the valuations, investors often bid up the shares of such companies precisely because of their expectations (hopes) for continued strong growth.

Lower Left

This is where all of the planets are out of alignment. It is the home of bad companies with lousy valuations. We would color it red, meaning "Danger—Do Not Enter." Very few (or no) legitimate investment candidates will be found here. If we recommended shorting stocks (which we do not), this would be the first place to look for them.

CHAPTER E-5

Timing

October. This is one of the peculiarly dangerous months to speculate in stocks in. The others are July, January, September, April, November, May, March, June, December, August, and February.
—Mark Twain

What Is Timing?

Timing means selecting the optimum *point in time* to make a transaction—to buy or to sell.

In the investment media, the most common uses of the word "timing" are rather narrow, because of two limiting characteristics that often go unstated:

- The time frames involved typically are short, a few days to a few months. This pertains to both how far back one looks for supporting data and how far into the future the resulting decision is expected to work.
- The reference is usually to "market timing," meaning movements of the whole market, rather than to individual-stock timing.

For reasons that will become clear, Sensible Stock Investors use the term "timing" in a considerably wider sense. For us, "timing" refers to long as well as short periods and to individual stocks as well as the whole market.

Picking the correct time to make an investment decision is often based on data called "indicators," which are key pieces of information considered likely to signal future performance. Anyone, of course, can tell in hindsight what the market *did*. The key to using timing as a successful tool lies in finding indicators that are reasonably predictive of the *future*. Because no person and no indicator can actually predict the future, the best use of timing is to influence, but not totally control, decisions.

Thus, for the Sensible Stock Investor, timing is just another tool in the toolkit. If you wish to sneak a glance ahead, we will employ a tool we call the Timing Outlook. A sample Timing Outlook can be found in Appendix I, Form 4.

To get a handle on timing, we employ indicators like the following:

- *Broad market performance:* We use a broad index (the S&P 500) as a proxy for the whole market. We look for market trends, which are generally consistent movements in one direction or the other. If we become convinced that an uptrend has been established, for example, we may posit that the trend is likely to continue, and therefore we are influenced in the direction of holding or buying stocks. If indicators suggest that the trend is about to reverse or has already reversed, we are influenced to sell.

- *Broad market valuation:* The valuation of the S&P 500 can be computed by aggregating the P/E's of the individual stocks in the index. If the market's valuation ratios get "too high" compared to their historical levels, we might conclude that the market is due for a fall and therefore be influenced to sell. If they get "too low," it points to the opposite conclusion, namely that it is an advantageous time to buy.

- *Individual stock performance:* This is like market timing (first bullet above), but for just an individual stock. It utilizes the same factors. Trends, once established, are presumed likely to continue unless contraindications appear.

- *Individual stock valuation:* This is the same as market valuation, except at the individual stock level. We have already seen (in Part D) that valuation plays a key role in Sensible Stock Investing's timing of stock purchases. We prefer favorable valuation when buying a stock. By the same token, if a stock that we own becomes overvalued (meaning that the market has set its expectations too high for the company's likely earnings growth), that can be an influence toward selling it.

- *The economy and corporate earnings:* At a macro level, a booming economy suggests that corporate earnings are generally going to do well and that therefore stock prices will go up: This is an influence to buy. A receding or slowing economy is an influence to sell. At the individual company level, healthy earnings growth suggests that a company is getting stronger and that its stock price will follow. A deceleration or reversal in earnings growth suggests the opposite.

- *Interest rates:* A booming economy, which is generally good for stocks (and therefore an influence to buy), can however be a precursor of inflation, which the Fed by law must try to control. The Fed's main weapon against inflation is to raise short-term interest rates, which usually slows down the economy, puts upward pressure on all interest rates, and makes interest-based investments more attractive. All of these effects are bad for the stock market, so rising interest rates are usually an influence to sell. Occasionally, and ironically, the market interprets the Fed's decision to raise interest rates as confirmation that the economy is getting better and that inflation will be held in check. When this happens, investor sentiment might actually become more positive toward the stock market for a short period of time.

Does Timing Work?

Timing—especially market timing—has a bad reputation in many quarters. For one thing, it is said, market timing is impossible, because the direction of the market cannot be predicted except by luck. People who believe this argue that any market timing is foolish and that the prudent investor simply buys solid companies and holds on to them for the long term. And in fact, several studies have concluded that many people who try to time the market usually get it wrong and end up buying high and selling low, the exact opposite of what they want.

Other studies have shown that stocks are a mediocre investment if you happen to be out of the market (because you timed yourself out) on the market's best days each year—implying, obviously, that the best course is to stay invested. Market timing, these advisers conclude, is just plain stupid. They say you should simply Buy-and-Hold index mutual funds, ride them through their ups and downs, and have faith that over long periods the market will return its historical 10 to 11 percent.

There is logic in the above reasoning. As we have seen earlier, it is axiomatic that on a daily basis the stock market is very nearly a random proposition. But common sense suggests flaws in the reasoning of those who totally discard timing:

- Their conclusions are almost always based on how market averages and indexes have performed, and we have already seen the dangers in drawing conclusions based on the historical performance of averages. Remember, all indexes are made up of a selection of stocks, and these stocks change over time, so behind the scenes, someone or some system is timing the movement of stocks into and out of the index itself.

- The impossibility of short-term timing (by the day or week) does not logically lead to a conclusion that timing must fail over longer periods of time (months or years). The fact that "daily timing" is random does not lead inevitably to the conclusion that timing over longer periods is also random. It's like concluding that Ted Williams was a bad hitter because he went 0-for-4 in one game. Trends that are invisible or hidden by "noise" over very short time periods may be clear over longer time periods. We know that certain macro factors—such as the direction of interest rates and the health of the overall economy—have fairly predictable effects on the stock market. Common sense suggests that the investor try to take advantage of that knowledge in a reasonable manner.

- When you are an individual investor, it is like running your own little business or mutual fund. You want to run it intelligently. Now, the excellent companies that you select do not ignore timing in running their own businesses. That is, they do not mindlessly charge ahead with relentless product introductions, marketing campaigns, acquisitions, and so on, regardless of the economy, interest rates, and their own industry's conditions. Instead, they study their markets, identify trends and changes in their industry, and adjust their actions through a continual process of strategic evaluation. They manage risks. They ask questions like, "When should we launch this new product?" and "Should we close down or divest this particular product line?" Why would you expect anything less of yourself as an investor? Why would you passively hang on to all your stocks during an extended period of obvious market decline, such as 2000–2002? It does not make sense.

- Even those perceived to be the most conservative stock investors—"value" investors—in fact practice timing, whether they acknowledge it or not. They practice timing at the individual stock level. They do it every time they decide not to purchase a stock because it does not meet their valuation criteria ("We're waiting for a better price"), decide to purchase a stock because it *does* meet their valuation criteria ("The price looks good right now"), or decide to sell a stock because it has met their target price ("We think this stock has had its run…we are very disciplined about selling when a stock hits our target price"). What can you call these actions *other* than timing?

- As for being out of the market at the wrong time, Laszlo Birinyi Jr. of Birinyi Associates (an investment research firm in Connecticut) has shown that being *in* the market on the *worst* trading days has much more of a negative impact on total performance than being out on the best days. As reported in *Money* (November 2003), Birinyi's analysis showed that if you were out of the S&P 500 on the five best trading days each year from 1966 to 2002 (and fully invested at all other times), you would have *lost* 90 percent of your money. But if you were out of the market on the five *worst* trading days each year over the same time span, you would have generated a 125,900 percent return. Once again, the importance of avoiding catastrophic losses is underscored as the real key to success in stock investing.

- As reported in his book *Ordinary People, Extraordinary Wealth* (2000), Ric Edelman notes the following: $10,000 invested in the market in 1927 and held there through 1998 would have become $21 million, or a 13.4 percent average annual return. But if someone were a *perfect* market timer (Edelman does not specify whether that is down to the day, week, month, or year) and sold those stocks just before they were about to go down and repurchased them just before they were to go up again, he or she would have increased the value of that $10,000 to $54 *trillion* at the end of 1998.

Faced with statistics such as these, doesn't it make sense that even if you cannot be *perfect* about timing, it is worth *trying* to find ways to ride advancing trends and to preserve capital (by holding it in cash) during declining trends? Given the vast potential difference in returns, that is the Sensible Stock Investor's conclusion: Over long periods, the use of timing techniques can help you reduce or avoid losses during falling markets and participate in gains during rising markets.

Therefore, we make timing a part of the Sensible Stock Investor's toolkit. In addition to utilizing knowledge about *a company* and *its stock's valuation* before we make a move, the Sensible Stock Investor will also utilize information about the economy, interest rates, the stock's individual performance, and the market itself to nudge up the quality of his or her investment decisions.

Note the familiar Sensible Stock Investing themes in this approach. First, we don't adopt an extreme point of view about timing but instead find a reasonable middle ground based on the evidence—we use it when it is useful, but we are not slaves to it. Second, timing is but one of the multiple perspectives we use to reach investment decisions, confident that a multifaceted approach is more likely to lead to better results.

Does Timing Lead to Too Much Trading?

One of the criticisms of timing is that it inevitably leads to heavy trading. But as we will see, the amount of trading that timing may induce depends on how *finely* you try to time. The smaller the time period that you examine for an investable trend, the more the trading, with the extreme being day traders who hold their stocks for only minutes or hours. Timing approaches that view time in bigger chunks (say at least a month or several months), or which use indicators that change less rapidly (such as long moving averages), generally lead to proportionately less trading. The trick is to find the happy medium where the benefits of timing outweigh the extra work and costs of doing it.

Our use of timing will not signal either the perfect time to buy or the perfect time to sell. No system can do that. Rather, our sensible goal will be to identify when the *odds are improved* of buying at lower prices and selling at higher ones. When we do a decent job with it, timing will help us capture the major portion of market uptrends and get us out during prolonged downturns.

In adopting our moderate approach to timing, we

- don't worry that many famous experts severely criticize any attempt at timing and paint timers as fools; and

- do what we can to intelligently apply what we believe are the usual effects of the economy, interest rates, and market trends to improve the quality of our investment decisions.

How Long Are We Talking About?

If we are going to use timing indicators, we must address how long a period is going to be of interest to us. We know that very short periods (an hour, a day) are not worth considering, but we don't know yet how long a period *is* worth considering.

This is an important issue, and the answer is not at all obvious. For example, it is generally agreed (in retrospect) that the stock market overall was in an extended bull run from 1982 to early 2000. During that period, the S&P 500 rose about 1100 percent in value. Does that mean it went up every day for 18+ years? No. Every week? No. Every month? No. Every year? There was only one slightly down year (1990, down 3.1 percent). But *within* three other years there were significant periods of sharp decline:

- August 1987 to December 1987—34% drop in the S&P 500

- July 1990 to October 1990—20% drop

- July 1998 to August 1998—19% drop

In addition to those "crashes," there were other numerous corrections (10 percent drops) that subsequently reversed themselves. And of course the whole nineteen-year bull market ended with the slow-motion but relentless decline of March 2000 to October 2002, which took the S&P 500's value down 49 percent and the NASDAQ Composite's down 76 percent. (Note to Buy-and-Holders: That 49 percent drop in the S&P 500—which is the basis of many index-based mutual funds—will take a *100 percent* increase to get back to even.)

In the literature, you will find extensive and contradictory statements of how long is the "right" time over which to measure such things as bull markets, bear markets, and what we might as well call investable trends. For example, perhaps the 1982–2000 period should not be viewed as a single extended bull market. Maybe it is better seen as two bull markets, separated by the 34 percent crash in 1987. Maybe it was four bull markets, interrupted by the three crashes listed above. Certainly investors who were able *at the time* to see finer gradations (and act correctly on them, both buying and selling) achieved far better investment results than those who simply rode the market straight through from 1982 to 2000, as good as that was.

The same question about what is the "right" length of time by which to measure a trend arises when the market is going down. The torturous erosion of 2000–2002 is now clearly a period where the bubble of the late 1990s was deflating. Certainly those investors who were astute enough to exit the market sometime during the erosion are glad they did compared to Buy-and Holders who rode it all the way down. But even *within* the 2000–2002 bear market, there were several significant periods (more than a month long) when the market went up. Do we want to measure time so short that we could call those investable trends?

Is there general agreement about *anything* when it comes to defining what is "long term" in the stock market? Actually, there is: 10 to 15 years. That is, it is difficult to find any credible literature that would not accept 10 to 15 years as long enough to count as "long-term" and therefore as qualified to establish an investable trend. Here are three recent sources that support this:

- The lead article in the February 2005 edition of *The Hulbert Financial Digest*, entitled "How Long Is the Long Term?" written by Mark Hulbert, concludes that 10 years qualifies as long-term. Hulbert's methodology was designed to identify the minimum length of time required to eliminate the element of luck in investment newsletter performance.

- *Bull, A History of the Boom, 1982–1999* (2003), by Maggie Mahar, cites extensive research that leads her to conclude that the market moves in 15- to 20-year cycles and has been doing so since 1882. That is, up cycles of 15 to 20 years are followed by down (or sideways) cycles of about the same length, which are then followed by another up cycle. (The only shorter cycle was the steep upward climb of 1922 to 1929 that preceded the Great Depression.)

- *Yes, You Can Time the Market* (2003), by Ben Stein and Phil DeMuth, citing extensive original research, reaches a 15-year answer to the question. In a nutshell, the book concludes that the S&P 500 index, when purchased at "low" valuations and held for 15 or more years, has always produced market-beating gains, no matter what happened in the interim. The authors identify low valuations as occurring any time the real S&P 500 dips below its 15-year moving average.

From a Sensible Stock Investing point of view, why try to cut it any finer than 10 to 15 years? For several reasons:

- A decade is a *long time* to wait for results. Although your lifetime investing horizon is longer than that, it is human nature to wish to see the fruits of your investments materialize before 10 to 15 years. Plus, you might need the money in the interim, meaning that you can't wait that long.

- Fifteen years is a long time to wait to *invest*. Under the Stein/DeMuth approach, for example, no stock investments should be made unless the real S&P 500 is below the 15-year moving average of one of several measures of valuation. Under this constraint, fewer than half the years qualified for stock investing over the last century.

- We know that the market has significant ups and downs that take place over much shorter periods of time than 15 years. *Bull* repeatedly suggests that any investment in the 1996–2000 time was foolish, because the market was already showing signs of being overvalued and would eventually come to a bad end. But really—the market (as measured by the S&P 500 index)—went *up* by a factor of almost 2½ from the start of 1996 to the end of 1999 (even including the short-lived 19 percent drop in 1998). Does that sound like a bad time to have been invested in the market? Does it sound like too short a time to be able to recognize a trend? Didn't it make sense for an investor to have tried to cash in on that incredible advance? It sure does, so long as he or she had a strategy for how to *get out* of the market near its peak in 2000.

So we need a "prediction horizon" for timing, just as we did for companies. While it is clear that the market is unpredictable over periods as short as a day or a week, let's work with the proposition that we can find indicators that give us a significantly better than random chance of being directionally correct about the market over periods of, say, more than a month. If we can find such indicators, we can improve the quality of our investment decisions without having to wait out 15-year cycles. These better decisions, in turn, will help us beat the market, our ultimate goal.

Sensible Market Timing Indicators

As stated earlier, "indicators" are key pieces of information that may be predictive of future performance. Thus, they are signals whether to buy, hold, or sell. We'd like to be more fully invested when the market is going up, and less fully invested—or entirely in cash—when the market is going down. Indicators can help us toward that goal.

Because we are individual investors who do not spend all day studying the market, the best indicators for us must be (1) readily available, (2) free, and (3) easily understood. It turns out that we can find such indicators without too much trouble.

All eight of the indicators discussed here meet those criteria. We will use these indicators in constructing a monthly Timing Outlook. A sample Timing Outlook is displayed in Appendix I, Form 4.

Four of our eight indicators are found on the Web site FundAdvice.com. Their indicators are presented in the form of green "up" arrows and red "down" arrows. Because those images are so clear, we will use that "arrow" approach for all of the indicators discussed here. The current status of the FundAdvice.com indicators is always available on their Web site. Furthermore, simply by signing up (at no charge), they will send you an e-mail whenever one of their indicators changes. We encourage you to sign up for those notifications.

1. Macro Economic Indicator

As we have seen earlier (Chapter B-3), the market tends to move ahead of the business cycle, because so many stock investors are trying to anticipate the business cycle, and they often get it right. GDP (Gross Domestic Product) is the measure of the overall economy—all the goods and services produced in the United States. The Fed's target growth rate for GDP appears to be around 3.5 to 4 percent per year. Anything in that range or higher we can consider to be strong economic growth (good for stocks), anything less than that (but above zero) is weak growth (not so good for stocks), and anything below zero (i.e., actual contraction of the economy) is considered to be recessionary if it persists (very bad for stocks).

With that in mind, it would be helpful to have a timing indicator with a historic record of projecting where the economy is going over the next few months. It turns out that there is such an indicator, The Conference Board's "Index of Leading Economic Indicators." This "Leading Index" used to be compiled by the U.S. Department of Commerce, but it was turned over to the Conference Board in late 1995. The so-called "Leading Index" is updated monthly, and the update is discussed in a press release available free at the Web site Conference-Board.org, under the tab labeled "Economics." The Index is also widely reported and discussed in the financial and popular press.

The Leading Index blends ten economic data elements that in the past have often been precursors of the broad economy. The Conference Board combines these ten indicators into a single number using a proprietary formula. The Leading Index is designed to signal coming peaks and troughs in the business cycle.

For us, what matters is not the Leading Index's absolute level, but rather its direction. If the Index is rising, that bodes well for the economy. If it is falling, that suggests a slowdown is ahead.

A simple timing indicator can be created from the Conference Board's monthly press release. If the Index rises for three (or more) consecutive months, it merits a green "up" arrow. If it falls for three or more consecutive months, give it a red "down" arrow. If it keeps fluctuating without going three straight months up or down, give it a neutral "sideways" arrow.

As is our practice throughout Sensible Stock Investing, we use a point system to quantify timing indicators. For each indicator, a green "up" arrow gets +10 points, a neutral "sideways" arrow gets +5 points, and a red "down" arrow gets 0 points. The points will be aggregated and interpreted on our monthly Timing Outlooks as explained a little later.

2. Interest Rate Indicators

Stable or declining interest rates are usually good news for the stock market, while rising interest rates usually are not. We can take advantage of this correlation to create simple interest rate market-timing indicators. One is our own, while the other comes from FundAdvice.com.

Interest Rate Indicator #1: While not all interest rates are determined by the Fed—there are separate bond and mortgage markets in which interest rates are free to find their own levels—most interest rates' *directions of change* eventually match what the Fed does in setting the short-term interest rates that it controls. That is, when the Fed lowers its interest rates, most other interest rates follow downward, and when the Fed raises its rates, most other rates trend upward. Generally speaking, a rate around 4 percent is considered to be "neutral." So it is a combination of the actual Fed rate plus the direction the Fed is moving it (or leaving it alone) that seems to influence the stock market.

We can use this knowledge to create a simple interest rate indicator:

*   If the current rate is 3.5 percent or below *and* the Fed lowers rates (by any amount), our market indicator is a green "up" arrow (+10 points). By lowering rates well below "neutral," the Fed is clearly trying to boost the economy.

*   Similarly, if the Fed lowers rates (from any starting point) *three times in a row*, the indicator is also a green "up" arrow. Again, the Fed is clearly trying to boost the economy. (The Fed meets eight times per year.)

*   If the current rate is 4.5 percent or above *and* the Fed raises it (by any amount), our indicator is a red "down" arrow (which gets 0 points on our rating system). By raising rates well above "neutral," the Fed is clearly trying to slow things down and fight inflation. A slowing economy's overall impact on the market is likely to be negative.

*   Similarly, if the Fed raises rates *three times in a row*, no matter what the starting point, the indicator is a red "down" arrow. The Fed is clearly trying to cool down the economy.

*   Under any other conditions, the indicator is "sideways," or neutral (+5 points).

Interest Rate Indicator #2: A second interest rate indicator is one of the four indicators available from FundAdvice.com. Their indicator does not look directly at what the Fed is doing but rather at rates in the corporate bond market. (The complete formula is explained on the FundAdvice.com Web site.) Their indicator is either green "up" (+10 points for us) or red "down" (0 points). It has no neutral position. According to the Web site, this indicator changes only about once per year on average.

3. Market Valuation Indicators

Market Valuation Indicator #1: A variety of research studies have attempted to determine what is the long-term "average" valuation of the market. The studies have used different methodologies, covered different time periods, employed different ways of defining "the market," and examined different valuation ratios (with the trailing P/E ratio being most common).

Fortunately, most of the studies end up in approximately the same place: They conclude that the long-term average valuation of the market is in the neighborhood of a trailing P/E of 16–18. In recent years, the market's average P/E has been climbing. For example, see YesYouCanTimetheMarket.com, which shows the most recent 15-year moving average of the S&P 500 hovering around 20.

Let's use 20 as our benchmark for a "normal" P/E for the market in current times. Then, leaving 10 percent as a cushion for a safety zone on either side, we will say that:

- a market with a P/E under 18 is "undervalued," poised to go up, and gets a green "up" arrow (+10 points);

- a market with a P/E between 18 and 22 is "fairly valued" and gets a neutral "sideways" arrow (+5 points); and

- a market with a P/E over 22 is "overvalued," poised to go down, and gets a red "down" arrow (no points).

The P/E of the S&P 500 is available at most financial Web sites, updated to the day. (You can often find it displayed beside each stock's individual P/E for comparison purposes.) It also appears on the YesYouCanTimetheMarket.com Web site, updated to the end of the preceding month.

One might question why we do not use *forward* P/E ratios here, since we are supposed to be peering ahead in time. One simple answer is that forward P/E ratios have not been correlated to market movements, even though the concept sounds sensible. Another is that forward P/E ratios involve estimates of earnings rather than actual reported data. If the use of trailing P/E ratios is a deficiency, the next indicator makes up for it.

Market Valuation Indicator #2: The stock and mutual fund research company Morningstar makes available another easy-to-use market valuation indicator. They maintain a free graph on their Web site showing the aggregate ratio of their "fair value estimates" of all the stocks that they cover to the actual prices of those stocks. Their graph shows directly whether they consider their universe of stocks to be undervalued or over-valued. Their universe of stocks is large enough that we can consider it to be a proxy for the whole market. Again, let's use a 10 percent cushion for safety: If the graph is within 10 percent of "fair value," give it a neutral sideways arrow (+5 points). If the graph shows the market more than 10 percent overvalued, give it a red "down" arrow (0 points), while more than 10 percent undervalued earns a green "up" arrow (+10 points). The graph can be found at Morningstar.com. Click on "Markets" and then on "Market Valuation Graph."

4. Market Trend Indicators

As we saw in the chapter on momentum (Chapter E-4), we presume that a market trend, once established, is likely to continue until contrary data appears. Thus, we will be influenced to buy when the market is on the way up and sell when it is on the way down.

We need an indicator that signals market trends. Happily, three such indicators are available to the individual investor at FundAdvice.com.

Market Trend Indicator #1: This is a basic trend identifier based on the simple moving average of the S&P 500 Index. Under this system (which is explained in more detail on the FundAdvice.com Web site), a green "up" arrow is generated when the Index crosses (upward) through its 150-day moving average. A red "down" arrow is generated when the Index moves (downward) through the 150-day moving average *and* falls 2 percent or more below it. This indicator generates about three to four new signals per year. It supports our ground rule that a trend should be fairly well established before acting upon it.

Market Trend Indicator #2: FundAdvice.com has a second trend model based on "breadth" of stocks rising or falling on the NASDAQ. "Breadth" is the ratio of stocks going up to stocks going down. In a rising market we expect more stocks to be rising than falling, while the opposite is true in a falling market. The FundAdvice.com model uses the NASDAQ's ratio of rising to falling stocks, with a cushion built in to keep the model from fluctuating too much. This indicator generates about seven new red or green signals per year. Note that the numerous switchbacks suggest that the NASDAQ has a high percentage of Type A stocks and is therefore pretty volatile.

Market Trend Indicator #3: Also from the FundAdvice.com Web site, the final market trend indicator is similar to #2, but it uses breadth on the NYSE instead of the NASDAQ. It generates a little more than three new signals per year on average (about half the NASDAQ—the NYSE is less volatile).

Using the Timing Indicators

So we have identified eight timing signals. Since the Sensible Stock Investor is dealing in individual stocks, not indexes, we need to relate those market indicators to our own decisions to buy, hold, or sell individual stocks. Our goal is to improve the odds of making successful "buy low, sell high" decisions. We want to be very conservative when the market is in a downward trend. While we want to ride rising stocks as far as possible, we protect ourselves on the downside by using trailing sell-stop orders.

Here, then, is how to use the timing indicators. First, keep your record of the indicators up to date. For example, when the Fed raises or lowers interest rates (they meet eight times per year, and their decisions are widely reported), change that indicator immediately. Sign up for the free e-mails from FundAdvice.com, which tell you when any of their four indicators changes. Check the Conference Board Web site monthly, soon after its press release is posted (usually in the third week of the month—the release dates are posted on the Web site). At the same time you do that, check the S&P 500's valuation and Morningstar's graph too. That gives you all the data you need to complete your Timing Outlook. Again, see the sample in Appendix I, Form 4.

Second, use this simple scoring system to interpret what the indicators are telling you:

- For each indicator, red = 0, neutral = +5, and green = +10. Add them up and divide by 8 to find the average of the indicators. A perfect score would be 10.

- Divide the 0–10 range of possible scores into three parts. At the low end, consider the market to be overvalued if the timing score is below 4.0. If it is, be cautious. Set tighter sell-stops. Don't be overeager to invest cash.

- If the score is in the middle, 4.0 through 7.0, consider it neutral—the market is about fairly valued. Take a "normal" Sensible Stock Investor approach to buying and selling.

- At the upper end, if the timing score is over 7.0, that is a bullish indicator. It suggests that the market is undervalued. Be optimistic—but not irrational!

Thus, when you are considering whether to actually invest some of your "stock money," use the indicators to speed you up or slow you down. A timing score of over 7.0 suggests that you want more (or all) of your "stock money" actually in the market. Be willing to buy when you see a good opportunity. On the other hand, a score around 5 or 4 suggests that you want less of your "stock money" actually invested. Slow down your purchases and demand better valuations before you buy. Be willing to let some of your money rest in cash until the indicators improve.

On the sell side, use the indicators to tighten or loosen your standing stop-loss orders. Particularly use the timing score to protect against losses. If the timing score is 4.0 or less, tighten your stop-loss levels; that is, set them closer to the actual current prices of your stocks. So if your regular stop-loss percentage on a stock is 15 percent, consider tightening it to 10 percent or even less. This will have the effect of taking more money out of the market, because it will make it more likely that the stop-loss orders are actually triggered. This is what you want when the market is generally falling.

The Presidential Cycle

There is one other timing consideration you may wish to use, although we do not incorporate it here. Historically, the third year of each four-year presidential cycle is by far the best for stocks. As reported in *SmartMoney* (March 2004), the average annual total return for the S&P 500 from 1952 to 2003 has been about 6 percent in year one of the presidential cycle, 8 percent in year two, 23 percent in year three, and 11 percent in year four. The theory is that in the third year, the administration emphasizes economic stimuli to gain favor for the coming election campaign. And as a matter of fact, in the most recent cycle, year three (2003) produced a gain of 26 percent and year four (2004) produced 9 percent, just about matching the historical figures.

Timing Summary

Because timing is just one facet of our multidimensional approach to Sensible Stock Investing, we will use these indicators to influence (but not absolutely determine) our buy, hold, and sell decisions.

Let's illustrate this with an example. Check out the sample Timing Outlook in Appendix I, Form 4. From that sample, here was the situation on January 23, 2006:

- **Conference Board Index of Leading Economic Indicators:** After going up and down for about a year, this indicator finally put together three straight months of growth. Thus it got a green "up" arrow. **+10**

- **Fed interest rate indicator:** On 12/13/05, the Fed raised rates 1/4 percent for its thirteenth consecutive meeting, to 4.25 percent. Their accompanying statement seemed to soften their stance on how much longer this will go on, but that does not save this from being a red arrow down. **+0**

- **FundAdvice.com's interest rate indicator** (their #2 indicator) has been red for about a year. **+0**

- **Morningstar's S&P 500 P/E ratio** rose from 21.1 to 21.9, still in the neutral range. **+5**

- **Morningstar's Market Valuation Graph** rose from about 6 percent overvalued to 7 percent overvalued, remaining neutral. **+5**

- **FundAdvice's S&P 500 trend indicator** (their #1 indicator) has been green since 11/1/05. **+10**

- **FundAdvice's NASDAQ breadth indicator** (their #3 indicator) has been oscillating regularly, most recently turning green. **+10**

- **FundAdvice's NYSE breadth indicator** (their #4 indicator) turned green 11/8/05. **+10**

So we have four greens, two neutrals, and two reds—a mixed bag. If we average out the point values, we get 6.3, in the middle range, suggesting that the market is just about fairly valued.

Here's how to interpret those results:

- In terms of using these indicators to set sell-stops, at a level of 6.3 we should be setting our sell triggers right around their "default" percentages. The mixed bag of indicators suggests neither a strong headwind nor a strong tailwind from the market on particular stocks. The actual stop-loss point for each stock is subject, of course, to unique factors pertaining to the individual stock.

- In terms of investing new cash, or reinvesting cash obtained when a price drop has triggered a sale, our neutral score suggests that we should exercise about a normal amount of caution. We should be willing to invest new cash if we identify a promising opportunity, but we will not feel a need to be fully invested. Cash is fine if good opportunities are not apparent.

CHAPTER E-6

Concentration and Diversification

How Many Stocks Should You Own?

How many stocks you have in your portfolio is a fundamental issue in any stock investing strategy. As we have seen repeatedly in developing our Sensible Stock Investing principles, the possible answers range from one extreme to the other. You can opt to own just one stock, "several" stocks (say 5 to 20), "a lot" of stocks (say 50 or more), or "every" stock in the market (as you would get—sort of—if you simply purchased a broad index mutual fund).

Although Andrew Carnegie once famously said, "Concentrate: Put all your eggs in one basket, and watch that basket," no credible financial adviser advises putting all your money into just one stock. Remember the unfortunate employees of Enron, many of whom had the bulk of their retirement money in Enron stock and saw it wiped out when the company collapsed. The risk of a one-basket strategy is just too high. The potential reward may be huge, but the risk of near total loss renders it an empty strategy.

At the other end of the scale, *many* financial advisers advocate a high level of diversification, and an important school of investment philosophy advocates "owning the market" by owning broad index funds rather than individual stocks. Since our goal is to beat the market, owning the market obviously will not work. So we must address the issue of just how many stocks make up a Sensible Stock Investing portfolio.

The correct point on the spectrum is to hold a portfolio of between 5 and 15 stocks, perhaps 20 at most. If they are truly your best ideas, and they are performing well, it is better to add your new "stock money" to them rather than keep buying different stocks. As your holdings creep beyond 20 stocks, that may be a sign that you are unsure of choices already made—that's why you keep buying different things. If a new opportunity absolutely cries out for investment, consider selling one of your worst-performing stocks rather than adding to the total number of stocks you own, so that you keep your total portfolio under about 20 or so individual stocks.

How Much Should You Diversify?

Note: The discussion here concerns diversification across *stocks only*. It does not address the allocation of all of your investable money across the spectrum of *asset classes*—cash, bonds, and stocks. Here, we are only talking about how you distribute your "stock money."

Diversification is related to but is not the same as how many stocks you own. After all, you could own 50 technology stocks. You would have lots of stocks, but you would not be diversified.

Rather, diversification refers to what *kinds* of stocks you own, in the sense of their being different from each other along some meaningful scale. Clearly, diversification implies owning more than one or two stocks. But that number does not have to be overly large. A 10- or 15-stock portfolio can be surprisingly diversified, depending on what stocks are in it.

"Diversify, diversify, diversify" is practically a mantra in the popular financial media, and it is promulgated reflexively by many investment advisers. But is it really good advice, especially if taken to extremes? Let's forget the dogma for a moment and take a commonsense look.

Statistically speaking, the more you diversify, the more likely you are to get market-average returns. Since the whole goal of Sensible Stock Investing is to beat the market, then by definition we've got to focus on stocks that do better than average. The more stocks you pick in an attempt to diversify, the less likely they are to outperform the market in the aggregate, because your combined holdings become more *like* the market.

In addition, the mantra is based on a Buy-*and*-Hold mentality. Diversification does provide protection of sorts when different parts of the market are underperforming. But we have a more direct way of protecting ourselves: through our disciplined sell-stop system.

That said, common sense suggests that a certain level of diversification is advisable, because it ameliorates "stock selection risk"—the risk that you have picked some bad stocks. So the sensible approach to diversification is to do it, but in moderation.

There are lots of scales along which diversification can be considered. You can spread your money

- across various *sizes* of companies, such as large-cap vs. mid-cap vs. small-cap;
- across *industries* or *major sectors of the economy*;
- based on *stock type,* that is, among Types A, B, D, and M stocks;
- based on *country of origin*;
- between stocks in *emerging* markets versus stocks in *mature* markets;
- between old-line *stalwart companies* and exciting *new companies*.

Because of our emphasis on the evaluation of *individual* stocks, Sensible Stock Investing's position is simply to stay away from the extremes. We suggest that you not put all your eggs in a single basket but also that you not "diversify, diversify, diversify" either. So:

- Don't overstress diversification. Your money should be concentrated in the most desirable opportunities. Remember, you are protected on the downside by your sell-stops. Don't be afraid to be "overweighted" in one or two industries if you feel they offer the best opportunities. And don't be afraid to ignore certain industries entirely.

- But don't understress diversification either. Do not put all your eggs in one basket. Instead, shoot for a "well-rounded" portfolio within the stocks that you own. Diversify across the various dimensions listed earlier, focusing always on your best ideas and opportunities.

You might also consider setting up a couple of different portfolios that have different strategic objectives. Risk can then be managed by owning portfolios that have different basic characteristics. For example, you might have one portfolio that tilts toward Type A stocks (and therefore toward volatility, excitement, high growth potential, more risk, and probably a higher rate of trading), and another which tilts toward Type B and D stocks (and therefore toward less volatility, less trading, less attention, and a higher percentage of your returns coming from dividends). In fact, that is exactly how the two demonstration portfolios in this book are constructed (see Part F). Even if you have multiple portfolios, however, the maximum number of stocks should stay at or below 15, maybe 20 at the outside.

Summary

So we have established four Sensible Stock Investing principles regarding the number of stocks to own and the question of diversification:

- Limit your portfolio to between 5 and 15 stocks.

- Don't put all your eggs in one basket. Probably no more than 25 percent of your stock money should be in any single stock, but don't sell a winner that is still winning.

- Make your portfolio "well-rounded" within the 5- to 15-stock target.

- Consider having more than one portfolio, each governed by different objectives and strategies. The total number of stocks in all portfolios, however, should still adhere to the 5- to 15-stock guideline, perhaps 20 at most.

CHAPTER E-7

Articulating Your Stock Investment Strategy

Insanity: doing the same thing over and over again and expecting different results.
—Albert Einstein

Run Your Investing Like a Business

Any well-run company has long-term objectives or goals, backed up by thoughtful strategies and programs that management thinks will achieve the goals. So too should your "personal investing company." In other words, the Sensible Stock Investor runs his or her investing activities like a business. Think of it as (Your Name) Investment Company.

There is no one right way to invest in stocks. But you should have your strategies down. The whole idea for having strategies is to implement them. They remind you of your investment goals and how you intend to achieve them. They take those fleeting temptations to bounce from one approach to another out of the equation. The strategic point of view is long-term, your investing as seen from an eye in the sky. You want an approach that is going to work for a long time—even if it involves active short-term trading.

Write Out Your "Constitutional Documents"

Operating in a true businesslike fashion, the Sensible Stock Investor writes out his or her stock investment objectives, plus the strategies and tactics designed to meet those objectives. You can call these whatever you like: your "Investment Policy Statement," your "Stock Investment Mission and Strategies," your "Stock Profile Declaration," whatever. They are Your Investment Company's "constitutional documents," the highest-level statements of your mission, objectives, approach, and expected results. Writing them out is an important step to committing yourself to disciplined investing.

Once written, they do not have to be rigid or unchanging. You should visit these fundamental statements from time to time (say annually), making adjustments both as your life progresses and as you learn more and become a better investor. Reconsidering your fundamental objectives and strategies will help keep you anchored emotionally. If worrying about the market is keeping you up at night or distracting you from your work or relationships, then you have not adopted a strategy that is right for you.

Investing should be fun, and a game player's attitude helps to do it well. That said, building wealth for your future should be taken seriously. You should manage it in a coolly rational fashion. Be dispassionate. In Your Investment Company, you do not have to worry about difficult human factors (like laying people off), so you can afford to be totally businesslike.

Universal Strategies

Your chosen portfolio management path should be governed by your overall time horizon, the inherent riskiness or speculativeness of certain approaches, your tolerance for risk, the time you have (or wish) to spend managing your investments, the interest you have in the process, and so on.

As a starting point, you need to draw certain lines. You have to say what you will and will not do under *any* circumstances. The lines you draw here represent the outer edges of Your Investment Company's strategies.

For the purposes of this book, I have drawn the following lines. These always apply. Of course, if any of these general approaches do not suit you—because they sound too risky or too restrictive—feel free to change them to suit yourself. Remember, it's *Your* Investment Company.

In Sensible Stock Investing, as universal rules, we will not do the following:

- Invest in any company that has never shown a profit
- Invest in "pink sheet" companies (companies that do not meet minimum SEC or major stock exchange requirements and trade only "over the counter")
- Use margin
- Short stocks
- Use options, futures, or any other "derivative" investments
- Invest in tobacco companies

However, we will, when appropriate and prudent, do the following:

- Purchase stock in any size company, so long as it meets our general criteria for company quality and valuation.
- Own about 5 to 15 stocks total.
- Aim for well-roundedness without mindlessly pursuing diversification.

- Allow up to 25 percent of a portfolio's money to be invested in a single stock, more if that stock is a continuing winner.
- Allow up to 100 percent of our "stock money" to be invested or in cash, depending on market conditions.
- Maintain a Shopping List of desirable opportunities to be ready when new money becomes available and market conditions are good.
- Use our Easy-Rate™ Stock Rating Sheet system of company scores and stock valuations, plus simple timing techniques from our Timing Outlooks, to improve the quality of our decisions.
- Invest in any type of stock: A, B, D, E, or M.
- Use trailing sell-stops to protect against losses and lock in gains. If a stock starts off badly, cut losses early at no more than 10 percent below purchase price.
- Sell any stock that underperforms the market for two years, even if other selling criteria are not present.
- Review each stock in the portfolio quarterly for continued suitability. Replace stocks as appropriate.
- Review these objectives, strategies, and approaches once per year and adjust them for changed circumstances, new knowledge, and the like.

Two Sample Portfolios

A unique feature of this book is that we have established two *real-money* (i.e., not hypothetical) portfolios to demonstrate the application of Sensible Stock Investing's principles. These portfolios are discussed fully in Part F, but to illustrate the articulation of stock investment objectives and strategies, here are the "constitutions" for these two portfolios.

Portfolio A: "Exciting" Portfolio

General Description: This portfolio is designed to profit mostly from capital gains (i.e., price rises in the stocks that it contains).

Investment Objectives:

- Never drop back more than 10 percent from any value the portfolio attains.
- Attain at least an 8 percent annualized return over every three-year period.
- Beat the S&P 500 in total return over every three-year period.

Strategies/Tactics to Meet the Objectives:

- Follow all "universal" strategies.
- Invest in and trade stocks that are likely to appreciate in value faster than the S&P 500, which is to say primarily Types A, A-B, and M stocks.

- Maintain a well-rounded portfolio of 5 to 10 stocks.

- Except for occasional Type M (momentum) stocks, invest only in companies that score highly on our company ranking and valuation criteria, that is, that appear in the upper-right quadrant of our Sensible Stock Opportunities Map™.

- Share price must be greater than $4 at time of purchase.

- Again excepting Type M stocks, buy when Timing Outlook conditions are "neutral" or better and when the individual stock displays at least one month of upward price momentum at the time of purchase.

- Manage the portfolio's risk according to the general precepts of Sensible Stock Investing.

- Sell any stock when its company score drops significantly, when its stock performance deteriorates significantly, or when other selling criteria of Sensible Stock Investing appear.

- Set trailing sell-stop prices appropriately for each stock. Reset stops at least once per week.

- Any stock that is sold off (by hitting its sell-stop) *and* which lost money is ineligible for repurchase for one year. (The presumption is that our analytical approach did not work well for this company/stock.) If a stock that *made* money sells off, it is eligible for repurchase at any time.

Portfolio B: "Boring" Portfolio

General Description: This portfolio is designed to profit from a blend of capital gains and dividends.

Investment Objectives:

- Never drop back more than 10 percent from any value the portfolio attains.

- Attain at least a 7 percent positive annualized return over every three-year period.

- Beat the S&P 500 in total return every three-year period.

Strategies/Tactics to Meet Objective:

- Follow all "universal" strategies.

- Invest primarily in Type B and D companies with dividend yields, at time of purchase, that exceed the S&P 500's average current yield (or about 1.7 percent or more). High-yielding ETFs (Type E's) also qualify. Purchase no Type A or M companies.

- Aim for a well-rounded portfolio, but feel free to overweight industries (such as real estate and utilities) and special types of companies (such as REITs and Master Limited Partnerships) that typically have high dividend rates.

- Do not automatically reinvest dividends in the companies that issue them. Bring the money into the portfolio in the form of cash, and reinvest that cash according to the objectives and strategies of the portfolio.

- Buy only when companies have "Fair +" or better valuations.

Risk Management

As you can see, these Sensible Stock Investing strategies place a lot of emphasis on the reduction of risk, even in an inherently riskier portfolio such as Portfolio A. We see in the strategies (including the universal strategies) such techniques as the following:

- Not buying on margin
- Not shorting stocks
- Not using options or other derivative investments
- Not buying stock in profitless companies
- Using trailing sell-stops
- Cutting losses early if a stock gets off to a poor start

This heavy attention to risk management comports with our general approach that the first rule in making money is not to lose money.

Some advisers posit that, if you have a "long time" until, say, retirement, you can tolerate significant losses (say 15 percent) in any one year, because you have lots of years to make up the loss. Well, maybe. Isn't a better approach the one advocated here, which confronts losses directly and controls them actively? Again, this is a difference between Buy-and-Hold passivity and Sensible Stock Investing.

Comparing Your Strategies to Mutual Funds

Mutual funds "compete," in a sense, for your stock investment dollars. If you cannot do better on your own than you could in a mutual fund, why spend the time and energy to invest directly in stocks yourself?

To help answer that question, compare and contrast the two sets of strategies above to what you typically see in a mutual fund prospectus:

- No mutual fund would ever suggest that it will never lose more than 10 percent of its value. But Your Investment Company can certainly set this objective. (A mutual fund, by comparison, is likely to say something like, "This fund's total return may fluctuate significantly, and an investor can lose money over short or even long periods.")
- No mutual fund company would ever say it will beat the S&P 500 (or any index) at all, let alone over the difficult criteria of *every* three-year period. But we can. (An index mutual fund, by contrast, is likely to say, "The fund seeks to track the performance of XYZ Benchmark Index.")
- No mutual fund company would ever say that no matter what the S&P 500 does, it will generate a positive return. But we can set that as a goal and even designate the return.

Mutual funds are limited, of course, in what they can promise to customers. Some of the limitations are spelled out in laws and regulations; others are merely prudent (to avoid lawsuits, for example). Mutual funds do not and cannot guarantee results. So we need to cut them some slack in comparing their objectives and strategies to our own.

That said, however, real businesses set "stretch" goals all the time. You should set stretch goals for Your Investment Company. They will make you think harder about how you are going to achieve them. They will lead you to construct better strategies and be more disciplined about sticking to them.

CHAPTER E-8

When to Buy

Wait for a good pitch to hit.
—Ted Williams

General Principles

Remember, the basic idea in Sensible Stock Investing is to make money by owning stocks whose returns exceed those of the market. Our benchmark for "the market" is the S&P 500 Stock Index.

Knowing what to buy is only part of the winning formula. Knowing *when* to buy is equally essential. Buying at a "good" price greatly increases the potential return of the stock. One of the cool things about stock investing is that if you have the patience to wait, the market's natural volatility will, sooner or later, create favorable buying opportunities for many companies you are interested in. Smart investors use price corrections—valuation pullbacks—to get good prices on stocks they want to buy. Then they pull the trigger.

Picking the best time to buy a stock, of course, is subject to all the risks of timing that we saw in Chapter E-5. Ideally, we would like to be able to buy precisely at times when great individual stock valuations coincide with a market bottom. In the real world, the best we can hope to do is get close to each. We can improve the odds, but we will never be perfect.

We use three tools to help decide when to buy: valuation, market timing, and stock charting.

Using Valuation in the Decision to Buy a Stock

As we saw in Part D, valuation—while not an element in deciding whether a company is an excellent company—is *key* to improving the odds that the company's stock is likely to outperform the market.

Some investment advisers—usually of the "growth at any cost" or "perma-bull" persuasion—all but ignore valuation. They figure that if you are buying the stock of a great company, it doesn't matter what you pay for it. It will go up. Advice like this tends to crescendo during extended bull markets and then dies down (or disappears) during bear markets. It was deafening during the bubble expansion of the late 1990s and then vanished during the erosion of 2000–2002, with financial magazines switching from articles like "Aren't You On Board Yet?" to "Valuation Is Back!"

Meanwhile, other experts are at the opposite extreme, seeming to look *solely* at valuation in picking stocks, and only buying stocks when they are "cheap." Their advice tends to get drowned out during extended bull markets or bubbles, and with good reason, because their approach significantly underperforms the market during those periods.

Usually, Sensible Stock Investing lands around the middle of these kinds of disputes. But we are not in the middle on this one: Except when you are considering a Type M (momentum) stock, there is a strong bias in favor of using valuation to help decide when to buy. Here's why: It is simply mathematically true that if you can purchase a good stock at a lower price, your gains over the years will be multiplied, because the miracle of compounding will be magnified. The longer you hold the stock, the more the magnification effect if its price continues to rise.

Consider this example: Let's hypothesize that, because of usual market volatility, the price of a desirable company fluctuates between $50 and $70 over the course of a year, and you could buy it at any time during that year because you have the money on hand. But because the company's earnings are steadily increasing, the stock begins a fairly steady climb, to $70 at the end of Year 1, $80 in Year 2, and so on for five years.

Let's look at two scenarios: You buy it at either $50 or $60 during that first year:

Importance of Initial Price in Total Return

Year	Price at End of Year	Total Return If Bought @ $50	Total Return If Bought @ $60	Return This Year (Either at $50 or $60)
1	$70	40%	17%	40% or 17%
2	$80	60%	33%	14%
3	$90	80%	50%	13%
4	$100	100%	67%	11%
5	$110	120%	83%	11%

Look at the two "Total Return" columns (highlighted). You can see that the total return at a purchase price of $50 is *significantly* better than at $60 and that the gap between the two returns actually *widens* as time goes on. At the end of five years, a $10,000 investment at $50 is worth $22,000, while the same investment at $60 has become just $18,370.

This result holds true even though in Years 2 through 5 there is no *annual* difference in performance (as shown in the last column). The percentage return each year after Year 1 is the same no matter what you originally paid for the stock. This, of course, is because at the beginning of each subsequent year, the price of the stock is the same no matter what you paid for it in the first place. So the percentage gain on the stock is the same every year except the year of purchase.

What does that mean? It means that the *entire difference in overall performance is a function of the price you originally paid for the stock.*

This may strike you as nonintuitive, especially because the percentage return is the same in all years except the first (the year of purchase). Shouldn't that bring things closer to parity the more years you own the stock? From the table above, we know that it doesn't. The total-return gap actually *widens* with each succeeding year. Why does that happen? It happens because

- *you have more shares* if you originally bought at $50 rather than $60; and
- *your first year's "extra" gains compound.*

To illustrate this in dollars, let's look again at the original $10,000 investment. At $50, you bought 200 shares; at $60 you bought 167 shares. As time goes on, here are their respective values under the same scenario as above:

Importance of Initial Price in Dollars

Year	Price at End of Year	200 Shares @ $50 Price	167 Shares @ $60 Price	Difference
1	$70	$14,000	$11,690	$2310
2	$80	$16,000	$13,360	$2640
3	$90	$18,000	$15,030	$2970
4	$100	$20,000	$16,700	$3300
5	$110	$22,000	$18,370	$3630

By the way, please note that the extra $3630 at the end of Year 5 represents an *additional* 36 percent return on your original $10,000 investment compared to if you bought the stock at $60.

Using Market Timing in Your Decision to Buy a Stock

We discussed the use of market timing indicators in Chapter E-5. You should put this information to use in making buying decisions: The best time to buy is when the majority of market indicators are positive (green "up" arrows), which suggests that the market is due for (or is already in) a rising period. The ideal confluence, of course, is when your individual stock has a favorable valuation *and* your market timing indicators point toward an up-trending market.

Conversely, if the market indicators generally are unfavorable, the Sensible Stock Investor will exercise caution. Even if you have the cash available and the stock's valuation looks good, an unfavorable market is not usually the best time to buy a stock. In fact, it is a time to tighten up your sell-stops. You can follow a hard-and-fast rule of no buying when the market looks bearish, or you can be a little more relaxed about it by moving into a more cautious mode but not banning buying entirely. (Some stocks do go up even during an overall bear market. This might be a time to restrict yourself to Type M momentum plays.)

If you do purchase a stock during unfavorable market conditions, you might seek additional protection by making your initial investment smaller (say half of what your usual investment amount is) as a hedge against the increased possibility that your stock will be pulled down along with the others if there is a market slide. If it's a non-momentum stock, you can demand that it have a Good+ or Excellent valuation rating before taking the plunge.

Using the Stock's Chart in Your Decision to Buy a Stock

The final Sensible Stock Investing piece of the "when to buy" puzzle can be gleaned from the stock's chart. Charts not only help you to take emotion out of play, but they also help you identify the optimum time to press the "buy" button.

Here's what to do:

- Print out the stock's chart for the past year, using a high-low "bar" chart format.
- With a ruler, draw a line that connects three or more highs (exactly if possible, but extremely close will do) and another line that connects three or more lows. There may be more than one of each kind of line on the chart. These lines are called "trendlines."
- The best trendlines extend over longer time periods, indicating that the trend has been persistent. We are interested in a recent trend that has lasted at least a month—we want our purchase to get off to a good start, particularly because we are going to cut losses quickly if the stock moves in the wrong direction.
- If an "upper trendline" and a "lower trendline" are roughly parallel, they form a "channel." Extend those lines to the right of the chart, past the actual data—this "future" part of the channel indicates what the chart is suggesting might happen next.

Now we have a tool we can use. If the channel is sloping upward, the stock continues to be a candidate for purchase, because the stock has been hitting *higher* highs and *higher* lows. Look at where the stock's current price lies within the channel. We already know that the stock is favorably valued. We also know that stock prices bounce around. The best time to purchase the stock is when it has very recently bounced off the lower trendline. In this case, the chart is suggesting that the stock is headed for the upper trendline. That's what we want. The closer the stock is to the *upper* trendline, the more wary you should be. That's because its next move is likely to bounce *down* off that trendline.

Occasionally, you will have difficulty fitting a straight trendline to a chart, but you will notice that for a relatively long time, the stock's actual price has stayed above its 50-day or 200-day moving average. That is just about as good a situation. The moving-average line itself shows the stock's upward momentum clearly. The generally rising prices are pulling the trendline (which is a trailing average) up along with them. Such a stock is displaying strength.

Buy?

So the answer to "when to buy" is when all four conditions are favorable:

- The company has a high Easy-Rate™ score.
- The stock's valuation is favorable.
- The most recent Timing Outlook suggests that the market is in a general uptrend or at least is neutral.
- The stock's chart is favorable.

At this point, you have done about all you can to stack the odds in your favor. You know you have an excellent company. You believe it has a favorable valuation. Market conditions seem positive. And the stock's own volatility seems to have put the price in a favorable short-term position. You are ready to buy.

What if all of the conditions are not favorable? Clearly, the safest answer is to wait until they are. Does that mean that sometimes you'll miss out on what could turn out to be a great purchase? Sure. But the most sensible practice, as in poker, is to "play tight." Don't give in on your starting requirements. Put your money into only the best opportunities.

Use a Shopping List

Here is one last simple tool to keep track of opportunities. Create a Shopping List of those companies that you would really like to own. The Shopping List is a by-product of your Easy-Rate Sheets. It identifies the best opportunities you have identified. Update the list every month or so. Between formal updates, you can handwrite in the data for new companies you research that score highly enough to make the list. (The Shopping List is discussed in more detail in Chapter F-2, and a sample Shopping List appears in Appendix I, Form 3.)

Each time you have some money to invest in stocks, check out the Shopping List and figure out which company best meets all the criteria we have discussed. Follow all the steps. If the valuation is good, then look at your Timing Outlook and finally at the stock's chart. If all the pieces look favorable, you are probably ready to push the "Buy" button.

Of course, there will be other times when everything looks overvalued to you, market conditions are not favorable, and the stock you have your eye on has been moving sideways or falling. These are the times that you want to be in Type C—cash—with your stock money. *Don't* push the button. Hang on to your money until better valuations and market conditions come along.

Be disciplined. Excepting Type M (momentum) stocks, buying at an advantageous price is so important to overall performance that you should simply make it a rule that you will not purchase a stock unless all buying conditions are working in your favor. Stay rational. Avoid wanting a stock so badly that you ignore the four conditions.

CHAPTER E-9

When to Sell

Even being right three or four times out of ten should yield a person a fortune if they have the sense to cut losses quickly.

—Bernard Baruch

So, Do You Sell Each Stock after One or Two Years?

If we're Buying-to-Hold with an intent to select companies that have above-average prospects for one to two years, does that mean we're going to sell each of our stocks after the one- or two-year period is up? Or that we're going to hold every stock we select for between one and two years?

Of course not. A preconceived holding period of any length doesn't make sense.

- For one thing, some of your stocks will still be good investments—outperforming the market—well beyond one or two years. Some stocks outperform the market for many years running. If your winners continue winning, you'll want to keep them for as long as they are successful.

- On the other hand, some of your stock selections won't pan out. Unless sold, they not only will fail to outperform the market but also may sink below where you purchased them. Perhaps the whole market will tank, taking your stocks with it. Holding on to such stocks in the hope that they will catch back up is usually a low-percentage proposition. The recommendation here is to get out if your losses approach 10 percent in any stock position. Using sell-stops as described in Chapter E-2 does this for you automatically and without emotion. Holding on to such a stock means that you are not only losing money outright but also that you are suffering the opportunity cost of not being able to put that money into a better place, either into a more promising stock or in cash.

- Finally, there is a middle area between the two extremes of stocks that are obvious winners and obvious losers. There may be times when holding on to an underperforming stock is the smartest thing to do, so long as it is not losing significant money. You may be absolutely correct about a stock's valuation, the company's prospects, and the long-term direction of the stock's price. You may just be premature as to *when* the upward movement in its price will come. In the interim, the stock may just move sideways, without ever hitting its selling trigger. In such a case, selling the stock would turn out to be a bad decision. As we saw in the strategic statements for our demonstration portfolios, our general approach is to give a stock two years to start paying off, provided that it does not set off a sell-stop or any other selling trigger. If it is still going nowhere after two years, sell it.

How often you sell tends to turn on two factors:

- *What types of stocks you buy.* Type A's are the most volatile and will normally lead to the most trading. Precisely because of that volatility, they will take occasional dips that trigger your sell-stop orders. Type D's are the least volatile and will lead to the least trading. You may even decide not to have sell-stops under them, relying instead solely on periodic Portfolio Reviews for suitableness. Type B's fall somewhere in between.
- *Market conditions.* Bad patches in the market will sometimes cause you to sell out of positions sooner than you would have if market conditions were more favorable.

So it becomes impossible to predict how long you'll hold on to any particular stock. But the actual *length* of ownership is not really the target here, nor is holding your turnover rate to some particular percentage. Rather, the relevant goal is to maximize your gains and minimize your losses, so that your investing performance makes money and outperforms the market. Sometimes that will lead to fairly frequent trading, and at other times it will mean you go months without making a move.

Optimizing Your Selling Decisions

For most individual investors, the decision whether to sell a stock is the hardest decision in stock investing.

Follow one hard-and-fast rule: Sell a new purchase before losing 10 percent in it.

Beyond that, it starts out sounding simple: The old saw is "Sell your losers and let your winners run." Right, obviously. But how do you *know*? Clearly, it's easy to list your winners and losers up until right now. But that's not what this particular decision is about. This one is about future events—unknowable by definition.

Get used to it: It's impossible to truly know. Figuring out when to sell a stock is one of investment's biggest challenges. First, let's consider the "sell your losers" part:

- Say the stock really is "a loser." It has lost money from the very beginning, or after a promising start it is now losing its gains back. And, despite what you thought when you bought it, it looks like it has entered a phase when it is going to continue to go down—say because the company's prospects appear to have changed for the worse and the market is in a prolonged dry spell. Well, you obviously don't want to continue to own the stock. You want to be out of it, moving the proceeds to some better place (which may simply be cash). And you want to reach that decision in a timely fashion to avoid suffering increasing losses. *Don't* fall prey to the common human foible of refusing to admit that you placed a losing bet. (A poker player would say, "Don't chase.") Accept the situation, sell the stock, and move on.

- But, even if your stock is falling in price (or going perpetually sideways), you don't want to *prematurely* reach a decision that you made a mistake in buying it or that its prospects have reversed from bright to lousy. It may not, in fact, be a "loser." It may already have gained significant value for you. Your positive outlook on the company and its stock may be fundamentally correct, and the optimal decision may be to give the stock sufficient time to reach its likely profitable destination. A stock in a short-term stall can become a long-term winner. So this points in the direction of being patient, with a bias toward holding rather than selling.

The difference between these two scenarios, of course, is being able to distinguish a *real* loser from a company/stock that's just going through a bad patch.

The Sensible Stock Investing approach to "sell your losers" is a combination of guidelines:

- Cut off actual losses at 10 percent or less.
- Once a stock has made at least 10 percent for you, you should never lose any part of your original investment.
- Consider giving stocks that have already made money for you a little more leeway to go backward, so long as the *stock's* prospects and the *market's* prospects continue to look favorable. You control this by widening your sell-stops.

So much for selling your losers. Now let's consider the "let your winners run" part:

- If a stock is truly a "winner," meaning that it has made significant money for you and looks like it is going to continue to do so, you obviously want to continue to own it. This points in the direction of being patient about selling decisions and guarding against premature decisions that the stock has "had its run." Indeed, perhaps you should buy more if you have cash available and don't see reasons that the stock is likely to slow down.

- You want to let a winner run even if its price is going up as part of a bubble. Note here that this is a *very* difficult situation to call, especially if the stock is particularly volatile, as bubbling stocks often are. You don't want to prematurely decide to get out of a stock solely because it has overshot its "fair" value. If a stock is in a bubble, it *will* overshoot its "fair" value—that's what a bubble is. But as a Sensible Stock Investor you want to take advantage of that for as long as you can—even though you are *convinced* that it is a bubble and that the valuation is not sustainable. Many "value" investors missed out on the great bull market of 1997–1999, because by 1996 many stock valuations looked unsustainable, and "value" investors sold on that basis. They were fundamentally right—stocks *were* bubbling and those valuations *were* unsustainable—but the bursting of the bubble did not come until 2000! Selling out in 1996 was *not* the optimum decision.

The Sensible Stock Investing selling guidelines for "let your winners run" can be summarized as follows:

- Once a stock truly has been a winner for you (let's define that as having gained 15 to 20 percent since you bought it), give it enough room for routine volatility before you sell it. This is to preserve your *upside potential* if the stock stalls out a little before resuming its forward momentum.

- Define "enough room" in an appropriate way for the stock and the market conditions. Factors that push you in the direction of more room would include a continuing high rating on the company itself, continuing good valuation of the stock (that is, its price has not outpaced its earnings), continued upward overall price trend (even if bumpy), and a neutral or favorable market outlook. Factors that push you in the direction of less room would be the opposites of those.

- *Don't sell* based solely on a worry that the stock has somehow "used up" its potential by going up in price. Dominant companies can keep growing earnings for years.

- Don't set a "target price" and sell if your stock reaches that price. If the market wants to continue to take that price up, let it. You can protect yourself on the downside with a sell-stop. Tighten the sell-stop if that makes you more comfortable.

The Sensible Stock Investing approach is to use all the tools at your disposal to make judgments about selling:

- Market indicators (which should get you out ahead of or very early in general bear markets and bursting bubbles)

- Individual stock valuations (which should make you wary if they get too high)

- Patterns as revealed on stock charts (which should make you wary if an upward channel gets violated to the downside)

- Rational selling rules that you actually follow (setting aside pride, ego, fear, and any other unhelpful emotions)—a rule-based strategy helps you avoid heavy losses and lowers the risk of your portfolio

- An unwavering determination to avoid any loss over 10 percent (even if that means selling a stock the day after you bought it)

And finally, let's accept that no matter what analytics we apply, we are going to make some selling mistakes, just as we make some buying mistakes. The real strategic goal is to improve as much as we can the percentage and degree of success of correct decisions, to stack the odds as much in our favor as possible.

Buy to Hold…or, Buy and Monitor

The Sensible Stock Investing strategy for making sell decisions can be accurately summarized as Buy-*to*-Hold. This means that your *intent*, when buying a stock, is to hold it for a long time, perhaps "forever," but that intent is rebuttable. It is not a hard-and-fast rule.

With the exception of Type M (momentum) stocks, your *intent* when you purchase a stock is not to sell it quickly for fast profits, but to hold it for as long as the stock performs decently and appears to have excellent prospects. This may be many years if the company was well selected, the market cooperates, the reasons that made it a good choice hold up, the stock isn't too volatile, and the company itself doesn't screw up.

But circumstances may change, or you may realize that your original selection was flawed, in which case the presumption in favor of holding on to the stock will be overcome by other evidence. You become aware of such evidence by periodically reviewing your portfolio and market conditions. Thus, another name for the Sensible Stock Investing strategy is "Buy and Monitor." At a minimum, we recommend that you review all your holdings quarterly to be sure they still deserve a place in your portfolio. This "Portfolio Review" is in addition to your more frequent adjustments of sell-stops to trail an upwardly moving price. Portfolio Reviews are discussed in detail in Chapter F-2, and an example of a Portfolio Review can be found in Appendix I, Form 5.

Reasons to Sell

The reasons to sell a stock are legion. They break down into four categories:

1. Reasons having to do with the company
2. Reasons having to do with the stock's or the market's performance
3. Reasons having to do with your portfolio
4. Reasons personal to you

Let's explore these in turn. As we do, remember that most of the actual selling under Sensible Stock Investing occurs because a stock has hit a previously established sell-stop order, triggering the sale. You predetermine the stop price. So most of the following "reasons to sell" are really *reasons to set the stop price tighter* to the current price—giving the stock less wiggle room. This protects you on the downside, but if the stock surprises you and goes up, you won't have sold the stock prematurely. A few of the reasons discussed herein are cause to sell immediately without waiting to trigger a sell-stop order. These special cases will be called out.

By the way, one of the main precepts of Buy-and-Hold investing is the avoidance of triggering taxable events. That *is* an advantage of not selling *when a stock is going up.* But avoiding losses and protecting gains is so important to your overall returns that tax avoidance is an insufficient reason to hold *when you are losing money.* While taxes are definitely a factor in determining your net returns, don't forget that the point of investing in the first place is to make money. Don't be tax phobic. You must pay taxes to take profits. The object of the pursuit is to take profits. You would not take a lower-paying job just to lower your income taxes, would you? Same way in investing: Capital gains are something we *want* to have.

1. Reasons to Sell Having to Do with the Company

The following are the most important signals that a *company* is no longer worthy of holding in your portfolio, presented in the approximate order they tend to occur:

Flawed Original Purchase Decision

Numerous investment psychology studies have shown that many people have the tendency to hold on to losing investments, because they don't want to admit or regret having made a mistake. They want to give the investment time to "make it back," which would validate their original decision to buy. This makes no sense to me—I've never had any trouble dumping losers—but if you find yourself thinking this way, do what you can to fight the tendency. Bad investments should be undone.

Deteriorating Company Outlook

Companies can and do change. Type A's change more often than others, but even in mature companies, change happens. So despite your best efforts to select companies that will be superior performers for one to two years or more, sometimes your company will suffer a negative change. This will show up in a declining company Easy-Rate™ score. Some examples:

- The company's Story score may go down. This may occur for one of the following reasons:

    1. The company loses its franchise dominance, market leadership, or the like.

    2. Its business model—which looked so fine before—suddenly looks flawed or obsolete.

    3. Competitors may overtake the company. A competitor may start a price war that hurts all the companies in the industry, bringing everybody's earnings down.

    4. Technology may commoditize or marginalize a company's product.

    5. Your company's entire industry may start to buckle because of technological or demographic changes. The industry might start down the path of irrelevancy. Cars made buggywhips obsolete, and DVDs have marginalized VCRs. Eastman Kodak in 2003 overhauled its entire corporate strategy because of what digital photography was doing to its film and processing businesses. It slashed its dividend 70 percent, instantly converting itself from a Type D to a Type A or B company.

    6. Your company may do something really stupid. Dumb, ego-driven acquisitions sometimes fall under this category.

    7. The company's revered CEO or founder might announce his or her retirement or bolt to another company. If the departing CEO is a Hall of Fame type leader, there is not much reason to believe his or her replacement will do as well as the Hall of Famer. In fact, the star leader may be getting out *because* he or she sees that the business is about to tumble.

    8. A company riding a cyclical wave may see that wave reverse. An example might be an oil company whose fortunes depend on the price of oil—over which the company has little control, because of OPEC.

- The company's financials may slide.

  1. For a fast-growing company, the time to sell may be when it gets out of adolescence and into adulthood. The company may go from rapid growth to slower growth. With rare exceptions, companies cannot grow rapidly forever.

  2. Remember that stock prices generally follow earnings *growth,* so a slowdown in financial growth often signals a slowdown or reversal in the stock's performance. This can happen even though the company may be accomplishing magnificent things. Earnings may still be growing at a wonderful rate—say 20 percent—but if that is a reduction from former years when they grew 45 percent, the stock's P/E ratio—and therefore its price—will invariably adjust itself downward to reflect investors' declining expectations. In particularly skittish industries—like technology—a slowdown in *revenue* growth (or even a tepid *forecast* about revenue growth) may trigger a slide in the stock itself, as investors fear that the revenue slowdown portends an earnings slowdown.

You monitor these factors, of course, by periodically re-rating the company. It is a good practice to update each Easy-Rate Sheet for owned stocks when you conduct Portfolio Reviews. In the example above, the earnings slide from 45 percent to 20 percent alone would cost the company 4 rating points: 3 for the magnitude of the change, and another because the most recent year's rate has probably sunk significantly from the three-year average. There may be concomitant slides in the company's revenue growth rate, its ROE, and so on, costing it more points. The rating system will bring all this to your attention.

If a stock's prospects are sliding, logic suggests that the market's expectations will be sliding too, meaning that the stock's P/E multiple will decline. The stock will get the double whammy of a declining P/E ratio on top of declining earnings growth. You'd best exit while this happens, which means setting a tighter sell-stop on the stock if not selling it outright. You may well wish to re-enter the stock once the valuation adjustment process has run its course, which could take anywhere from a few months to a few years. After all, it still may be a great company, just transitioning from a high-growth to slow-growth business.

Sudden Change in Dividend Policy

We have seen the importance of dividends both in evaluating a company (Chapter C-9) and in valuing its stock (Chapter D-4). A company's downward change in dividend policy can be a telegraph of bad news coming. In the case of Type D stocks, whose principal reason for ownership is the dividends, perhaps you should sell without waiting, or at least significantly tighten your sell-stop, if the dividends are cut or decelerate significantly. With utility stocks or REITs, normally you can expect a dividend increase every year. Sell any such stock—or severely tighten the sell-stop—if the company does not raise its dividend regularly in line with its earnings.

Untrustworthy Management

Do not tolerate deceit from management. A company violating this standard is an outright sell, and you shouldn't waste any time once you find out. Don't wait for your sell-stop to be triggered—just sell.

Less-than-honest management can rear its head in many forms, including criminal acts, bad accounting, and antitrust violations. News that a company is under investigation by the SEC, any other regulatory body, or a state's attorney general is usually significant. Resignation of the CFO or CEO under any sort of bad publicity is almost always a bad sign.

Significant Legal Difficulties

Take a hard look at the stock if it gets into a legal bind, or many of them. Look in the "Legal Matters" disclosure in the annual report. If management says the outcome is not expected to adversely affect the company in a material way, things may be OK. Also be aware in the news if a major litigation has been announced against the company. Consider these to be cautionary flags, perhaps warranting the tightening of the sell-stop if it appears they will hang over the company for a long time.

Mergers and Acquisitions

When one of your companies is involved in a merger or acquisition, you should reevaluate the resulting company or companies. If the new entity does not comport with your investment principles, a sell may be in order.

Example: AOL's announcement in early 2000 of its intent to acquire Time Warner. AOL went from being a focused, fast-growing Internet provider and information-rich "portal" to a huge diversified media conglomerate. Remember, *stock price* growth has nothing to do with *company size* growth. It has to do with *earnings growth.* In this case, many investors could not figure out how combining a youthful high-growth company (AOL) with a mature slower-growing company (Time Warner) could be good for the stock. And many investors did, in fact, sell AOL after this announcement, and to this date they have not been sorry they did. On January 3, 2000, just before the announcement of the merger, AOL's price was $83 per share. At this writing (February 2006), the stock is around $18 a share, or 21 percent of its former self. Using the "makeup" table displayed in Chapter E-2, the stock will need to go up almost 400 percent to regain its former price. Think that will happen anytime soon?

Ironically, as the AOL—Time Warner story spun out in 2003, it was the AOL division that turned out to have business problems and growth reversal, and to have employed questionable accounting practices, while the "old economy" Time Warner divisions kept churning profitably ahead. As you probably know, in 2003 "AOL" was dropped from the company name. The company readopted "Time Warner" and went back to using its former ticker symbol. It has been trying to resuscitate its AOL division ever since.

Creation of Tracking Stocks

Tracking stocks are created by companies to "track" the performance of a particular division or subsidiary, without actually spinning it off. In other words, the stock of the main company still exists, but a new stock is created representing the subsidiary's business. The main company still owns and controls the subsidiary. The idea is to "unlock the value" of the subsidiary and give investors access to it separately via the tracking stock.

Frankly, it is difficult to know how to evaluate tracking stocks. What exactly does one represent? If you already own the main company and it creates a tracking stock for the best component of its business, that doesn't sound like good news for the main stock.

Whether you buy a tracking stock is subject to its own individual analysis, just as any other purchase decision would be. You may well find that putting a value on the tracking stock defies analysis. You may have no idea, for example, how the main company is going to allocate companywide costs to the division being tracked.

2. Reasons to Sell Based on Market or Individual Stock Performance

Occasional underperformance is a normal part of the game for any stock. The issue is what (if anything) to do about it. Sensible Stock Investing posits that underperformance should only be tolerated up to a point, which you, the investor, determine. You "enforce" your determination by setting sell-stops in advance (when you are thinking most clearly). So the question becomes, how do you determine the "proper" point at which to set the sell-stop triggers?

Stock Initially Loses 5 to 10 Percent from Purchase Price

As discussed elsewhere, any stock is on probation until its stop price clears its purchase price. The initial sell-stop should be set 5 to 10 percent below the purchase price. I typically use 8 percent.

Unfortunately, once every great while, this means that the stock is sold (i.e., the trigger point is hit) just a few days after you bought it. But if a stock begins going backward, that may be a warning sign that something *fundamental* is changing about the company, and the market is simply recognizing it before you. It may also be a warning sign that, for whatever reason, the market is lowering its sentiment and changing its behavior toward your stock. The initial 5 to 10 percent sell-stop enforces the "don't lose money" part of our overall strategy.

Stock Survives Initial Probationary Period

What do you do with a stock after it is off probation? The typical example will be that we've held the stock for a few weeks or months, things have gone OK, and the stock is up, say, 20 percent from our purchase price. The question is, how far below the current price should we set the selling triggers?

The distance to leave between the stock's current price and its sell-stop price will not be the same for each stock that you own. Rather, it is situational, depending on things like how much of a paper profit you already have in the stock, your degree of conviction in the continued upside potential for the company, its current valuation, its chart, and current market conditions.

Stop-loss levels can be set in one of two ways:

- At a percentage below the current price
- On the basis of the stock's chart

The following two subsections summarize the factors to take into account in setting stop-loss percentage triggers. The text envisions a 15 percent "default" percentage. That is, we are presuming that a 15 percent paper drop in value is acceptable to you. Of course, if you want, you can adjust the figures to default to 10 percent, 12 percent, or whatever you think is better than 15 percent. You might do this if you have a lower or higher tolerance for volatility.

In no instance should you set a stop-loss trigger so loosely that you could lose money in a stock that has already gained enough to come off probation. So even if your default stop-loss trigger would be set at 15 percent for a particular stock, don't actually set it there until it has gained 15 percent from your purchase price. Once a stock is off probation, you should never lose money on it.

Reasons for Looser Sell-Stops Based on Performance

These are the main reasons you might want to *loosen* your sell-stop—that is, give the stock a little more room for volatility.

- *Bull market:* Market indicators suggest an upward trend in the market as a whole. Such markets are often a little more volatile than normal, so more wiggle room may be in order. (20 percent)
- *High-conviction stock:* The stock is highly rated on all counts, and you *really* believe in the long-term potential of the stock. You just can't tell when it will take off, so you're willing to give the stock extra room for volatility while it finds itself. However, do not kid yourself on this category. You must be able, with conviction, to articulate solid reasons to place a stock in this category. (20 percent or more)
- *High reward possibilities:* The stock is volatile, and you want to give it plenty of wiggle room, because you are convinced that there is potential for *considerable* upside gains, and you're willing to tolerate considerable volatility. This is essentially a "bet" on a Type A stock, the kind you might make, for example, on a stock in an industry in which you are truly an expert. That is a "high-conviction" stock *for you*, because of your expertise. (up to 30 percent)
- *Blue chip/core holding:* These are most likely to be slow, steady performers and to fall into the category commonly called "defensive" stocks. They are the Type B's—large-cap, supposedly recession-proof stocks. You are willing to give such a stock room to wander, figuring that long-term it is very safe. Ask yourself, "In five years, is this stock almost certainly going to be higher than it is now?" This is the closest the Sensible Investor gets to a Buy-and-Hold strategy. (20 to 40 percent, or no stop-loss order at all). Be careful with these, though, because a "safe" or "bellwether" stock can drift downward for years, right out of the money entirely.

Reasons for Tighter Sell-Stops Based on Performance

These are reasons that you might want to *tighten* your sell-stops.

• *Bear market*: Market indicators suggest a downward trend in the market as a whole. (5 to 10 percent)

• *Well-rated company but mediocre-performing stock:* The stock has very good Company and Valuation scores, but it has performed indifferently since you bought it, and you're no longer very sure about its long-term upside. For the period you've owned it, it has not behaved the way you think it should, and maybe you're growing a little tired of its act. Give it a short leash in the hope that it either will start living up to its potential or sell off. (5 to 10 percent)

• *Stock is way up:* You want to lock away some of your gains. Maybe it will help you sleep better, knowing that no matter what happens from here on out, you will have a great profit from your original invest-ment. It still looks good, but you want to take some money off the table. (5 to 10 percent on part of your holdings) Notice here that we are *not* recommending selling solely because the stock has hit a particular target price: It may keep going up! You can both preserve a shot at further gains and protect some paper gains with a tight sell-stop.

• *Extremely overvalued stock:* Similar to the previous item, but it doesn't "still look good," because the company has achieved an unsustainably high valuation. Such a stock clearly has increased risk for a significant drop. It is "priced for perfection" (meaning it will plunge at the first sign of bad news), and it will be highly sensitive to overall market downturns. When the pullback starts, you want to preserve as much of your gain as possible. This can also pertain to any stock you purchased as a Type M (momen-tum) stock. (3 to 8 percent)

• *Already hit one stop-loss trigger:* You originally set two triggers, each covering half of what you own. You did this as a hedge. The second trigger should be only a small percentage below the first. Because it's already hit one stop-loss trigger, it's already had its "correction." (2 to 5 percent)

• *You want to reduce or close out your position:* When you've decided to get out of a stock for any reason, rather than sell it outright, you might use a very tight sell-stop to squeeze out any remaining gains that the market might have in store for it. (2 to 5 percent) If you are going to need the money at a specific time (as for a house down payment), you might tighten the percentage a little each week as your due day approaches. This is a lot of fun in a bull market, squeezing every last penny out of a stock before you have to sell it to get the cash.

Non-percentage Approaches to Setting Stop-Loss Triggers

Stop prices can be set in other ways than selecting a percentage below the current price: by using trendlines and channels from the stock's chart. To do this, simply set the stop price at the value of the lower trendline at the far right of the chart. (You might allow a 1 or 2 percent cushion from this price.) The idea, of course, is that if the channel is an accurate predictor of future performance, the stock's actual price will not exit the channel—as the price falls toward the lower trendline, it will "bounce" up off the trendline and stay within the channel.

If you use this method of setting a trigger, I suggest that you update the stop price at the end of each week, printing out a new chart, redrawing the channel, and determining the new price. In this way, your stop price will keep moving up (the channel is presumably ascending), thus "trailing" the actual price, as we want it to.

A variation on using trendlines is to use moving average lines. You may notice, for example, that a stock, while volatile, never seems to drop below its 50-day or 200-day moving average. In that case, you can just use the moving average line as the sell-stop. Again, update it every week or two.

3.   Reasons to Sell Based on Portfolio Allocation

We have seen earlier that

- the optimum number of stocks to hold is about 5 to 15;
- it is a good idea to have some degree of well-roundedness in your holdings; and
- you probably do not want to have more than 25 percent of your money tied up in one particular stock.

All of these factors are designed to give you the market-beating potential of concentration while holding risk to a reasonable level. With this background in mind, let's look at valid reasons for selling based on the makeup of your portfolio.

Better Place to Put Your Money

There may be times when you discover a great new investment opportunity, but you don't have any additional cash to invest. If this happens, it will be necessary to reevaluate your holdings to decide whether it makes sense to sell all or part of one in order to raise the money needed for your new opportunity.

This is not a simple decision. Commissions and capital gains taxes must be considered. It is possible that after figuring them in, your "better idea" doesn't really hold much promise for better returns. The capital gains tax, in particular, is a difficult obstacle to overcome. At 15 percent capital gains rate, for example, you have to believe not only that your new investment will perform better over the next one to two years than the stock you already have, but also that it will regain the 15 percent tax you paid. How strongly do you believe that the new stock is *that* much better?

Here are some of the factors to look at in comparing the relative attractiveness of the new opportunity to the one you already own:

- The likely return of the new opportunity compared to what you already own. If, for example, you believe that the new stock has the potential to return 40 percent *more* than an existing holding over the one- to two-year prediction horizon, consider making the swap.

- If the current stock has already returned significantly for you, consider raising cash for the new purchase by selling part but not all of the current holding. This approach is also a hedge against being wrong, because it leaves you with a remaining stake in the current stock.

- Try rating all your holdings on the well-known "Scale of 1 to 10." You might swap a new 8 for an old 4. On the other hand, you probably don't want to swap a new 6 for an old 4—the margin of improvement is simply not great enough.

To Rebalance Your Portfolio

Sometimes, one stock will substantially outperform all the others in your portfolio. In doing so, that one holding may grow over time to become a substantial portion of your stock money. Should you sell some of it? Probably. In fact, the maximum proportion that a single stock may occupy should be specified in the "constitutional documents" for your portfolio.

Selling part of an "overgrown" position is a form of hedging, because disproportionate positions in a single stock increase the nascent risk of the portfolio. You can do it in one of two ways.

- Tighten up the sell-stop on a portion of the position. This lets you squeeze as much out of it as possible, then sell off at any hiccup.

- Address the situation directly, without waiting for a sell-stop to come into play. For example, if a single holding represents an overwhelming percentage of your portfolio (greater than, say, 30 to 40 percent), you may feel uncomfortable tying such a high percentage of your overall results to a single stock. If that is how you feel, sell off a portion of the stock to bring its proportion down under 25 percent.

You Own Too Many Stocks

Elsewhere, we've discussed how many stocks you should own, and we decided that the commonsense answer is somewhere between 5 and 15. But picking stocks is fun, and after you've been investing for some time, you may find that you own more stocks than you want or can follow effectively. You don't need as many companies as you've got.

In this case, sell your weakest stocks after one of your quarterly Portfolio Reviews to bring your total number down to 15.

4.   Reasons to Sell Personal to You

Last but not least, we come to reasons that are personal to you. Any of these can supersede all of the other guidelines.

You Need the Money

This may sound self-evident, but for completeness we list it here. If you need the money—to live on in retirement, for college tuition, for the down payment on a house, for a family emergency—this is a valid reason to sell. When you are in this situation, use it as an opportunity to prune your losers, your lowest-conviction stocks, or overgrown positions.

For Peace of Mind

Your peace of mind is always a valid reason to sell. This gets to your quality of life, your feelings, and your subconscious tolerance for risk. It is entirely personal.

While successful investing is an essentially rational exercise, it should also be fun. Therefore, an investment that is making you nervous is in fact sending you a "sell" signal. For example, if you've invested for many years and have saved up and feel it's time to take some money off the table, do it—put it someplace with less risk. If you can't sleep at night because of the volatility of an investment, or you don't want so much of your net worth tied up in the stock market, these are valid reasons to sell.

To Lock in Tax Losses

Under our tax laws, capital losses can be used to offset capital gains, thus reducing the taxes you owe by reducing the total income they are figured on. This can sometimes be a valid reason to sell a stock. Selling at a loss lets Uncle Sam absorb some of your loss.

Toward the end of the year, therefore, many investors sell losing positions. This gives them losses to offset capital gains.

This book is not a tax manual, so you should look elsewhere for exactly how these rules work, or consult your tax adviser.

CHAPTER E-10

Summary of Portfolio Management

There has been a lot of material in this Part E on managing your portfolio, so here is a quick checklist of the most important points.

1. Probably the most important rule about making money is: don't lose it.

2. Therefore, take consistent and prudent precautions to manage risk. Most of the points in this checklist concern risk management.

3. Write out the "constitutional documents" for your stock investing: State your goals, how you expect to achieve them, what kinds of stocks you will purchase, and your strategies for buying and selling.

4. Understand the different types of stocks. Stick to types that you are comfortable with, because each stock you own requires its own amount of attention and management. The types are: A (Alpha males), most suited to active management and sometimes requiring frequent trading; B (Big), more suited to moderate management and less trading; D (Dividend), which normally require little management and trading; E (Exchange-traded funds), which must be treated as momentum stocks because there is no other way to analyze them; and M (Momentum), which require close monitoring.

5. When market conditions are bad or you can't find any attractive opportunities, don't be afraid to hold a significant portion of your "stock money" in cash. Sometimes, 100 percent cash is better than any amount in the market.

6. Use timing indicators to help optimize your buy, hold, and sell decisions. Spend a few minutes to update your Timing Outlook monthly, or whenever anything happens (such as an interest rate change) which impacts one of your indicators.

7. Don't use margin.

8. Don't short stocks.

9. Except for exchange-traded funds (Type E) and momentum stocks (Type M), limit your purchases to highly rated companies with favorable valuations. Use a Shopping List, updated periodically, to keep track of stocks you may be interested in owning.

10. Generally, purchase stocks when they are on an uptrend rather than a downtrend.

11. Sell your losers and let your winners run.

12. Use trailing sell-stops. Keep moving them up as the stock's price moves up. Set your sell-stops either as suitable percentages or as derived from stock charts.

13. Never lose more than 10 percent on a stock.

14. Limit the total number of stocks you own to between five and 15 (or 20 at the very maximum).

15. Conduct a Portfolio Review quarterly. Update the Easy-Rate Sheet for each stock that you own. Review each one's performance and outlook to determine whether it still deserves a place in your portfolio.

16. Don't allow any single stock to comprise more than 25 percent of your portfolio, unless it is still going up and you have a tight stop-loss on it.

17. Keep up with the important news on your stocks, but don't let "noise" fool you.

18. Follow the cockroach theory: If really bad news comes out about one of your stocks (such as the CEO or CFO resigning under suspicious circumstances), sell the stock immediately. There's likely to be more bad news shortly.

PART F.   BUILDING A REAL PORTFOLIO

Chapter F-1.   Getting Started

Chapter F-2.   Evolution of Sensible Tools

Chapter F-3.   Real-Life Buying and Selling

Chapter F-4.   Focusing the Portfolios on Different Missions

Chapter F-5.   Actual Results

Chapter F-6.   Lessons Learned

CHAPTER F-1

Getting Started

Two Portfolios

This book has been developed from research that I originally did for my own use, beginning in the mid-1990s. The research included my own investing experiences, magazine articles, books, pundits on TV, newspaper and web articles, and scholarly papers.

When I first started investing in stocks, I was getting confused. Much investment literature is inconsistent. Some of what I read or heard did not even seem logical, going against both common sense and my own growing experience. I decided to explore why that was, sort through and organize the different ideas, and try to develop a coherent picture of how the market works and how to invest in stocks intelligently. The result is this book.

From the time in 2000 that I began writing, I realized that any theories I developed would need a real stock portfolio to illustrate and validate them. I personally do not believe that any advice on stock investing is credible unless it is backed by a bona-fide illustrative *real-time* portfolio. It is remarkable how much investment advice is churned out that leaves the reader or viewer wondering, "Well, how did it turn out?" Magazines print articles about stocks to invest in, but there are few follow-up articles or only sketchy anecdotal ones. Investment web sites do the same thing, investment newsletters do it, books do it, and TV and radio do it. As a result, the individual investor is left in the dark on what the advice actually would have accomplished, in real dollars and in real time.

Without a real portfolio, any writer can spin the results to look more favorable than they would if actual investments were made. For example, an adviser may claim that its "highest-rated" stocks over the years have outperformed the S&P 500, ignoring that at any given time they have scores of stocks with the highest rating, stocks move constantly onto and off of their list, and realistically no individual investor would have been able to create a portfolio from them.

Sometimes the purveyors of investment advice create "model" portfolios, but they leave out commissions or other transaction costs, the management of which is an important element of successful investing. Occasionally follow-up articles seem to mention only successes but no failures. "Winning picks" are duly noted, but you're not sure whether some picks crashed and burned. Or all picks are mentioned, but one cannot see how a total portfolio actually would have performed.

And almost *never* do original or follow-up articles point out the mathematical fact that going down 20 percent (last year) followed by going up 20 percent (this year) does not get you back to where you started. You lose 4 percent in the round trip.

Credibility, therefore, requires a record of investing real dollars in real time, including commissions or other fees. The record will reveal how the investment scheme actually did, blending the blowups with the successes to tell the full story.

For this book, not one but two portfolios were created. They exist, contain real dollars invested in actual accounts, and do not ignore commissions. I started the first portfolio in 2001 and the second in 2002, and I have managed them as I was writing the book. The portfolios have been educational as well as profitable, and I have worked the lessons into the book.

Real investing is different from constructing model portfolios. I wanted to truly reflect the decision processes, emotions, rationality, and irrationality that a human being goes through when he or she is investing in the stock market, and do it under the pressure of knowing that the results would be published.

The first of the portfolios was funded with $50,000 on April 1, 2001. So the first portfolio is, as of this writing, approaching its fifth birthday. It has lived through a recession, the 9/11 tragedy, the last two years of a bear market, a war, the 2003 bull market (or bear-market rally, depending on who's talking), Enron, other corporate and accounting scandals, the dividend tax cut of 2003, the mutual fund scandals of 2004, 14 consecutive interest-rate hikes by the Fed, and the "sideways" markets of 2004–2005. That's quite a cross-section of investing conditions.

The second portfolio was instituted a year later, April 1, 2002, with $40,000 real dollars. Both portfolios are in accounts maintained at E-Trade. No other money is intermingled with the "book portfolios."

Originally, the two portfolios were just two versions of the same thing, without distinct roles. But in mid-2003, I gave them different missions regarding types of stocks and trading strategies. The focus of the first portfolio was turned toward capital gains (Types A, some B, and M stocks). Portfolio 2 was refocused onto dividend-paying stocks (Types B and D), as I came to more fully appreciate the role of dividends in total returns at about the same time that the Federal government lowered the tax rate on most dividends to 15 percent.

In retrospect, early 2001 was a lousy time to start a stock portfolio. The recession was going on (I had not yet fleshed out this book's ideas about timing), and (unpredictably) the 9/11 tragedy was just a few months away. Early 2002 was also not a good time to start the second portfolio, as 2002 absorbed the steepest market losses from the bubble deflation. So in the timing of their creation, mistakes were made. You learn from your mistakes. All in all, the portfolios have been invaluable tools for creating, refining, and applying the ideas behind Sensible Stock Investing.

More details about these portfolios are available on this book's Web site, SensibleStocks.com.

The Historical Context

As stated above, 2001 was not the greatest time to start a stock portfolio. To frame the picture, we really need to back all the way up to 1990.

The 1990s saw the longest uninterrupted stretch of economic growth in the country's history. Although the decade began with an almost-forgotten recession, by 1992 the economy was rolling along strongly with an expansion that lasted almost without interruption for eight years, capped off by the Internet and technology boom of 1997–1999.

The Internet and technology companies epitomized what many were calling the "New Economy." Its opposite was the "Old Economy," backwaters of manufacturing, services, and things like mining, which, not apparently having anything to do with technology, were decidedly non-sexy and hardly worth looking at as investments, thought many.

The economy was not the only thing that surged forward during the 1990s. The decade also achieved history's greatest nine-year leap in the stock market. The great bull market was powered by the boom in technology stocks. In 1999 alone, the "tech-heavy NASDAQ" flew up a stunning 86 percent. The same year, even the Old Economy Dow grew by 25 percent. The people running the Dow modernized it by dropping three ancient stocks and replacing them with contemporary success stories Microsoft, Intel, and Home Depot. The inclusion of Microsoft and Intel represented the first time that NASDAQ stocks appeared in the Dow, and they also reflected the growing recognition of the influence of technology companies in the economy.

But then came 2000, and the wonderful stock investment decade came to a screeching halt. The S&P 500 fell more than 9 percent, its first yearly decline since 1990. The NASDAQ fell 39 percent, wiping out most of its gain from the previous year. (Again illustrating the anti-miracle of negative compounding: 86 percent gain followed by 39 percent loss equals just 13 percent gain—not the 40 percent+ gain that may be intuitive.)

The economy went into reverse too. Finally feeling the effects of a series of Fed interest-rate hikes begun in mid-1999, by the fourth quarter of 2000 the economy was decelerating rapidly. As the year came to an end, many economists were debating whether the economy was actually in or entering a recession (i.e., contracting)—which it was. Bonds overall provided better returns than stocks in 2000, an unusual but not unknown occurrence. It would happen again in 2001 and 2002. It was widely reported that the S&P 500 had never fallen three years in a row. This time, it would.

The year 2000 started out OK. In February, the U.S. economy completed its ninth consecutive year of growth (a record). On the stock-market side, by March most broad stock indexes were at all-time highs, with technology stocks leading the way.

The reversal came abruptly. The NASDAQ fell 34 percent in five weeks after reaching its March high. Then there were intermittent rallies during a volatile year—including 13 increases of 5 percent or more in a single day (the epitome of "bear market rallies")—but overall the trend was decidedly down. By the end of 2000, the NASDAQ had fallen 51 percent from its March high, and 39 percent for the year.

What happened to cause this?

- A Fed series of interest rate hikes finally took hold in the last quarter of 2000, choking the economy with breathtaking speed. Altogether, the Fed raised rates six times in about a year, with the increases totaling nearly 2 percent. That braked the annual growth rate of the economy down to about 1 percent in Q4, the lowest in more than five years.

- Unrelated to what the Fed was doing, oil and gas prices skyrocketed, raising the *actual* rate of inflation, contributing to the *fear* of inflation, and cutting profits in energy-*dependent* industries (while conversely bringing sky-high profits to many energy-*producing* companies).

- Investor sentiment about stocks reversed, from glee and optimism to FUD (fear, uncertainty, and doubt). Indeed, by Q4 2000, hundreds of companies were falling short of earnings expectations and issuing earnings and revenue warnings all over the place. Selling pressure replaced buying pressure, driving stock prices down and down.

- Corporate spending for information technology (IT) products and services slowed abruptly. There were two main reasons. First, companies had upped their IT spending wildly in fear of the Y2K danger (remember that?), spending billions to find and replace "old code" in their legacy programs or to replace the programs altogether. When January 1, 2000 came and went without incident, this spending simply stopped. Second, as the economy was slowing, firms began looking for ways to trim their operating and capital budgets. IT was a real target for cuts, because it had just been getting all the money, and companies felt the need to turn their attention elsewhere. Formerly routine corporate policies—like replacing PCs every three years—were reexamined and in many cases thrown out the window.

- Finally, the Internet bubble simply burst. Many dot-com companies spiraled downward so fast you could hardly follow the news. Their capital dried up, their employees left voluntarily or were fired, and their business models were exposed as hopelessly flawed—they had no way to make a profit. Their stocks followed suit. The New Economy, it turned out, had to play by Old Economy rules. The premier old rule—make a profit—was no longer overlooked by investors, who began dumping dot-com stocks at breathtaking speeds. Some companies lost 80 to 90 percent or more of their market value, and hundreds went out of business.

As 2001 began, these trends continued. During the first quarter, the economy grew at essentially a zero rate. Despite an occasional day or two of strength, the stock market continued to march downward, with the

Dow and NASDAQ hitting lows in a terrific flameout on Monday, March 12, 2001—almost exactly a year after they had hit their all-time highs. The fall in the NASDAQ was unprecedented: It had closed above *5000* in March 2000, but closed March 12, 2001 below *2000*—a stunning 60 percent fall. All its gains of 1999 and some of 1998's had been wiped out. Trillions of dollars of investor wealth simply disappeared. Two days later, the Dow fell over 300 more points, closing below 10,000 for the first time in well over a year. While it moved up and down over the next couple weeks, the movement in both bellwether indexes was downward in the aggregate.

Good or Bad Time to Start a Stock Portfolio?

As luck would have it, this was just when I was planning to start the first portfolio for this book. Remember, at the time, I did not have the benefit of the timing indicators which are now part of the Sensible Stock Investing system and which would have warned me to go slow or hold off.

In the absence of timing indicators, many signs seemed positive.

- Because the stock market tends to be predictive, it is often thought that one of the best times to invest in stocks is when the economy is at low ebb, in anticipation of an economic turnaround and a sure-to-come growth phase of the business cycle. (This is the theory behind "contrarian" investing—go against the flow.)

- The bear market had been going for about 12 months. It was widely reported that is a fairly typical length for a bear market.

- The Fed had reversed course on interest rates, beginning to cut them as its concerns shifted from preventing inflation to preventing a recession. By the end of 2001, rates would be cut an unprecedented 11 times.

We now know that these positive signs were misleading. The impact of the Fed cuts would not kick in until after a significant time lag. The economy went into recession. The market would continue to fall (overall) for three years running.

But I did not know this. So I went ahead and started the Sensible Stock Investing portfolio. From the time the portfolio was started in April 2001, the S&P 500 would drift (or crash) from 1160 to as low as 841 at the end of February 2003, a 27 percent drop. So the biggest lesson learned during the first two years of the portfolio was to have the discipline to stay in cash when market conditions are unfavorable. Our timing indicators now help us tell whether conditions are favorable or unfavorable. Cash is now enshrined as a Type C "stock," in other words a good place to be when the market is tanking.

The Original Portfolio Begins

Initially, to create a good *demonstration* portfolio, I established the following simple ground rules:

- To use the S&P 500 as the benchmark. That's what we are trying to beat.

- To never add money to the account (except for dividends received). That makes the portfolio's gains and losses simple to compute.

- To start the portfolio at the beginning of a quarter, again to make comparisons easier. Q2 2001 began on April 1. That's April Fool's Day, which perhaps should have been a warning.

April 1 was actually a Sunday, so my first day for potential buying was Monday April 2. The value of the S&P 500 at the end of trading the preceding Friday was 1160. That's the starting benchmark. It is hard to believe, but it took almost 3½ years, until November 4, 2004, for the S&P 500 to finally regain that starting level of 1160. Quick preview: By that time, the portfolio's value was up 10 percent—way better than the benchmark.

The Second Portfolio Begins

Essentially, the decision to begin the second portfolio faced the same "wall of worry" that the first one did. It was a year later, and the economy appeared to be climbing out of the recession of 2001. After a strong run-up in the wake of the September 11 tragedies, the market basically moved sideways. The S&P 500 finished 2001 at 1148. Three months later (at the end of March 2002) it stood at 1147. The Fed had set a record with its 11 interest rate cuts, and the pundits were already looking forward to the reversal of this course and the first tightening (raising) of rates. (The pundits were premature. The Fed would not raise rates again until mid-2004.)

Still not having the benefit of the timing indicators, I rated April 2002 as an OK time to begin Portfolio 2. So, it was funded with $40,000 on April 1, 2002. Its ground rules were similar to those for the first portfolio.

The value of the S&P 500 at the beginning of the second account was 1147, so that's the starting benchmark for Portfolio 2, a little below the starting value for Portfolio 1. This time, it took about 2½ years, until November 3, 2004, for the S&P 500 to approximately regain that initial level. Another preview: By that time, Portfolio 2's value was up 17 percent. Sensible Stock Investing was working, even in abysmal market conditions!

CHAPTER F-2

Evolution of Sensible Tools

Easy-Rate™ Stock Rating Sheets (Appendix I, Forms 1 and 2)

It was clear from the beginning that—to keep investing sensible and fact-based rather than impulsive and emotional—certain tools would be needed.

The first tool is the Easy-Rate™ Stock Rating Sheet, an example of which appears in Appendix I, Form 1. There is nothing particularly inventive about single-page stock digests. "Snapshot" sheets are pretty common in investing. What makes ours unique is the special brew of information.

The Easy-Rate™ Sheet illustrates the use of separate scores for the *excellence of a company* and the *valuation of its stock*. Both scoring systems have been refined over the years, and indeed they still undergo continual reexamination. Around the time Portfolio 1 was begun, the maximum number of points a *company* could score was about 35. There are more factors in use now, and the total number of points available is 63.

The original *valuation* system used a simple Good-Fair-Poor scale. The more extreme valuations "Excellent" and "Bubble" were added later, as was the numerical scoring system to arrive at the valuations. Now, the use of numerical scores for rating both companies and stock valuations presents a parallel structure, with both systems easy to use and understand.

In Sensible Stock Investing, no stock is purchased without first creating an Easy-Rate Sheet for it. In practice, I keep the sheets strung alphabetically together as one long Word document in my PC. I also keep a printed set in a three-ring binder, with three tabs:

- Owned stocks
- Shopping List stocks (the Shopping List is discussed below)
- Everything else

An individual investor cannot follow hundreds of companies. I keep the number of active Easy-Rate Sheets under 100. Stock and company information, of course, is dynamic. Important financial information changes at least quarterly (when earnings are announced), and valuation information changes daily (as the stock's price fluctuates). Analyzing companies and valuing stocks takes some time, to be sure, but it is well within the reach of the individual investor. It can be fun, and it is a joy when you discover an excellent company with a favorable valuation and a decent chart. Here is about how much time it takes to maintain reasonable records:

- I like to update the Easy-Rate sheets for the stocks I own every three months. For 15 stocks, that takes about 4 hours. The updates are necessary for the Portfolio Reviews discussed later in this chapter.

- I update the Easy-Rate Sheets for stocks on my Shopping List at least every six months. For 25 stocks, that takes 6 to 7 hours. In between, as new stocks are evaluated which score highly enough to make the Shopping List, I just handwrite them in. If it gets too messy, I prepare a new Shopping List, with the new stock integrated into it.

- I try to analyze two to three new companies each month. That takes about an hour each. The new sheets then get filed behind the correct tab in the binder. If it scores highly enough, the stock and its scores are also hand-written onto the existing Shopping List.

By the way, new company ideas can come from many sources:

- *Companies that make or sell the products that you yourself use and like.* This is the classic "buy what you know" approach of famed investor Peter Lynch.

- *Companies featured in well-reasoned articles.* Popular magazines like *Money, SmartMoney,* and *Fortune,* and newspapers like the *Wall Street Journal* and the *New York Times,* often carry feature articles that go into depth and can give you great insights into a company's Story, including its industry, market share, and the like. Your local paper may profile a local company that is not widely known.

- *Companies that you screen for.* Stock screening tools are available on *Yahoo, MSN Money,* and several other financial Web sites. Your online brokerage probably has a screening tool in its "Research" section. To screen for stocks, plug in the same criteria that we use in evaluating companies. Use mid-level values for the screening variables, to avoid missing companies falling a little short on just one or two criteria. If you set all the variables to the values required to get maximum credit on our scoring system, the screen will return zero companies! No company is perfect. Of course, you can adjust the screening criteria any way that you wish.

- *Tips.* Stock tips, of course, have a very bad reputation, and it is obviously foolish to invest solely on the basis of a tip. But the Sensible Stock Investor does not invest in any stock without subjecting it to all of our tests, so you can treat tips dispassionately, as just another source of a potentially good idea. I consider anything short of a feature article or complete analyst's report as a "tip," so this category includes not only what you hear at the water cooler but also thumbnail sketches or brief articles, stocks touted on TV by a pundit or CEO, stocks that appear in lists of good-performing stocks or widely-held stocks, stocks that are on a brokerage's "recommended list," and the like. Once you get started, you'll have many more stock ideas than you have time to check them out.

If you are writing-phobic, take a look at the Story Questionnaire in Appendix I, Form 2. If you answer the questions on that form, you will basically have the stock's Story completed.

The Shopping List (Appendix I, Form 3)

As concise and useful as the Easy-Rate Sheets are, it is useful to condense the information further to guide you when you are actually buying and selling stocks. That's the purpose of the Shopping List. The Shopping List is derived from your Easy-Rate Sheets. It is a list of companies you might be interested in buying.

A sample Shopping List appears in Appendix I, Form 3.

The Shopping List can be as simple or complex as you want to make it. At the simple end, it would just be a list of your highest-rated companies. That's how I started.

Later on, my Shopping List became more sophisticated. As shown in the sample, each Shopping List now contains four sub-lists, each with a different purpose. In fact, the beauty of the Shopping List system is that you can make special sub-lists to emphasize any factor you choose. My Shopping List currently consists of these four sub-lists:

- Sub-List 1: Best Total Score. The total score is the sum of the company score and valuation score. Because of the way our point system is constructed, the company and valuation scores are on roughly equal footing in their ability to influence the total score. Thus, this sub-list is essentially a display of the upper right quadrant of the Sensible Stock Opportunities Map (displayed at the end of Chapter E-4). These stocks are the best opportunities overall—the highest scoring companies with the best valuations. I usually limit this sub-list to the highest 20 scores (plus ties). In the sample Shopping List in Appendix I, Form 3, the list of Top 20 overall scores required 53 or more total points (company score plus valuation score).

- Sub-List 2: Best Company Score. This is based on company scores only. It represents the upper half of the Map, so it includes both the best opportunities overall plus potential momentum opportunities—that is, high-scoring companies which do not have great valuations but that may nevertheless be enjoying good momentum in the market. In the sample Shopping List in Appendix I, Form 3, the Top 20 company scores are represented, which required a company score of 31 or more points when the list was created.

- Sub-List 3: Best Valuation Score. This sub-list represents the right side of the Map—stocks with the best valuations (no matter what their company score). For rigor, I include only stocks that have valuation scores of "Good" or better—which requires 23 or more valuation points. This sub-list is often short, because most good companies do not have Good or better valuations very often. In the sample Shopping List in Appendix I, Form 3, 16 companies made this sub-list.

- Sub-List 4: Best Dividend Stocks. I love this sub-list. It is the basis for most of Portfolio 2. Creating it takes just a little extra work. First, only companies with current yields that exceed the S&P 500's average are eligible. Each of those companies is given a composite score consisting of the sum of their overall score plus an extra dividend weighting. The dividend weighting is the stock's current yield multiplied by 4 (rounded to the nearest integer). So a stock yielding 2.3 percent gets an extra dividend weighting of 9 points. Stocks often turn up on this list that do not appear on the other sub-lists. Several stocks that have performed well for our portfolios, such as Kinder Morgan Energy Partners, Bank of America, Exxon Mobil, Chevron Texaco, and GE all were purchased because they popped up on this list.

I update my Shopping List on a continuing basis (handwriting in changes as Easy-Rate Sheets are updated or created), and reprint the formal document, with changes incorporated, several times a year just to keep things neat. Altogether, maintaining a Shopping List takes only a few hours per year, well worth the time spent. I try to make sure that any stock on the Shopping List has an Easy-Rate Sheet that is never more than 6 months old.

Timing Outlook (Appendix I, Form 4)

The Timing Outlook is a simple tool that summarizes the timing indicators described in Chapter E-5. It takes about a half hour, and it is best done monthly. The third Thursday of the month (when the Conference Board usually releases its new Index of Leading Economic Indicators) is usually a good time. Between full updates, you can handwrite in and recalculate the effect of changes in other indicators, such as Fed interest rate changes, as they happen.

A sample Timing Outlook is displayed in Appendix I, Form 4.

Portfolio Reviews (Appendix I, Form 5)

The final tool is the Portfolio Review. A sample is displayed in Appendix I, Form 5.

This is where you take a step back and view your portfolio through a wide-angle lens. Between these formal reviews, the other mechanisms—updating your sell-stops, updating your Easy-Rate Sheets for owned stocks, completing the monthly Timing Outlook, and keeping your Shopping List current—keep your portfolio sort of on automatic pilot.

However, every three or six months, it is a good idea to take a bird's-eye view of your holdings. The idea behind every Portfolio Review is to distance yourself from the daily and weekly noise and reassess your portfolio strategically. The Portfolio Review combines information about the company behind each stock, its valuation, and general market conditions. Ask questions like:

- What is the current outlook for the market? (Consult your most recent Timing Outlook.)
- Has the portfolio gotten out of balance in some way—too much of one stock, too much cash for market conditions, not well rounded enough? If so, you may want to do some buying or selling to restore the balance you want.
- Has anything changed about the fundamental outlook of each company? You'll discover this when you update the Easy-Rate™ Stock Rating Sheets. If a company's outlook has changed, does anything need to be done about it?

- Does each stock in your portfolio still deserve its place there? How has the stock performed, and what meaning does that have? Has every holding kept at least even with the market over the past two years? Has any company's rating slipped badly such that it is far less attractive than when you bought it? Does each company still satisfy the reasons you bought it? You may want to tighten or loosen sell-stops as a result of these questions.

- What is the current valuation of the company? Do your stop-loss limits make sense given that valuation and current market conditions?

- Does your Shopping List contain candidates that now seem far more attractive than current holdings? Want to make a swap or two? Your incumbent stocks "defend their records" as to why they should be held. Your Shopping List stocks "make their case" why they should be purchased. Don't forget to take into account the likely tax aspects of selling in order to make a swap—this puts a heavier burden on potential new buys.

- Do any of the stocks you sold deserve reconsideration? Was selling them a mistake?

- Should any changes be made because of personal conditions in your life?

The Portfolio Review counteracts inertia. You want to get the best results you can from Your Investment Company. While all of our other mechanisms do let things run on autopilot, over time there can be an almost imperceptible drift away from best practices. The Portfolio Review helps you to catch and correct those.

Since you are taking a wide-angle strategic look, the Portfolio Review is also a good time to reexamine the "constitutional documents" for your stock investing. Review your goals and strategies. Is there anything you think should be changed in your overall approach? Change it and update your strategic documents.

A complete Portfolio Review should take a couple of hours to complete.

Summary of Sensible Stock Investing Tools

So these are the tools for the individual Sensible Stock Investor to use in managing real-life portfolios:

Tools and Time Required for Sensible Stock Investing

Tool or Activity	Purpose	Frequency	Time per Year
Easy-Rate™ Stock Rating Sheets	One-page snapshot showing important factors about company and its stock's valuation. Summed up in Total Company Rating Score and Total Valuation Score. Keep total number of active Sheets to a manageable number (probably fewer than 100).	Update quarterly for owned stocks. Update semiannually for Shopping List stocks. Create 2 to 3 new sheets per month. Periodically clean out stocks with "no hope."	50 hours
Shopping List	Summary of the most attractive investment possibilities from various points of view.	Update formally monthly or at least quarterly. Update informally on continuing basis as Rating Sheets are updated or new ones are created.	20 hours
Timing Outlook	Summary of timing indicators and short-term market outlook. Provides basis for tightening or loosening sell-stops as well as setting direction for holding cash vs. being in the market.	Monthly	6 hours
Portfolio Reviews	Formal review of owned stocks for performance, continued suitability, balance, and diversity.	Quarterly, after earnings season (February, May, August, November)	8 hours
Update sell-stops	Continual process of adjusting sell-stops as stock prices move up, so that they "trail" the stock's actual price.	Daily or weekly	20 hours
Constitutional documents	Outline objectives and strategies for portfolio(s)	Update annually	2 hours

In summary, the individual investor can employ a sensible, "tight" investment methodology in a little over 100 hours per year—or about 9 hours per month. That seems like a reasonable time expenditure for Your Investment Company. If you really enjoy the process, you can spend more time at it—researching new stock ideas, updating sell-stops daily, and the like. On the other hand, if you are not willing to spend the 100 hours per year, owning individual stocks (rather than mutual funds) may not be for you.

CHAPTER F-3

Real-Life Buying and Selling

Life can only be understood backwards, but it must be lived forward.
—Søren Kierkegaard

This chapter is not a diary of all the purchases and sales in both portfolios—that would take too long. Instead, let's focus on a few illustrative experiences that have contributed most heavily to the refinement of Sensible Stock Investing's principles.

After researching my first batch of stocks, I determined that my first two purchases would be Berkshire Hathaway and Symantec, which were the only two stocks that turned in "Good" valuation ratings among the first that I analyzed. So I bought about $5000 worth of Berkshire and about $3000 of Symantec on Monday morning, April 2, 2001, and the Sensible Stock Investing portfolio was on its way.

Notice that in today's world of computerized trading, old concepts like "round lots" (that is, blocks of 100 shares) have lost essentially all of their meaning. To hit the dollar targets, I bought just 4 shares of Berkshire and 70 shares of Symantec, without having to pay extra commissions for "odd lots."

Each stock got off to a positive start, while the market itself bounced around, and the commentators were still arguing over whether we were in or entering a recession, whether the Fed would lower interest rates further at their next meeting, and so on.

If you watch this stuff daily, it can either be interesting (like toggling among myriad football games on the satellite) or it can drive you crazy. The spectrum of opinions rendered in an average day on CNBC and Bloomberg is mind-boggling.

Psychologically, within a month I was already having trouble staying disciplined. Rather than taking a year or more to invest the $50,000 stake, as I originally thought I would, by the end of the first month I purchased four more stocks (Citigroup, Sawtek, Kerr-McGee, and Tyco). Almost $32,000 was already invested. It didn't help on the discipline front that the stock market was really powering forward and so were my stocks. The portfolio gained 9 percent in its first month; it seemed like the good old days were back already. This is an interesting psychological phenomenon: It feels incorrect to be on the sidelines ("in cash") when the market's going up. I was already getting quite itchy to invest the rest of the money. Commentators were reporting that the market had clearly "hit bottom." But it hadn't. "The bottom" was still more than *two years* away. Virtually no one had figured out that we were coming out of a bubble of such historic proportions that it would take many, many months of price declines to bring valuations back to historically sensible levels. Few recognized how far technology prices were out of line or that, before the deflation was over, some of these stocks would lose 70 to 80 to 90 percent of their value.

Handling an Acquisition

Early on, the portfolio offered a lesson in what to do when one of the companies you own is acquired. In mid-May, Sawtek, which had been doing fabulously (up over 50 percent), was offered to be acquired by an outfit named Triquint Semiconductors. When a company offers to purchase another company, they normally offer a premium over the existing stock price (say 30 percent or so). That is an inducement to gain board and shareholder approval. As you would expect, this usually causes the price of the target company to rise accordingly, as many investors now consider the offering price to *define* the value of the target company, and they become willing to purchase shares of the target company at prices *approaching* that valuation.

I say "approaching," because usually the target company's stock price does not quite reach the acquisition offer price. This reflects investors' recognition of the risk that the deal will not go through. Sawtek's board could reject it, regulators could block it, or something else may go wrong.

The offer for Sawtek caused its shares to explode upward to catch up to the offering price, running them up even faster than they had been, which was pretty good anyway. Eventually, Sawtek would reach a point 90 percent higher than when I bought it, in just a couple of months.

TriQuint's offer was not all positive news, however. It introduced at least three major uncertainties:

*   The offer was made in Triquint *shares*, not cash. In other words, Triquint was using its shares as currency. This meant that the actual value of the offer would hop around as the price of Triquint hopped around. Furthermore, Triquint's normal volatility might be exacerbated by the acquisition offer itself, as Triquint's current shareholders evaluate what *they* think of this move by management. If they think it is dumb, they might pile out of Triquint's shares, lowering their prices, and thereby lowering the value of the offer. Triquint's volatility essentially became Sawtek's.
*   I did not know anything about Triquint. If I held onto Sawtek through the deal's closing, I would become an owner of Triquint. Sawtek would disappear. (Had the offer been made in cash, conversely, I would just have received the money.) So Triquint, which had not been on my radar screen, had to be checked out. It might be an overvalued lousy company. On the other hand, it might be a great company fairly valued. You cannot tell until you do the research.

- The deal might collapse. If this happens, it would make the value of Sawtek very questionable. Was it really worth the offering price? Was the former price correct? Something in between? The risk was that the price of Sawtek could collapse.

With all this in mind, the sensible thing to do was to tighten the stop-loss order for Sawtek to protect at least some of the unexpected paper gains from the offer. I tightened it from 40 to 25 percent. (Nowadays, I would tighten it to just a couple of percent.) The idea still was to leave plenty of room for both "normal" volatility and for the price to go up further, as it might if another suitor stepped in and a bidding war broke out.

I got a chance to look into Triquint a few days later, and I did not like what I saw: It was a semiconductor company with lots of debt. Then coincidentally *in a single day* a host of bad news came out about the semiconductor industry and about Triquint. Its stock plunged, and a good portion of my 90 percent gain in Sawtek was lost as it sold off at the 25 percent stop-loss point. Since I did not want to own Triquint, at some point I would have sold Sawtek anyway. Postscript: The companies merged. The new Triquint continued to plunge steadily over the next three years, practically to nothing. At this writing, February 2006, its price is about $5.00, off a high of over $50 in 2000. That's a 90 percent drop, not untypical of what can happen to a bubble stock when the bubble pops.

Are there other ways I could have handled the situation? Sure.

- I could have sold Sawtek as soon as I heard about the acquisition. But my thinking in setting the stop-loss order was that Sawtek might go up *more*. And for a while it did, by a couple thousand dollars at one point.
- I could have set a stop-loss order right at (or very near) the current price of Sawtek as soon as I heard about the acquisition. That would have given me the benefit of any upside after the announcement, but gotten me out of the stock if it began to go down. That's what I would do now.

Lesson learned: Immediately set a stop-loss order just below the run-up price after the announcement of an acquisition offer for a stock that you own. This protects practically all of your gains from the offer, but leaves you in possession of the stock in case something sends it up even more (such as a competing offer from another company once the world finds out your company is "in play.")

Learning about a "Bear Market Rally"

In the first couple months after April 1, 2001, the Dow Jones Industrial Average surged 2000 points (21 percent) from its March 22 closing "bottom." The NASDAQ gained 40 percent since its April 4 low.

Was irrational exuberance back at work? Yes. The market was in what is known as a "bear market rally." What this means is that while the *overall* market trend was decidedly downwards, nevertheless for a short period of time, the market rallied. As we learned in our discussion of market trends, you cannot tell the difference in real time between short-term blips and the beginning of long-term trends. You can only see the patterns afterwards. In the meantime, you have to make your decisions in real time.

A bear market rally is a short-lived event embedded in a long-term trend. Note that a falling stock price in the face of lower earnings results in little change in valuation. If both P and E decline proportionately, the P/E ratio does not change very much. Looking at the NASDAQ as a whole, for example, its P/E ratio hit 150 in March 2000. Despite the prices of tech stocks plummeting, its P/E still stood at 131 a year later.

Lesson: To deflate a bubble, *valuations* must decline to sensible levels. Price declines, by themselves, do not pop a bubble. What are "sensible levels"? Some would say valuations must drop to historical averages (like 17 for the S&P 500), while others argue that to fully deflate a bubble, valuations must decline even below that (say to 15 or 12), thus wringing out even the most tenacious irrationally exuberant investors. Whatever the case, in early-to-mid 2001, neither condition had been reached by a long shot.

Watching Your Portfolio

In the early days, I watched my portfolio every day (except when on vacation). I still do. *Many* advisers say that is too close inspecting, because you are more prone to react to the insignificant bits of news that flow throughout every day. That is probably true for many people, but I still do it because I find it to be fun. There is a sports-competition mentality about it: You root for your stocks to do well, and for the market itself to go up (because that usually helps your individual stocks). The Sensible Stock Investor is protected from emotional dumb decisions by following the investment strategies, principles, and rules of Sensible Stock Investing.

On a typical day, a $50,000 portfolio goes up or down a few hundred bucks (that is, less than 1 percent). On its best day, our portfolio has gone up over $1800, and on its worst day it has been down about $1000.

Tech Collapse—and Lessons from It

We know now that the technology sector was really collapsing in 2001 and would continue to do so in 2002. Somewhat to my embarrassment for purposes of this book—and the Buy-to-Hold philosophy—all of the portfolio's tech stocks sold off (that is, they hit their 40 percent sell-stops) during the middle of 2001.

Lesson: Tech stocks are unique. They are *really* volatile, even when near "fair" prices. There is just something about technology companies and their stocks that gets investors' juices flowing. The stocks tend to trade at high valuation ratios, even when the companies are not performing well. They tend to overreact to news. They are the epitome of Type A stocks.

Another lesson: Tech is cyclical. Many experts denied this during the New Economy era, but the fact of the matter is that most tech profits come from corporate (not consumer) spending. Much of corporate spending is discretionary, and when any company slows down, cutting its tech spending is one of the first things in its tool kit to improve its performance numbers.

The tech stock situation also is a vivid example of the portfolio management conundrum between buying and "just" holding, or accepting the more frequent trading that inevitably results from selling to stop the damage when your stocks slide. There seem to be two diametrically opposed conclusions that could logically be drawn:

- Don't set *any* volatility "window." If the company is a good one, and its stock was fairly priced, it will come back. This is the essence of true Buy-*and*-Hold thinking. But: If you've made a mistake, and your stock drops 40 to 50 percent, what is the probability that it will not only recover that 40 to 50 percent, but will go on to post significant gains? Does the fact that your stock drops 40 to 50 percent itself *tell you* that you made a mistake in picking it? Again, you can't tell until much later. Maybe the answer differs between Type-A (high-volatility) stocks and Type B or D (lower-volatility) stocks. Perhaps they deserve different rule sets for buying and selling.

- Set *tight* volatility windows—perhaps as low as 8 or 10 percent.

What is the most sensible conclusion? Certainly, reasonable minds can differ. William J. O'Neil, the publisher of *Investor's Business Daily,* recommends allowing only an 8 percent downside when investing—if your stock loses 8 percent, get out. On the other hand, there are many Buy-and-Hold investors who line up much closer to the other end of the spectrum. An interesting note, though: Buy-and-Hold works a lot better in a positive market environment. Holding onto many of the stocks on the original Shopping List would have resulted in huge paper losses that have not been recovered even to the present day.

Cataclysmic Events—September 11, 2001

The terrorist attacks on September 11, 2001 presented an unprecedented situation, being a foreign attack on the continental U.S. Of course, the biggest impact was the human devastation. A surreal weirdness settled over the country as we watched the developing news, witnessed the World Trade Center towers collapse, and agonized over the plight of the victims and rescuers.

The stock markets—which had been in a protracted decline anyway—were closed for the rest of the week after the Tuesday attacks, to reopen again the following Monday. That allowed time to consider what the financial impact of the attacks might be. Therefore, while the markets were closed, I conducted a careful Portfolio Review.

Although at the time I tried to make the best Portfolio Review I could, in the end it cost money. That is because, in anticipation of a steep market drop when the markets reopened, I installed tightened sell-stops. Nearly all of them were triggered—some for significant losses—when the markets reopened. I ignored copious information—or more accurately, had trouble believing in the emotions after the attacks—that historically the market recovers pretty quickly from cataclysmic events. What I should have done is *removed* all the sell-stops and ridden it out. The first day of trading, unsurprisingly, brought a tremendous sell-off, reflecting the general anxiety after the attacks. Both the Dow and the NASDAQ plunged about 7 percent. Several of the stop-loss orders were executed at well under the stop price, because some stocks *opened* far below their closing prices from the week before.

Setting the stop-loss orders was a mistake, an emotional decision. I was correct in predicting what the stocks would do—sell off. The mistake came in:

* Not believing that the markets would rebound so quickly after the terrorist attacks; and

* Underestimating how far below their last closing price many stocks would open, guaranteeing huge losses when the sell-stops were triggered.

The lesson, of course, is that when a true cataclysmic event occurs, hang onto your stocks, they will more than likely recover and the market will return to its pre-event level. The following table is illustrative.

Market Reactions to Catastrophes

Event	Reaction Period	Dow during Reaction Period	Dow 6 Months Later	Dow 1 Year Later	Dow 2 Years Later
Pearl Harbor	12/6-10/1941	–7%	–10%	–1%	+14%
Cuban Missile Crisis	10/19-27/1962	+1%	+24%	+30%	+51%
Market Crash of 1987	10/2-19/1987	–34%	+15%	+23%	+54%
Iraq Invades Kuwait	8/1-2/1990	–1%	–5%	+5%	+18%
World Trade Center Bombing	2/26-27/1993	–1%	+9%	+14%	+18%
Oklahoma City Bombing	4/19-20/1995	+1%	+13%	+31%	+57%
9-11-2001	9/11-17/2001	–7%	+19%	–8%	+16%

CHAPTER F-4

Focusing the Portfolios on Different Missions

As has been stated, in the beginning the two portfolios were really not distinguishable. They used the same basic strategies, the same Shopping List, and so on. The differences in their holdings were more the result of judgment calls at particular times and the vagaries of when cash was available for investing in each portfolio.

In mid-2003, I decided to turn Portfolio 2 into a dividend-focused portfolio. I did this for several reasons:

• I wanted to make the portfolios different, so they could demonstrate different things and teach different lessons.

• Dividends seemed to be growing in importance. This was partly spurred by the dividend tax cut (to a 15 percent maximum rate), making dividends one of the least-taxed forms of income anywhere.

• Spurred by the tax change, more companies were starting dividend programs, and companies that already had them were expanding them.

• I like the contribution to overall returns that high-dividend stocks provide.

• I like some of the typical characteristics of dividend-paying stocks—such as lower volatility, the stream of cash in my hand, and their own usually strong cash positions.

With Portfolio 2 being focused on dividend-paying stocks, I decided to tilt Portfolio 1 toward stocks whose rewards would come mostly from capital gains. Thus, distinct missions were established for the two portfolios. Essentially, Portfolio 1 (dubbed "The Exciting Portfolio") focuses on capital gains, high-growth stocks, and close portfolio management. It invests in Types A, B, and M stocks. Portfolio 2 ("The Boring Portfolio") focuses on strong companies with good to great dividend yields combined with the expectation of at least some capital growth. It invests in Types B and D stocks.

The difference in approach between the two portfolios leads to a difference in expectations. For example, because The Exciting Portfolio is "price increase" oriented, we ask a little more from it: annualized gains of 8 percent versus 7 percent for The Boring Portfolio. We set the bar higher for Portfolio 1 because we expect

Portfolio 2 to be "safer": Dividend-paying stocks usually come with less downside risk than the stocks of non-dividend-payers.

Some readers may think we have set the performance bar too low for both portfolios by using hurdle rates of 8 percent and 7 percent, given the S&P 500's historical return of 10 percent or so per year. Actually, the hurdle goals are tougher than they sound: We are expecting these portfolios to return that much over every three-year period *no matter what the S&P 500 does,* even if the index loses money. In addition, both portfolios are expected to beat the S&P 500's performance, so if the index achieves its historical 10 to 11 percent performance (or more), that becomes the hurdle rate for both portfolios, and the rates of 8 percent and 7 percent become moot.

In addition, we have set a performance goal almost never seen elsewhere: Neither portfolio is *ever* expected to fall back more than 10 percent from any value it attains.

CHAPTER F-5

Actual Results

How the Portfolios' Performance Is Analyzed

Because we never add or withdraw money from either portfolio, their performance is easy to analyze. The math is simple: Either portfolio's total value at any time can be compared to:

- the initial stake—to get total performance to date;
- the previous month's value—to get monthly performance; and
- the value at the beginning of the current year—to get year-to-date performance.

The same comparisons can be made with respect to the S&P 500 Stock Index in order to compare portfolio performance to "the market."

The summary tables later in this chapter show our actual results. I keep more complete tables showing every stock purchase and sale, plus month-end totals for each portfolio's dollar value and the benchmark S&P 500 Stock Index. The complete tables are too long to print here. More information is available on our Web site, SensibleStocks.com. The condensed tables below show year-end results for each year of each portfolio's existence.

Note well: Unlike most of what you read or hear on TV, these portfolios *do* count transaction costs. Most TV talking heads and magazine articles conveniently ignore these costs when talking about how their stock picks have done. But believe me, transaction costs are very much part of your real investing life, as are taxes. Any way you can lower your transaction costs (by paying lower commissions, holding down the number of trades, or taking advantage of promotions by a broker—such as receiving *x* number of free trades for opening an account) works in your favor.

Here are a few additional notes about performance checking:

- The first portfolio, opened at E-Trade in 2001, was credited with a promotional $150 which E-Trade was offering at the time. Crediting that money to the portfolio may sound like cheating, but it is in fact what happened in real life. Sometimes you get good deals. At the time, E-Trade generally charged $15 per trade, so it was like getting 10 free trades. If I had signed up with a broker that charged only $8 per trade, I would have been getting credit for that, too, in the form of lower transaction costs.

- Each portfolio is credited with any dividends received (that is, dividends go into the brokerage account). Dividends are not automatically reinvested in the company that issued them; they come into the account as cash. Until such time as they are invested, they stay in cash.

- Each portfolio is also credited with the account's sweep interest each month. Sweep interest is almost universal in brokerage accounts and therefore also reflects real-life investing. Most of the time, a portion of each portfolio is in cash. The interest earned on this cash (small though it is) is properly counted as part of the portfolio's return. Exactly the same reasoning would apply if I decided to park that cash in a money-market fund or bond fund temporarily while deciding on individual stocks to purchase.

- The return on each account is figured on the total original dollars placed in the account, not only on the money actually invested in stocks. In other words, if I keep some money in cash, it still counts as part of the stake against which we are measuring performance. Again, this reflects real life investing. Depicting the *whole portfolio's* return as equal to the return *on only the dollars invested* would misleadingly inflate the returns depicted. The picture we're looking for is, how did we do with the $50,000 in Portfolio 1 and the $40,000 in Portfolio 2?

Of course, most real-life portfolios have money added or withdrawn from time to time. Doing that here would just complicate the calculations. In all other respects, the demonstration portfolios are like any portfolio at an online brokerage.

So how have the two portfolios done? The following sections tell the story.

Portfolio 1's Performance

Portfolio Number 1

Date	Description	Port Value $	S&P 500 Stock Index Value	Port Change % for Year	S&P 500 Change % for Year	Total Port Change %	Total S&P 500 Change %
4/1/01	Initial deposit to account	$50,000	1160				
12/31/01	2001's performance (9 months)	44,991	1148	−10%	−1%	−10%	−1%
12/31/02	2002's performance for the year	41,492	880	−8%	−23%	−17%	−24%
12/31/03	2003's performance for the year	47,040	1112	+13%	+26%	−6%	−4%
12/31/04	2004's performance for the year	59,868	1212	+27%	+9%	+20%	+4%
12/31/05	2005's performance for the year	59,849	1248	−0%	+3%	+20%	+8%
1/31/06	2006's performance (1 month)	61,568	1280	+3%	+3%	+23%	+10%

Notice how the portfolio's relative performance to "the market" (as represented by the S&P 500 Stock Index) has improved as:

- Experience has been gained;
- More conservative sell-stop orders have been used; and
- The portfolio was given a more defined focus in 2003.

Notice also that these results are "scalable" to any size portfolio, since the measuring stick is percentage gain. So, for example, if we'd started off with $500,000 rather than $50,000, the portfolio would have ten times more (i.e., $615,568) in it. Either way, it is a total gain of 23 percent. Overall, this port has better than doubled the market.

Portfolio 2's Performance

Portfolio Number 2

Date	Description	Port Value $	S&P 500 Stock Index Value	Port Change % for Year	S&P 500 Change % for Year	Total Port Change %	Total S&P 500 Change %
4/1/02	Initial deposit to account	$40,000	1147				
12/31/02	2002's performance (9 months)	30,759	880	−23%	−23%	−23%	−23%
12/31/03	2003's performance for the year	41,582	1112	+35%	+26%	+4%	−3%
12/31/04	2004's performance for the year	47,975	1212	+15%	+9%	+20%	+6%
12/31/05	2005's performance for the year	50,262	1248	+5%	+3%	+26%	+9%
1/31/06	2006's performance (1 month)	50,477	1280	+0%	+3%	+26%	+12%

Portfolio 2, begun in April 2002, got off to a terrible start, beginning as it did during the most severe part of the bursting market bubble. After one year, the portfolio was down 23 percent (equal to the market). But 2003 saw a dramatic turnaround as the portfolio became focused on its newly defined mission of concentrating on dividend-paying stocks. It has outperformed the market steadily since then. Over its life, it has better than doubled the market.

Performance versus Objectives

Since the mid-2003 mission definitions, each portfolio has had specific performance objectives. Have these been accomplished? Let's look at each portfolio.

Investment Objectives for Portfolio 1:

- *No matter what the S&P 500's return (even if negative), attain at least 8 percent positive annualized return over every three-year period.* Even though the objective did not exist until 2003, the portfolio's annualized return can be computed for each full year following the completion of its third year of existence from the port's inception in April 2001. For the three-year period ending April 2004, the annualized return was –0.9 percent, reflecting the terrible start the portfolio got off to during the market collapse of 2000–2002. For the three-year period ending April 2005, the annualized return was 12.6 percent, beating the target easily.

- *Beat the S&P 500 in total return over every three-year period.* This has been attained. For the first three-year period ending in 4/2004, the portfolio outperformed the index by –17 to –27 percent. For the second period ending in 4/2005, the portfolio beat the index by +22 to +3 percent.

- *Never drop back more than 10 percent from any value the portfolio attains.* This was not accomplished in the portfolio's early days, but it has been accomplished since the objective was established in mid-2003. In fact, the largest decline since the beginning of 2003 has been about 5 percent. The use of conservative sell-stops makes me confident that this objective will continue to be accomplished in the future.

It is worth talking about one objective that could have been established but was not. That would be holding the turnover rate in the portfolio to some set percentage each year. Mutual funds are often judged on this criterion, with lower turnover rates automatically considered better. It is true that lower turnover rates hold down transaction costs, but that does not mean that your performance will be "better." Sometimes, trading (buying or selling) a stock is the very action that makes performance "better."

If your account is with an online broker that charges $5 or $7 per trade, your transaction costs will be low anyway. For example, if you hold 10 stocks in a $50,000 portfolio, and make two "round trips" per year in every holding, that would be 40 trades and a 200 percent turnover rate. That sounds way too high. But at $5 per trade, that's just $200 in trading costs, or 0.4 percent. It is also true that trading stocks triggers taxable events. If the event is a loss, that loss can be used to offset gains when tax time comes. If the event is a gain, it makes common sense to be *happy* that you have a gain you can pay taxes on. After all, that's the whole point, right?

We have seen the overwhelming importance of avoiding outsize losses in any stock portfolio. We do that by using sell-stops for day-to-day protection and by conducting quarterly Portfolio Reviews for making strategic decisions. The turnover rate of the portfolio therefore becomes a by-product of the decisions we make in selecting stocks and making hold-or-sell decisions, not the other way around. Over time, the avoidance of outsize losses will be far more important to performance than keeping portfolio turnover below some predetermined amount. In the end, total performance as measured by compounded annual returns is all that matters. Spending lightly on transaction costs, while desirable, is just one element in achieving total performance. That said, *all other things being equal,* a lower turnover rate is preferable to a higher one, both for holding down costs and because it's a lot less work.

Investment Objectives for Portfolio 2:

- *No matter what the S&P 500 does, return at least 7 percent annually over every three-year period.* This objective was set in mid-2003, but we can look at the record for the three-year period from the portfolio's inception in April 2002 through April 2005. During that time, the portfolio returned 30 percent, or 9.1 percent annualized. This exceeds the goal.

- *Beat the S&P 500 in total return over every three-year period.* During its first three-year period (April 2002 through April 2005), this portfolio beat the S&P 500 Stock Index by +28 percent to +3 percent.

- *Never drop back more than 10 percent from any value the portfolio attains.* This objective was established in mid-2003. There was a 10 percent drop in April 2004 when the Fed began raising interest rates and the port's REIT lineup got clobbered. That aside, this portfolio tends to be less volatile than the first portfolio, given the nature of its dividend-paying holdings. I am confident that this objective will continue to be accomplished in the future.

CHAPTER F-6

Lessons Learned

When I first started these portfolios, I knew they would be good teaching/learning vehicles, as well as demonstrations of what Sensible Stock Investing can do. However, they have been even more valuable than I anticipated. Here's why:

- The tech crash and interest-rate-raising by the Fed in 2000 created a full-blown recession in 2001, providing opportunities for investment lessons during all phases of the economic cycle. (I already knew how to manage a portfolio through boom times, namely the late 1990s, when my personal investments routinely returned between 150 and 200 percent of the S&P 500.)

- The recession became a start-and-stop, slow-moving affair, lasting much longer than most pundits predicted. Indeed, the recession was already underway for several months in 2001 while the experts were arguing whether we were "heading into" a recession. Finally, after the events of September 11, essentially everybody conceded that either a recession would happen, or that we were already in one. In point of fact, we had been in one for six months. Recessions, like stock market trends, are hard to identify in real time.

- I did not fully appreciate the necessity of containing losses when I began this portfolio. This blind spot was an artifact of not having had many losses to contain during the preceding several years. That extremely important lesson has been thoroughly learned, and Sensible Stock Investing now contains a heavy dose of loss-control and risk-management techniques that are easily applied by the individual investor.

- I did the wrong things in the immediate aftermath of the September 11 tragedies. History predicted that the stock market would "crash" for a short while, and then would recover back to where it had been, if not better. That is exactly what happened. But rather than sit tight and let the momentary crash-and-recovery occur, I sold most of the portfolio, either via stop-loss orders that were immediately triggered when the market reopened on September 17 or by placing outright sell orders on stocks that I thought (erroneously) would be permanently and adversely affected by the tragedies. In a few trading days, I had lots of cash and few stocks, and essentially had to start the first portfolio over. To make matters worse, the selling prices I got were terrible, usually well below my stop prices.

With that background in mind, here are the major lessons learned from the Sensible Stock Investing portfolios:

1. Invest When Market Conditions Are Favorable; Hold on to Your Cash When They Are Not

It is now clear that starting the first portfolio in April 2001 was a mistake, because the bubble was deflating. Having started the portfolio, it was a mistake to become fully invested so fast. I was irrationally exuberant. This is perhaps the most important lesson of Sensible Stock Investing, because it underscores the importance of holding losses in check. The probabilities of selecting stocks in 2001 that had favorable odds of making money over the next couple of years were not very high. Sensible Stock Investing's timing tools now provide a method for helping determine when is a good time to invest and when is not.

2. Market Values, Over Time, Tend to Revert to the Mean

Most theorists believe that stock valuations—or for that matter any of a variety of financial or social data measured over time—tend to return to their long-run patterns. Thus, for example, if stock valuations stray very far from historical averages—such as in a bubble situation—they will at some point return to their long-run averages. It's not finance, per se—it's human nature. The market is a social institution.

We saw this and learned the lesson in the first portfolio, which was mistakenly begun when the stock market, while deflating, was still in the bubble of the late 1990s. While stock *prices* had declined quite a bit from their early-2000 highs by the time the portfolio was started in April 2001, *valuations*—not just prices—must decline to sensible levels in order to deflate a bubble. Price declines, by themselves, do not let the air out of a bubble, because the price declines may simply be tracking earnings declines.

3. Take Careful Advantage of Bear Market Rallies

The principles just stated do not mean that you cannot make money during a bear market rally. After all, it is a rally, and such rallies can last for months, long enough to make some serious money. Just be careful that you recognize the fragility of the situation and act appropriately: Pick companies carefully, be sure that their valuations are favorable (or that you know why you can ignore them), be sure of the upward trend, and most important, be ready to get out quick when the rally fizzles.

4. Some Stocks Go Up Even during Bear Markets

Even during the extended bear market bubble deflation of 2000–2002, some stocks thrived. It is an old Wall Street adage that there is always money to be made somewhere. One classic example is housing stocks. When the economy is in trouble and the Fed is lowering interest rates to try to pump it up, many people take advantage of the lower rates to purchase houses and lock in low-interest mortgages. Many homebuilders did just fine during the 2000–2002 bear market.

5.   Practice Risk Management

Risk management as practiced in Sensible Stock Investing has two elements: (1) containing losses; and (2) taking gains before they slide back out of your grasp. Methods include:

*   Laying out the "constitutional documents" that define your goals, strategies, and techniques for stock investing.
*   Buying stocks only for sound, articulable reasons—usually including the excellence of the company, the attractiveness of its stock's valuation, and its current price strength.
*   Using trailing stop-loss orders and updating them regularly as prices change.
*   Investigating stock charts to confirm positive trends and gain confidence in their likely continuation.
*   Updating your Timing Outlook monthly—this helps you decide how wide a berth to give your trailing sell-stops, and it also helps you calibrate how quickly (or even whether) you want to move available cash into the market.
*   Conducting Portfolio Reviews every quarter for a strategic, wide-angle perspective.
*   Paying attention to news about your holdings, so you can react if necessary to *critical* news (but not "noise") about one of your stocks.
*   Employing simple hedging techniques. *Selling* is the ultimate, and most direct, hedging technique, literally taking profits off the table or getting out of a losing position.
*   Quickly cutting off initial losses on a newly purchased stock at 5 to 10 percent.

6.   Match Your Buy-Sell-Hold Strategy to the Types of Stocks You Own

The Sensible Stock Investor recognizes that there are different *types* of stocks (see Chapter E-3), and he or she utilizes hold-or-sell rules that are appropriate to the types owned. Volatile Type A stocks are best suited to aggressive loss-avoidance and profit-maximizing rules, which is another way of saying potentially frequent trading. On the other hand, less volatile Type B and Type D stocks tend to allow a more relaxed attitude toward trading.

7.   Select Stocks That Fit You

This is a corollary to the lesson just stated. In your stock-selection process, limit yourself to purchasing stocks that suit you: your personality; your comfort with risk; the amount of time you have to watch, study, and react to price changes and fundamental changes at each company; and so on. If you want to be a Buy-and-Hold investor, don't mess around with Type A stocks. Conversely, if you want to have a shot at making a killing on a small, little-known company that could grow from Haloid to Xerox, concentrate on smallish Type A firms. You may want to establish separate portfolios for different investment goals, as we have done in the two portfolios in this book.

8.   Protect All Gains If an Acquisition Offer Is Made for Your Company

Recall the Triquint/Sawtek incident described earlier. The most sensible thing to do when an acquisition offer is made for a company that you own, and which causes the price of your company to run up close to the announced acquisition price, is to set a stop-loss order just beneath the acquisition price (say 1 to 2 percent under, or $1 under). This protects the paper profit you have made simply because of the offer. If for some reason the offer falls through, you'll get most of the money you would have received had it been completed. If higher offers then come in from other potential acquirers, that will push your stock's price higher (and you should reset the sell-stop to reflect that). If the offer is made in the acquiring company's stock (rather than cash), research the new company to decide if you would like to own it, because that's what will happen if the acquisition is completed while you still own shares of your original company. If you don't want to own the acquiring company, be sure to sell your company before the deal is finalized.

9.   Sit Tight during External Catastrophes

History teaches that the stock market usually recovers its former levels within a few weeks or months after a tragedy. The market usually overreacts to sudden negative cataclysmic events. Fortunately this is a lesson that only needs to be applied a couple of times during most lifetimes. The lesson of history is that the financial machinery of the USA is very resilient.

So, in the event of a cataclysmic event, *remove* your sell-stops if you can get to them in time. In a time of crisis, have confidence that the financial system will rebound quickly after an initial extreme downdraft. Sell-stop orders are an intelligent tool during "normal" times. But they do not work well in times of national crisis.

10.   The Business Cycle Rules

The term "business cycle" implies something regular, like a sine wave that moves up and down continuously and smoothly. It is not that; at least it is not regular. But history teaches that business activity *does* move up and down, ebbing and flowing according to macroeconomic factors that are capable of overwhelming practically all megatrends, industry cycles, and so on. When the money supply contracts, business activity slows or contracts, and there is no use fighting it or wishing it were not so. It is so. The next time you hear someone say (for example) that technology stocks are in a class by themselves and immune from the business cycle, do not believe it.

11.   Don't Buy Any Stock That Does Not Fit Your Criteria

Once you have your constitutional documents, goals, and strategies set, follow them. The whole idea behind taking a strategic approach is so that you can follow it. Trust your research and analysis. Apply your own criteria. If you feel compelled to make an exception, ask yourself whether that means you need to tweak your strategies and rules. If not, only make an exception if you can articulate the reasons for it. That will give you something to refer back to when you conduct Portfolio Reviews.

12.   *Aim for Low Portfolio Turnover, but Do Not Let It Rule Your Investment Decisions*

Low turnover is generally a good thing, because it reduces transaction costs and avoids taxable events. That said, it is not the most important goal on the Sensible Stock Investor's agenda. High returns and low risk are the most important goals, and we have seen how they are enhanced significantly by avoiding large losses. Therefore, we recommend conducting Portfolio Reviews two or four times per year, in which you explain to yourself again what conditions would cause you to sell each stock. The way to implement your rational approach is to place trailing stop-loss orders underneath most of your stocks. If the stop-loss orders (or other selling criteria) are hit, then sell the stocks. Inevitably, that will create a higher portfolio turnover rate than a straight Buy-and-Hold approach. However, in the end, controlling losses will do far more for your total returns than holding down your trading costs. All of this assumes, of course, that your trades cost $5 to $10 or so, not the $100-and-up of traditional brokers.

13.   *Have a Strategy for Cash*

As you manage your portfolio, you will sell some stocks and have cash as a result. Have a strategy for what you are going to do with that cash: Reinvest it immediately? Let it sit in your account's "sweep" feature (at low interest rates)? Reinvest it slowly, or according to some logical approach that you are comfortable with? Whatever it is, you should have a strategy for cash. Notice that an element of this strategy will probably be to take into account what your Timing Outlook tells you each month. In other words, a positive Timing Outlook should influence you to be less in cash and more in stocks, while a negative outlook tells you the opposite.

APPENDICES

APPENDIX I. **SAMPLE FORMS**

Form 1.   Easy-Rate™ Stock Rating Sheet

Form 2.   Company "Story" Questionnaire

Form 3.   Shopping List

Form 4.   Timing Outlook

Form 5.   Portfolio Review

APPENDIX II. **ANNUAL CALENDAR FOR THE SENSIBLE STOCK INVESTOR**

APPENDIX I

Sample Forms

SAMPLE FORM 1

Easy-Rate™ Stock Rating Sheet

PEPSICO

Ticker Symbol: PEP

Sector: Consumer

Company/Stock Type: B

Date of Rating: 1/29/06

Subsector/Industry: Drinks, snacks & foods

Cap: Large

Company Rating

The Story: Incorporated in 1919, PEP is one of world's largest beverage and snack companies, enjoying fruits of long turnaround begun in mid-1990s. Far more than a cola company, PEP produces and markets myriad of snacks, carbonated and noncarbonated beverages, and foods. Among its many top trademarks are Aquafina (#1 water brand), Aunt Jemima, Cap'n Crunch, Cheetos, Cracker Jack, Doritos, Frito-Lay, Fritos, Gatorade (80 percent market share), Golden Grain, Lay's, Life, Mountain Dew, Pepsi-Cola, Quaker, Rice-A-Roni, Ruffles, 7UP, Sierra Mist, Slice, SoBe (a leader in "new age" drinks), Tostitos, and Tropicana. 16 brands bring in >$1B each. Through partnership with Starbucks, dominates bottled-coffee market. PEP's customers include franchise bottlers, independent distributors, and retailers. Snack products bring in about 58 percent of total revenue; beverages about 37 percent; and Quaker Foods about 5 percent. International operations are growing efficiencies with scale and account for about 1/3 of revenue and profit. *Fortune* (2/2006) has called PEP one of best-run companies in world. ROE has exceeded 30 percent since 1997 without excessive debt. Profit margins have ramped up steadily since 1996. "Power of One" ad strategy encourages food and beverage divisions to work together. Steady dividend growth accelerated in 2005–2006. +7

EPS Growth Rate: 3-yr: 18% +3

Return on Equity: 28% +5

Revenue Growth Rate: 3-yr: 8% +1

Debt/Equity Ratio: 20% +4

Fortune **Admiration Rating:** <8.0 +2

Dividends: +10

COMPANY SCORE: 40

Future: 11% +1   **TTM> 3-yr:** --

Years ROE>15%: +5

TTM v 3-yr: --

Cashflow>Earnings? Yes

Analysts' Rating: 1.7 +2

Stock Valuation

Price/Earnings Current: 25 +3

PEG Ratio: 2.0 +3

Price/Sales: 3 +3

Dividend Yield: 1.7% +1

VALUATION SCORE: 17 = Fair

TOTAL SCORE: 57

P/E Forward: 22 +3

P/CF: 16 +3

Price/Book: 7 +1

SAMPLE FORM 2

Company "Story" Questionnaire

1. From a high macro level, what business is the company in? How does it make money?

2. How dominant is the company in its industry? How did it attain dominance? Does it enjoy an effective monopoly or near-monopoly? What is its market share? Is its dominant position being attacked or likely to be attacked on antitrust grounds?

3. Is it free of significant competition, and devoid of *likely* significant competition? What prevents competitors from taking customers away?

4. Is there any new or disruptive technology on the horizon that might obsolete the business or industry?

5. Is it protected by government regulation? Or if not protected, at least not subject to the likelihood of damaging regulation?

6. How are its competitive advantages protected (e.g., by patents, copyrights, etc.)?

7. Is it in a fast-growing, important industry, one with probable staying power for at least the next one to two years?

8. Is it insulated from rapid shifts in tastes or fashion?

9. Does it have a good strategy and a history of good execution?

10. Does it have pricing power? Why can't a competitor start and win a price war? Why do the company's customers accept price increases?

11. Is it fast growing for its size? Does management have a growth orientation?

12. Does it appear to have strong prospects for sustained earnings growth for the next few years?

13. Does it have strong and sustainable brands? Does management work to protect and enhance them?

14. Is it in a commodity business? If so, is it the low-cost producer?

15. Are there any significant questions about the excellence and integrity of its management?

16. Does it have significant litigation or potential legal liabilities?

17. Does it have good labor relations?

18. How strong are its fundamental financials (low debt, cash-strong, displaying good earnings growth, etc.)?

19. How does the executive team function? Does management display regard for shareholders, as through increasing dividends, share buyback programs, open and honest communications, and the like?

20. Is it riding a megatrend?

SAMPLE FORM 3

Shopping List

STOCK SHOPPING LIST
2/3/06

FOUR SUB-LISTS:

1. Best Total Score—Company And Valuation (>53 points)
2. Best Company Score (>30 points)
3. Best Valuation Score (>23 points = "Good" or better valuation)
4. Best Dividend Stocks

SUB-LIST 1: BEST TOTAL SCORE (>53 points)

STOCK	SECTOR	STOCK TYPE	COMPANY SCORE	VALUATION SCORE	TOTAL SCORE
Chevron Texaco	Energy	B	40	30	70
Occidental Petroleum	Energy	B	40	28	68
Exxon Mobil	Energy	B	41	23	64
Bank of America	Financial	B-D	33	29	62
Home Depot	Consumer	A-B	37	24	61
Wal-Mart	Consumer	A-B	36	24	60
Johnson & Johnson	Healthcare	B	39	21	60
Walgreen's	Consumer	A	40	19	59
General Electric	Conglomerate	A-B	33	26	59
Cummins	Industrial	B	28	30	58
Diebold	Business Services	A-B	31	26	57
PepsiCo	Consumer	B	40	17	57
UICI	Financial	A	29	27	56
Best Buy	Consumer	A	35	21	56
RC 2 Corp	Consumer	A	30	25	55
Biomet	Healthcare	A	36	19	55
Dell	Technology	A	36	19	55
Procter & Gamble	Consumer	B	37	17	54
RAIT Investment Trust	REIT	D	29	25	54
Kinder Morgan Energy Ptnrs	Energy	B-D	28	25	53

SUB-LIST 2: BEST COMPANY SCORE (>31 points)

STOCK	SECTOR	STOCK TYPE	TOTAL SCORE	COMPANY SCORE
Exxon Mobil	Energy	B	64	41
Walgreen's	Consumer	A	59	40
Chevron Texaco	Energy	B	70	40
PepsiCo	Consumer	B	57	40
Occidental Petroleum	Energy	B	68	40
Johnson & Johnson	Healthcare	B	60	39
Procter & Gamble	Consumer	B	54	37
Home Depot	Consumer	A-B	61	37
Chicos Fas	Consumer	A	46	37
Biomet	Healthcare	A	55	36
Wal-Mart	Consumer	A-B	60	36
Dell	Technology	A	55	36
Varian Medical	Healthcare	A	42	36
Chicago Mercantile	Financial	A	41	35
Best Buy	Consumer	A	56	35
Starbucks	Consumer	A	43	34
General Electric	Conglomerate	B	59	33
Bank of America	Financial	B-D	62	33
Google	Media	A	37	32
Diebold	Business Services	A-B	57	31

SUB-LIST 3: BEST VALUATION SCORE (>23 points = "Good" or better valuation)

STOCK	SECTOR	STOCK TYPE	TOTAL SCORE	VALUATION SCORE
Chevron Texaco	Energy	B	70	30 = Good+
Cummins	Industrial	A-B	58	30 = Good+
Bank of America	Financial	B	62	29 = Good+
Occidental Petroleum	Energy	B	68	28 = Good+
UICI	Financial	A	56	27 = Good
General Electric	Conglomerate	B	59	26 = Good
Diebold	Business Services	A-B	57	26 = Good
Beazer Homes	Consumer	A	51	26 = Good
RAIT Investment Trust	REIT	D	54	25 = Good
Kinder Morgan Energy Ptnrs	Energy	B-D	53	25 = Good
RC2 Corporation	Consumer	A	48	25 = Good
Home Depot	Cons. & Bus. Svcs.	A-B	61	24 = Good
Wal-Mart	Consumer	A-B	60	24 = Good
Pfizer	Healthcare	A-B	52	24 = Good
Valero Energy	Energy	A	50	24 = Good
Exxon Mobil	Energy	B	64	23 = Good

LIST 4: BEST DIVIDEND STOCKS

Based on Total Score + Dividend weighting = "Grand Total"

Dividend weighting calculated as dividend yield times 4, rounded to nearest whole number

Minimum dividend yield required = 1.7% (i.e., more than S&P 500's average dividend)

Minimum "Grand Total" required = 65 points

STOCK	SECTOR	TOTAL SCORE	DIVIDEND WEIGHTING	GRAND TOTAL
RAIT Investment Trust	REIT	54	9.0% = 36	90
Chevron Texaco	Energy	70	2.9% = 12	82
Bank of America	Financial	62	4.2% = 17	79
Kinder Morgan Energy Part.	Energy	53	6.5% = 26	79
Exxon Mobil	Energy	64	1.8% = 7	71
General Electric	Conglomerate	59	2.8% = 11	70
Buckeye Partners	Energy	44	6.3% = 25	69
Johnson & Johnson	Healthcare	60	2.1% = 8	68
Diebold	Business Svcs.	57	2.2% = 9	66
PepsiCo	Consumer	57	2.2% = 9	66

SAMPLE FORM 4

Timing Outlook

TIMING OUTLOOK

Date of This Outlook: 1/23/06
Date of Last Outlook: 12/1/05

----

1. Market Performance Since Last Outlook

S&P 500 last time: 1265
S&P 500 now: 1266
S&P 500 at beginning of year: 1248
S&P 500 YTD: +1%

----

2. Indicators

- **Conference Board Index of Leading Economic Indicators:** After going up and down for about a year, this indicator has finally put together 3 straight months of growth: October, November, and December. Green "up" arrow. **+10**

- **Fed interest rate indicator:** On 12/13, the Fed raised rates 1/4 percent for its 13th consecutive meeting, to 4.25 percent. Their accompanying statement seemed to soften their stance on how much longer this will go on. Greenspan will be replaced by Bernanke in February (one meeting from now). Red arrow down. **+0**

- **FundAdvice.com's interest rate indicator** (their #2 indicator) has been red for about a year. **+0**

- **Morningstar's S&P 500 P/E ratio** rose from 21.1 to 21.9. Still neutral. **+5**

- **Morningstar's Market Valuation Graph** rose from about 6 percent overvalued to 7 percent overvalued. Remains neutral. **+5**

- **FundAdvice's S&P 500 trend indicator** (their #1 indicator) has been green since 11/1/05. **+10**

- **FundAdvice's NASDAQ breadth indicator** (their #3 indicator) has been oscillating since June, with 9(!) flip-flops since then, including two this period. Presently green. **+10**

- **FundAdvice's NYSE breadth indicator** (their #4 indicator) turned green 11/8/05. **+10**

----

3. New Rating

Conclusion: The average of the indicators dropped from 5.6 last time to 3.1 during the period, but it has sprung back to **6.3** this time. This is well above mid-point but still in the neutral range. Sell-stops should be in "normal" positions, with a maximum cash position of 25 percent or so. Of course, demand favorable company ratings, valuations, and (or) clear momentum before investing.

SAMPLE FORM 5

Portfolio Review

Portfolio Review Q2 2005

Name of Portfolio: Type A & B Stocks

Date of Review: 6/7/05

Date of Last Review: 2/15/05

----

1. Performance Since Last Review

S&P 500 last time:1207

S&P 500 today: 1205

Change: –0%

Portfolio last time: $59,003

Portfolio now: $61,888

Change: +5%

----

2. Portfolio Changes Since Last Review

Stocks:

This port is now well into its second year focusing on Type A and B stocks. A higher turnover rate is expected in this portfolio than the "Type B & D" port. Because of the nature of its holdings, this portfolio tends to move forward in spurts, then fall back, then spurt forward again. Some highlights:

- Portfolio underperformed the market in 2003, +13 percent to +26 percent, and then outperformed the market in 2004, +27 percent to +9 percent. It is outperforming the market YTD through 5/31/05, +1 percent to –2 percent.

- Since last time: Sold Apple; Beazer Homes; Coventry Health; FBR; First Marblehead; and Penn National Gaming. Closure Medical was purchased by J&J for a snazzy 50 percent+ gain.

- Bought Chicago Mercantile; eBay; Google; PanAmSat Holdings; Pfizer; RC2 Corporation; and XLU (a utility ETF).

Cash:

$13,555, about 22% of portfolio. Latest Timing Outlook is at 4.4, or neutral. Cash position is OK, but could be lowered to about 15% of portfolio with one more attractive stock purchase.

----

3. Portfolio Status, Comments, and Actions

Stock	Date Bought	Price When Bought	Price Now	Commentary.	Action
CME	5/9/05 5/20/05	199.18 204.90	248.01	Up 23% in a month or less. Classic momentum success story. Since valuation is "Poor," maintain pretty tight sell-stop, guaranteeing at least 15% gain.	30 @ 7%
EBAY	5/25/05	38.08	38.01	Has bounced around in the couple weeks of ownership. Hold stop at 8% below purchase price.	150 @ 8% below purchase
GOOG	6/1/05	286.85	293.31	Has had a good first week of ownership. Since it has "Poor" valuation, keep tight leash on it.	20 @ 7%
PA	5/20/05	18.48	19.99	Up 8% in less than a month, a promising start for a momentum stock. Has no valuation, so also keep tight leash on it. Profit is already guaranteed.	350 @ 7%
PFE	5/17/05	28.14	28.08	Hopefully a long-term holding, although pharmaceuticals are notoriously skittish. Still under probationary 8% sell-stop.	200 @ 8% below purchase
PG	12/3/04	56.41	55.48	Top-25 company and probable long-term holding. Had misfortune of buying it just before it announced acquisition offer for Gillette, and it took the predictable tumble. Up a couple bucks since last review, still hasn't cleared its purchase price. Gillette acquisition fits long-range strategy well.	100 @ 8% below purchase.
RCRC	3/15/05	30.30	36.25	Has performed well since purchase 3 months ago, up 20%. Profit guaranteed.	180 @ 8%
XLU	5/02/05	30.22	30.66	First ETF purchased as a momentum play. "Boring" utilities have been going up slowly for about 3 years, with never more than a 3% drop. Off to a fair start, up 1% in a month.	150 @ 7%

APPENDIX II

Annual Calendar for the
Sensible Stock Investor

January

- Change sell-stops daily or weekly
- Portfolio Review, including update of Easy-Rate™ Stock Rating Sheets for all owned stocks
- Create Easy-Rate Sheets for one to four new stocks, add to Shopping List those that qualify
- Update Shopping List, including new Easy-Rate Sheets where necessary
- Timing Outlook
- Review and amend the "constitutional documents" for Your Investment Company

February

- Change sell-stops daily or weekly
- Create Easy-Rate Sheets for one to four new stocks, add to Shopping List those that qualify
- Update Shopping List, including new Easy-Rate Sheets where necessary
- Timing Outlook

March

- Change sell-stops daily or weekly
- Create Easy-Rate Sheets for one to four new stocks, add to Shopping List those that qualify
- Update Shopping List, including new Easy-Rate Sheets where necessary
- Timing Outlook

April

- Change sell-stops daily or weekly
- Portfolio Review, including update of Easy-Rate Sheets for all owned stocks

- Create Easy-Rate Sheets for one to four new stocks, add to Shopping List those that qualify
- Update Shopping List, including new Easy-Rate Sheets where necessary
- Timing Outlook

May

- Change sell-stops daily or weekly
- Create Easy-Rate Sheets for one to four new stocks, add to Shopping List those that qualify
- Update Shopping List, including new Easy-Rate Sheets where necessary
- Timing Outlook

June

- Change sell-stops daily or weekly
- Create Easy-Rate Sheets for one to four new stocks, add to Shopping List those that qualify
- Update Shopping List, including update of all Easy-Rate Sheets for stocks on Shopping List
- Timing Outlook

July

- Change sell-stops daily or weekly
- Portfolio Review, including update of Easy-Rate Sheets for all owned stocks
- Create Easy-Rate sheets for one to four new stocks, add to Shopping List those that qualify
- Update Shopping List, including new Easy-Rate Sheets where necessary
- Timing Outlook

August

- Change sell-stops daily or weekly
- Create Easy-Rate Sheets for one to four new stocks, add to Shopping List those that qualify
- Update Shopping List, including new Easy-Rate Sheets where necessary
- Timing Outlook

September

- Change sell-stops daily or weekly
- Create Easy-Rate Sheets for one to four new stocks, add to Shopping List those that qualify

- Update Shopping List, including new Easy-Rate Sheets where necessary
- Timing Outlook

October

- Change sell-stops daily or weekly
- Portfolio Review, including update of Easy-Rate Sheets for all owned stocks
- Create Easy-Rate Sheets for one to four new stocks, add to Shopping List those that qualify
- Update Shopping List, including new Easy-Rate Sheets where necessary
- Timing Outlook

November

- Change sell-stops daily or weekly
- Create Easy-Rate Sheets for one to four new stocks, add to Shopping List those that qualify
- Update Shopping List, including new Easy-Rate Sheets where necessary
- Timing Outlook

December

- Change sell-stops daily or weekly
- Create Easy-Rate Sheets for one to four new stocks, add to Shopping List those that qualify
- Update Shopping List, including update of all Easy-Rate Sheets for stocks on Shopping List
- Timing Outlook
- Update all active Easy-Rate Sheets
- Clean out "no hope" stocks from master document of Easy-Rate Sheets

About the Author

The author of the book is David Van Knapp. Dave is a successful individual stock investor. He ended his business career in 2001 to research and write this book, with the mission of helping other individual investors achieve better results. He is firmly convinced that famed investor Peter Lynch is correct when he says "the amateur investor has numerous built-in advantages that, if exploited, should result in his or her outperforming the experts, and also the market in general."

Dave's undergraduate degree, from Holy Cross College, is in physics. He worked for three years as a rocket scientist and systems engineer before heading for law school. Dave graduated with a JD degree from Georgetown University Law Center in 1974. He has also received formal business training in the MBA program at Rochester Institute of Technology and in the executive development program at INSEAD in Fontainebleau, France (one of the world's leading graduate business schools). His career has included positions as a legal analyst, writer, and editor; managing editor; editor-in-chief; general manager with profit-and-loss responsibilities; and executive-level business and strategy planner. His employer—a global information and publishing company—supplied both fundamental and analytical information to a variety of professional markets, including lawyers, accountants, and the investment community.

Dave's career experience makes him the ideal author for this book. He understands how public companies develop their strategies, are managed, deal with financial issues, and compete. As a published analyst and author, he has extensive experience in taking complex subjects, often involving contradictory points of view, and blending them into a reasonable and readable presentation.

Sensible Stock Investing began as "notes to self" when Dave was beginning his own stock investing years ago. As he continued his research and his notes grew, Dave realized how often individual investors face problems comprehending investment terminology, understanding what goes on in the markets, and sorting out seemingly irreconcilable inconsistencies among different "schools" of investing. He set out to solve these problems. This book was conceived and then developed over the course of five years after Dave realized that the problems he was solving could be of great help to other individual investors.

Sensible Stock Investing is the book Dave wishes he had when he began investing in stocks. He hopes and believes it will help both beginning and experienced individual investors with clear, innovative, fact-based investment strategies and methodologies.

Acknowledgments

I would like to express my special thanks to the following people for helping me complete the long journey that has resulted in the completion of this book.

David Hanssens: David is a former work colleague, an expert on strategy and decision-making, and an experienced investor. His big-picture comments on the book, especially on making it easily navigable for its intended audience, were invaluable and influenced the book's final structure.

Keith Holder: Keith is a CPA who makes his living trading stocks. By sheer coincidence, he is also a neighbor. His detailed comments and reality checks made me rethink some issues and alter my approach in subtle ways. His background as an editor meant that we spoke the same language as we traded ideas about the book.

Sue Van Knapp: My wife is a person of many wonderful talents. While she rose to an executive position with a major publisher, she began her career as a professional copyreader. She was the first person to read and comment on the original drafts of this book. Besides finding errors, her many suggestions helped make the book much more readable. I also owe Sue great thanks for her positive support and encouragement, especially as the book hit the home stretch.

I want to express my appreciation and thanks to a "virtual focus group" of friends and colleagues who come from a variety of backgrounds and reside across the country. "Meeting" via email, this Advisory Panel has helped me in innumerable ways, from testing potential titles to reacting to marketing concepts. Thanks to David, Keith, and Sue already mentioned, plus Ron Boller, Lock Bounds, Tom Bourne, Al Brazener, Jim Dayton, Bob Levin, Ron Manne, David Oliveiri, Don Thoes, and Tom Trenkner.

I would also like to thank Morningstar, Inc. for permission to use fundamental stock data from their Web site at Morningstar.com. This data appears in several places in the book, most prominently in the Easy-Rate™ Stock Rating Sheet displayed in Appendix I, Form 1. In regard to this data, Morningstar has asked me to include the following statement: © 2006 Morningstar, Inc. All Rights Reserved. The information contained herein: (1) is proprietary to Morningstar and/or its content providers; (2) may not be copied or distributed; and (3) is not warranted to be accurate, complete or timely. Neither Morningstar nor its content providers are responsible for any damages or losses arising from any use of this information. Past performance is no guarantee of future results.

Finally, my thanks to a person I never met. Tom Ainslie published *The Compleat Horseplayer* in 1966, and I discovered the paperback edition in 1969. It played right into my love of sports, problem solving, probabilities, and betting. On top of that, I admired its clear, straightforward writing. I got many ideas for this book—finding contenders, winnowing out the also-rans, bankroll management, and illustrating with an actual portfolio—from his book, which was one of many that he wrote on horse racing. Investing is betting in fancier clothes, and to the game theorist, the issues are identical. I don't think Mr. Ainslie knew about game theory, but his instincts were right. His book, which I first read long ago and have reread several times since, served as an inspiration for this one. Take what you know and share it with others—it sends positive energy around the planet.

Disclaimer &
Important Information

This book is for your personal use only, and its contents are protected by applicable copyright, patent, and trademark laws.

The information provided in this book is for general informational purposes only. It is not intended and under no circumstances should be construed as providing personal investment, tax, or legal advice or recommendations. The book also should not be construed as an offer to sell or the solicitation of an offer to buy, nor as a recommendation to buy, hold, or sell any security.

The author is not a registered investment advisor, a registered securities broker-dealer, or a certified financial planner, or otherwise licensed to give investment advice. All opinions, analyses, and information included herein are based on sources believed to be reliable, and the book has been written in good faith, but no representation or warranty of any kind, expressed or implied, is made, including but not limited to any representation or warranty concerning accuracy, completeness, correctness, timeliness, or appropriateness.

You are responsible for your own investment decisions, and each investor is solely responsible for analyzing and evaluating any information used or relied upon in making an investment decision. Prior to making any investment decision, you should thoroughly investigate the proposed investment, consider your personal situation, and consult with a qualified investment advisor. The information and opinions provided in this book should not be relied upon or used as a substitute for consultation with professional advisors.

The use of or reliance on the contents of this book is done solely at your own risk. No representation or warranty, expressed or implied, is made as to the accuracy, completeness, or correctness of this book's opinions, analyses, or information. Investment markets have inherent risks, there can be no guarantee of profits, and investors may lose money any time they invest in the stock market. Different types of investments involve varying degrees of risk, and there can be no assurance that any specific investment or strategy will be either suitable or profitable for a specific investment portfolio.

Past performance does not assure future returns. Therefore, no reader should assume that the performance of any investment approach discussed in this book will be profitable in the future, equal its past performance, or reach any performance objectives. The author shall have and accepts no liability of whatever nature in respect of any claim, damages, loss, or expense arising from or in connection with an investor's reliance on or use of this book.

In no event shall any reference to any third party or third party product or service be construed as an approval or endorsement by the author. In particular, the author does not endorse or recommend the services of any particular broker, dealer, mutual fund company, or information provider.

The author may now or in the future have positions in or trade the securities discussed in the book.

978-1-60528-010-3
1-60528-010-0

Made in the USA
Lexington, KY
04 December 2011